THEATRE ARTS
IN THE ELEMENTARY CLASSROOM

Grade Four through Grade Six

Second Edition

Barbara Salisbury Wills

ANCHORAGE PRESS, INC.
New Orleans, Louisiana

**Theatre Arts in the Elementary Classroom
Grade Four through Grade Six**

Second Edition

©Copyright, 1996, Barbara Salisbury Wills
©Copyright, 1996, Anchorage Press, Inc.

ISBN 0-87602-034-1

Graphic Design: Susan Russell
Illustration: Susan Monday

FOREWORD

Barbara Salisbury Wills, building on her training and extensive teaching experience, has now created two outstanding theatre arts textbooks for the elementary classroom teacher. My reading of the manuscript began in a large metropolitan airport waiting room. In the midst of the *Why, What, How?* chapter, the material came alive as three young children, two girls and one boy, began playing nearby. "This is my house," announced the boy as he ran about checking the seats, completely involved in his play, totally oblivious to the throng of people coming and going. The girls joined him in the house. They pantomimed kitchen utensils and discussed the meal they were preparing.

After a few minutes of play, one of the girls picked up a small stick of wood which she immediately turned into an airplane. The other children joined her on the floor and all three went on an imaginary flight, spontaneously describing the plane and the sights they were seeing. The adults looked on occasionally, always without comment. When the adults called the children to go on their separate ways, their dramatic play ended as abruptly as it had begun.

Obviously these were younger children, unaffected by adult expectations concerning their free dramatic play. By using the theatre arts activities in this text the teacher can guide older students to return to the more uninhibited, spontaneous creativity of their early school years. The older children bring longer attention spans, more maturity, and self control, qualities which enhance all of their drama activities.

Structured around the specific objectives or essential elements to be taught in kindergarten through sixth grade, the two volumes approach the subject of theatre arts in a manner not previously available in textbook form. Acting, playmaking/playwriting, and responding serve as the three essential elements for all grades. The charts on pages 28–29 detail these essential elements and activities by grade level.

At each grade, additional objectives and exercises are added to help teachers and students realize the major values and goals of theatre arts, including:

- helping the children to develop to their fullest potential in all areas of study
- helping children realize that the goal in the elementary school is not to put on a play for an audience, but to help them develop their imagination, creativity and appreciation of the art of theatre
- learning that theatre arts is a subject in its own right while also being used as an aid to all subjects in the curriculum

The keys to success in theatre arts activities are clearly presented by Salisbury Wills in very specific terms, such as control, discipline, warm-ups, cool downs, visualization, questions, organization, etc. Her knowledge of the child's interests and abilities by grade level is clearly demonstrated in her selection of appropriate material and activities. Shadow plays, puppet activities, delightful stories and formal plays are interspersed within the text. All are designed for classroom use. The activities range from those lasting a few minutes to full length sessions of thirty to sixty minutes.

Since many of the drama activities can be successfully repeated at different ages, Salisbury Wills gives a cross-reference guide for easy access to other level activities with information for simplifying or enriching given concepts.

For all age levels, the author, in Chapter Five, correlates drama with other subject areas including language, mathematics, and science. She also gives ideas for the use of drama with special populations from the academically gifted to the economically deprived.

Assessing the students' work in theatre arts is the subject of the last chapter. Here Salisbury Wills offers several options for the evaluation of the various types of theatre activities, including a checklist and rating scale guide. Emphasis is placed on measuring each student against his or her own potential with reference to the individual's progress, rather than comparing students against each other.

This book allows teachers with or without formal training in theatre arts to guide children to achieving their greatest potential in both curricular and extra-curricular theatre arts activities.

In a recent creative drama session with fourth grade students, the shyest, most withdrawn child in the class was found actively participating for the first time. She was clearly concentrating and revealing an imagination not previously noticed by the teacher. During the evaluation period the girl commented: "I was having so much fun, that I forgot to be afraid." Ideally, all teachers will use these excellent texts in the spirit of learning and sharing as they and the children have rewarding, creative fun. During these creative periods all children will benefit as they develop their concentration, imagination and knowledge of the world.

Equally important are the formal theatre experiences which the students have as audience members. Since students are often more familiar with television and film, Salisbury Wills uses these as a comparison and contrast to theatre. She also notes that theatre for children consists of adults (high school age and up) performing for children, for it is the script and the audience that make theatre for children, not the age of the actors.

To receive maximum educational benefit, the audience members should be prepared before seeing any production. The vicarious experiences of the young audience, through the lives of the characters of the story, be it comic or serious, encourage emotional and aesthetic growth.

After seeing effective productions, many children leave the theatre interested in playing out some of the scenes. They often spontaneously take on the characteristics of the major roles, roaring like a lion or strutting and bragging like the mischievous rogues as they leave the theatre. An analysis and discussion of the theatre experiences as well as recreating them in creative drama sessions are important classroom followup activities for audience members.

Salisbury Wills' texts are excellent guides to combining creative fun and serious work so that school children have exciting, memorable learning experiences in theatre arts.

Dr. Coleman A. Jennings
Department of Theatre and Dance
The University of Texas at Austin

INTRODUCTION

Geraldine Brain Siks
Professor Emeritus
University of Washington

Whatever you can do or dream you can,
*   begin it,*
Boldness has genius, power, and magic in
*   it*
Begin it now.

Goethe 1749–1832

Imagine you are a teacher who has never taught theatre arts in your classroom. You enjoy theatre. For several years you've wanted to share it with children, but you didn't know how to go about it. This past year a fellow teacher showed you the first edition of this book. You read the opening chapter and the chapter describing the procedure for teaching theatre arts in your grade. As you studied these chapters, they motivated you into action.

So you begin. And you did it! You guided your children into high-spirited theatre experiences by following Barbara Salisbury Wills' *Theatre Arts in the Elementary Classroom*. You found it comparatively easy with her curriculum guide. You marvelled at the children's concentration as each one figured out how to achieve an objective. Best of all, you witnessed the enthusiasm as children imagined and created believable action in the roles of such characters as a kind duke, a hungry beggar, a sorcerer and others. It's glorious to dream and imagine, isn't it? Even more so to carry out a dream.

Before Barbara developed the first editions of these two volumes, many theatre educators wondered if it could be done. How could a theatre textbook be written so it would harness children's physical and emotional energies? How could such a book fire children's imaginations and challenge their minds? How could a book stimulate enough enthusiasm to involve children in working together to solve dramatic problems? Drama is **action**. Theatre is of the moment. How could these essential qualities be captured in a book?

Barbara believed it could be done. She was committed to the idea of guiding teachers to teach theatre arts as a subject in its own right. She approached this challenge with her years of varied experience. Barbara is a master educator. She has taught children of all ages and she continues to conduct drama and theatre workshops in elementary and secondary schools. During these experiences, plus her university teaching, the vision of these books began to shape itself in her mind.

She used a conceptual approach to theatre arts to form the foundation for the format and content of the first edition. This approach involved children in the "fun" of doing drama while they gained concepts, expressive skills, and an initial grasp of the art of theatre. This approach reinforced the belief that a learner's knowledge of a subject is incomplete unless an intellectual understanding accompanies emotional enjoyment and skill proficiency. Barbara employed this approach in the belief that if teachers and children alike comprehend what is to be learned from each lesson, the learning will be appreciated and last longer.

The first edition was commended as excellent by leading theatre educators throughout the country. It was used by hundreds of classroom teachers and children in kindergarten through grade six. On the whole, the children responded enthusiastically. Teachers' responses were overwhelmingly favorable; many described the format as "teacher friendly." Read what three teachers had to say about the first edition:

> *"I have found your books to be very well organized, easy to understand, and easy to use. Thank you!"*
>
> *"[The lessons have] questions that enable the children to do good creative thinking and brainstorming."*
>
> *"As a Language Arts teacher, I am always looking for ways to bring subjects 'to life.' Thanks for opening new doors!"*

When the first edition found its way to children, Barbara, as her own best critic, re-examined the format and content. She questioned teachers as to what had worked and what needed improvement. Her persistent pursuit brings us two new volumes, revised, expanded and strengthened.

A few significant changes have been made in the opening chapter to clarify the conceptual approach, the essential elements and the teaching process. In response to teachers' comments, four specific additions to the format are incorporated in each grade level chapter. These include the following:

1. A list of ongoing dramatic behaviors addressed to the individual student for self-assessment is stated at the beginning of each grade level chapter.

2. Specific suggestions for assessment are included at the end of each lesson.

3. **Every** lesson uses the same teacher procedure — the creative drama process (introduce, plan, act, reflect/evaluate).

4. Related objectives from other subjects are listed for each lesson along with the drama objective.

New changes in content meet children's contemporary interests while challenging their abilities even more than in the first edition. Fifteen new pieces of delightful, dramatic literature have been added. These include tales from China, Nicaragua, Puerto Rico, Mexico, West Africa, Chile, Native America and Black America. Specific suggestions in many lessons are given as a follow up to dramatic involvement. These suggestions aim to motivate children to write character attributes, objectives and dialogue. Other suggestions focus on the writing of dramatic plots, new endings to stories, or entirely new stories.

In the *Grade Four Through Grade Six* book, students are guided to participate in the collaborative nature of theatre arts. This is done by the inclusion of lessons involving students in the related roles of playwright, designer and drama critic. Lessons such as "Swapping Scenarios," "Storyteller's Rap," "Lights, Camera, Action," and "Making Decisions" are both challenging and intriguing. Students are further challenged by guidelines encouraging them to assess their own progress in drama as individuals and as group members.

Imagine, if you will, the excitement and high rare mood in a classroom when children become involved in this kind of study. The revised edition of this book holds high appeal for both students and teachers in the joy of learning together.

PREFACE

The Second Edition of *Theatre Arts in the Elementary Classroom, Grade Four Through Grade Six,* like its predecessor, is directed to teachers who think they have limited experience using drama in the classroom. Prior to writing this edition, I surveyed as many teachers who used the original book as possible to find out what they liked and didn't like. The survey confirmed that most of the teachers used drama more than they realized. They found the lessons on sensory recall and rhythmic movement, for example, reassuringly familiar — they just didn't know they were "doing drama" before. The intent of this book is to familiarize teachers, who may or may not have used theatre arts activities before, with the goals, concepts and methodology of drama in the classroom.

The premise of this book, and of its companion volume for teachers of kindergarten through third grade, is that drama, as one of the fine arts, should be taught in the classroom as a subject in its own right. While theatre arts activities complement many aspects of child growth and development, they do so only because of the integrity of the art form itself. By becoming directly involved in the process of creating drama, children acquire an understanding of theatre arts, as well as an understanding of themselves and the society in which they live.

In 1994, the Consortium of Arts Education Associations developed the *National Standards for Arts Education*, which includes content and achievement standards for dance, music, theatre and the visual arts at three levels: K-4th grade, 5th-8th grade, and 9th-12th grade.* As the executive director of the American Alliance for Theatre & Education, I sat on the Coordinating Council and was very much involved in the development of the theatre standards. Although this book does not explicitly address each of the eight content standards written in the standards document, it does include them all in some way. The standards greatly influenced the recasting of the

---

*For information about ordering the *National Standards for Arts Education*, contact MENC Publications Sales, 1806 Robert Fulton Drive, Reston, VA 22091.

essential elements and concepts in this second edition.

The book is organized to provide very specific and practical help to teachers.

Chapter One, for example, is both theoretical and practical. It deals with the "nitty gritty" of drama, and provides tips about classroom management when teaching theatre arts lessons. A scope and sequence chart shows how various dramatic concepts develop sequentially over the years, from kindergarten through sixth grade. I have chosen three "essential elements" as organizing principles for the activities in the book. It has been my experience that states and school districts develop curriculum frameworks using a variety of different organizers or categories. The important point is not in individual labels, but rather in concepts which are the real building blocks of the art. No matter what you call them, when the elements of drama are combined effectively, they produce theatre that is powerful — theatre, whether formal or informal, which moves people to tears or laughter, theatre which lends insight about what it means to be human.

Chapters Two through Four are grade level chapters. Each grade has a chapter of its own, so that teachers will have ready access to useful materials. These materials are presented as lesson plans, with concepts, objectives, materials and procedures clearly stated, and graphically arranged so they can be easily followed. Often, specific questions and comments are written as if the teacher were speaking directly to the students. Such a format seems the clearest and most direct way to demonstrate the progression of each lesson; the comments, however, should not necessarily be followed verbatim. Each teacher will want to adjust and adapt the lessons according to his or her individual teaching style and the needs of specific classes.

Those familiar with the original book will notice some format changes in the grade level chapters. Based on the exceedingly positive response from teachers to the original format, I decided not only to retain the format but to expand on it to increase its usefulness. For example, teachers wanted to know how the lessons might tie directly into other subjects in the curriculum. Therefore, following the statement of the drama objective, there are lists of related objectives which the teacher may choose to reinforce in the lesson. Assessment is another area teachers are more and more concerned about. Although there is still a separate chapter on assessment, the end of each activity has one or more suggestions for assessing that particular activity. In addition, expectations for appropriate ongoing drama behaviors are listed in the opening of each grade level chapter.

As in the original book, the first lesson for each grade in Chapters Two through Four is called *Getting Started*. This lesson is designed to introduce drama in classes where the children have not previously participated in theatre arts activities. Even those who have had experience in drama, however, should find the lesson a good review.

After the introductory lesson, the lessons are grouped according to specific drama concepts, such as rhythmic movement, pantomime, sensory awareness, and others. Three or more lessons for each concept are presented, arranged from the simple to the more complex. Rather than teaching all the lessons under one concept before moving on to the next, however, I would encourage teachers to mix and match, for more variety. For example, a lesson may start with a movement activity followed by a sensory awareness activity or a pantomime lesson.

On the other hand, a given class might need or want more work in a certain concept — rhythmic movement, for example. In that case, the *Cross Reference Guide* at the beginning of the grade level chapter will be useful. The guide lists page numbers of other lessons dealing with the concept for the grade lower and the grade higher than the grade in question. There should be no concern about teaching lessons more than once — whether during the same year or in successive years. The lessons are open-ended so that each experience can be different. And, just as children enjoy hearing favorite stories over and over again, they will enjoy repeating favorite drama lessons several times.

As before, each story is printed in its entirety in the book, so the teacher doesn't need to search for the story in order to teach the lesson. Almost all the stories are new in this volume, and they represent several different cultures.

A number of the teachers surveyed indicated that the lessons for the fifth and sixth grades could be more challenging. Accordingly, substantial changes in previous lessons were made and materials were added which deal with playwriting, designing, and critiquing. The students I piloted the materials with were stimulated, challenged and pleased with their accomplishments, as was I.

One of the unique features of the grade level chapters continues to be the way in which the essential element labeled "responding and constructing meaning" is presented. The lessons are participatory in nature, just as they are for the other essential elements. Lessons in audience etiquette, for example, involve the students in practicing the proper behavior, rather than just talking about it. Lessons on analyzing certain aspects of a play are taught by working with a real script which the students use as a model to enact and analyze. Lessons on the similarities and differences among television, film and live theatre are taught by having the students use real or imagined cameras and viewfinders to demonstrate the differences. The lessons are intended to prepare them so they will be able to appreciate and understand the unique qualities of live theatre.

Chapter Five is different from the other chapters; it deals with using drama as a technique to teach other subjects, and to teach special student populations. Many teachers have found drama to be an effective tool to teach other curricular areas. Ideas relating drama to specific concepts in other subjects are described in this chapter. For maximum success in using drama as a teaching tool, the children should be quite familiar with the drama process itself. Only then should it be applied to other subjects. Drama is also a powerful tool to use with children who have special physical, mental or emotional needs. This chapter gives suggestions for ways to use drama with such children.

Teachers surveyed indicated that the recommendations in the Appendices were helpful. Consequently I have retained the *Idea Starters,* in Appendix A, in which potential drama activities are categorized by subjects such as "Seasons," "Senses" and more. Appendix B provides an updated, annotated list of children's literature suitable for dramatization. And Appendix C is an updated, annotated bibliography which can be useful for teachers who want to investigate additional resources.

Many people have contributed to this book and to its companion volume in very special ways. Countless children, university students and classroom teachers have acted as willing "guinea pigs" as I tried out materials with them. Their feedback, and that of drama specialists, has been invaluable, helping me to choose which ideas to retain, eliminate or add to this volume. Although space limitations prohibit my relating their specific contributions, special thanks to Sara Akers, Ellen Baltz, Laurence Binder, Kathleen Blum, Joan E. Brownrigg, Michael Cantrell, Shirley Trusty Corey, Brenda Cotto-Escalera, Ruth Denney, Susan Dickes, Jan Graves, Lucilla Iglehart, Jeannie Jackson, Carol Jones, Judy Matetzschk, Monica Michell, Lynn Murray, Thelma Pate, Nancy Prince, Sally Pritchard, Richard Runkel, Melanie Smith, Gayle Starr, Molly Tower, Jennifer Wydra, and David Yagow.

I wish to recognize, once again, two mentors who have influenced my philosophy and direction over the years. One is Geraldine Brain Siks, whose belief that children should be taught *about* drama, *through* drama, led her to distill concepts so they could be taught in the elementary classroom. I am honored that she agreed to write the Introduction to the 2nd Edition of this book. The other is Agnes Haaga, whose conviction that drama is inside everyone led her to develop a leadership style which brings release, joy, and knowledge about self and humankind to the participants. Together these two have opened doors to the joyful discipline of the art of drama. For that I thank them, as do generations of others.

In addition, I thank Coleman A. Jennings for writing the Foreword, Orlin Corey for his patience during the revisions, J. Robert Wills for his continuing support and encouragement, and my new "inspirations," grandchildren Emmett, Emily, Austin, Allison, Megan, and Roselie.

ACKNOWLEDGMENTS

"Fog" from *Chicago Poems,* copyright © 1916 by Holt, Rinehart and Winston, Inc. and renewed 1944 by Carl Sandburg. Reprinted by permission of Harcourt Brace Jovanovich, Inc.

Permission to adapt "The Squire's Bride," from *My Book House,* © The United Educators, Inc.

Permission to adapt "The Wind and Sun," from *The Fables of Aesop,* by Joseph Jacobs, copyright © 1964, MacMillan Co.

"The Stone in the Road" from *Stories to Dramatize* by Winifred Ward. Reprinted with permission from Anchorage Press, copyright © 1952, renewed 1980 and 1981.

"Why Mosquitoes Buzz in People's Ears," adapted by Monica Michell, reprinted with her kind permission.

Permission to adapt "Jack and the Northwind" from *Tarheel Tales* adapted by Tom Behm, copyright © 1976, by Anchorage Press.

"The Birds of Summer" from *Star Tales* by Gretchen Will Mayo. Copyright © 1987 by Gretchen Will Mayo. Reprinted with permission from Walker and Company.

"The Frog Who Wanted to be a Singer," and "Spread the Word: A Storyteller's Rap" by Linda Goss, from *Talk That Talk* edited by Linda Goss and Marian E. Barnes. Copyright © 1989 by Linda Goss and Marian E. Barnes. Reprinted by permission from Simon & Schuster, Inc.

Special appreciation to the following:
  Monica Michell for sharing her expertise about using drama in the museum;
  Charlotte T. Wooldridge for sharing her expertise about using drama with children from special populations;
  The Texas Education Agency for sharing their working documents on the assessment of theatre arts.

CONTENTS

Foreword by Coleman A. Jennings iii

Introduction by Geraldine Brain Siks vi

Preface ix

Acknowledgments xiv

Chapter I: Why? What? How? 1
    Background 2
    Theatre Elements and Concepts 6
    Creative Drama Process 18
    Strategies and Management 22
    Scope and Sequence 27

Chapter II: Grade Four 31
    Cross Reference Guide 33
    Getting Started 34
    Acting
        Movement
            Heavy and Light 37
            Eyes Ahead 39
            Falling Safely 40
            Shake It Up! 42
            Big Beach Ball 44
            Group Objects 45
        Sensory Awareness and Recall
            Listen and Imagine 46
            The Beach 47
            The Attic 48
        Pantomime
            Reaching for a Reason 50
            Sports 51
            Deep Sea Diving 52

Emotional Recall
   Remember a Time When..................................... 54
   It Depends... 55
Voice
   The Lost Kitten.. 56
   The Phone Call... 57
   Leave a Message 58

Playmaking / Playwriting
Pantomime and Dialogue 59
   Tug of War 59
Plot Structure 65
   The Birds of Summer...................................... 65
   Application of Plot...................................... 74
Characterization: Physical Attributes 76
   A Bushel of Thanks 76
Characterization: Objectives 84
   The Wind and the Sun 84
   Application of Character Objectives 88
Characterization: Dialogue 90
   The Stone in the Road.................................... 90
   Application of Character Dialogue 95
Shadow Play and Puppetry 97
   The Strange Visitor..................................... 97
   Why Mosquitoes Buzz in People's Ears 104

Responding and Constructing Meaning
   Applaud!.. 109
   Audience Etiquette...................................... 111
   Jack and the Northwest Wind............................. 113
   Seeing a Play.. 129
   Acting For a Camera 131

Chapter III: Grade Five...................................... 135

Cross Reference Guide 137
Getting Started 138
Acting
Movement
   Mirror Delay and Relay 140
   Concentrate! 141

    Cautiously 142
    Who Are You? 145
    Fire 146
Sensory Awareness and Recall
    Blind Walk 149
    Word Chain 150
    Mouth Watering! 152
    Smoke 153
Pantomime
    Cooperative Pantomime 155
    Pass the Space Substance, Please 157
    Adverb Game 158
Emotional Recall
    The Mood Changes 159
    Expressing Feelings 160
Voice
    "Come Here" 162
    Whisper 163
    Voices and Feelings 165
Playmaking / Playwriting
Pantomime
    The Stooges 166
Plot
    Conflict Caused By People 169
    Conflict Caused By the Environment 171
    Conflict Caused By Oneself 173
    Writing Scenarios 177
Characterization: Attitude
    The Frog Who Wanted To Be a Singer 180
    Getting Up In the Morning 189
    Attachment 191
Puppetry
    The Adventures Of 193
Responding and Constructing Meaning
    The Squire's Bride 197
    Seeing a Play 209
    The Same, But Different 211

Culminating Project
    Swapping Scenarios. 213
        The Scenario 214
        The Critique 216
        The Rewrite. 218
        The Performance. 219

Chapter IV: Grade Six. **223**
Cross Reference Guide 225
Getting Started 226
Acting
    Movement
        Diamonds 228
        Back and Forth 230
        Open and Close 231
        Color 233
    Sensory Awareness and Recall
        How Aware Are We? 237
        Shape Up! 239
        The Cave 240
        Reacting to a Sound 241
    Pantomime
        Where? 243
        Charade Pantomime 244
    Emotional Recall
        Waiting 245
        Something Happens 247
    Voice
        Gibberish. 249
        Timing 250
        Switching Stations. 252
        Storyteller's Rap 253
Playmaking/Playwriting
    Pantomime
        Music Sets the Mood 259
        Halloween 261

Plot

    Plot: Setting 263

    Plot: Time 265

    Who, Where, When 266

    Theme: What It Is Really About 268

Characterization: Speech and Dialogue

    Beyond Words 271

    Different Intentions 273

    Characters and Voices 274

    Move One Chair 277

    Walking With the Characters 279

    Crowds 282

Responding and Constructing Meaning

    The Hammer of Thor 285

    Seeing a Play 296

    Lights, Camera, Action! 299

Culminating Project

    Making Decisions 302

        Line 302

        Color Revisited 305

        Designers 306

        Playwrights 308

        Actors 311

Chapter V: Other Subjects; Other Populations 319

Subject Areas

    English Language Arts 320

    Mathematics 326

    Science 327

    Health 329

    Physical Education 329

    Fine Arts 330

    Social Studies 333

    Other Languages 338

Special Populations
    Children Who Are Academically Gifted 340
    Children With Learning Disabilities. 340
    Children With Physical Disabilities 341
    Children With Behavioral Problems. 343
    Children Who Are Economically Deprived 345

Chapter VI: Assessment 349
Evaluation Strategies. 350
Criteria Checklists. 352

Glossary of Terms 369

Appendices 375
Appendix A: Idea Starters 375
Appendix B: Children's Literature 380
    Anthologies and Collections 380
    Books for Intermediate Grades 383
Appendix C: Additional Resources. 386
    Creative Drama. 386
    Puppetry 389
    Special Populations. 390
    Music 391

Literature and Author Index 393

Chapter I:

WHY? WHAT? HOW?

"Well, I got concentration . . . You have to be right on top of things." (Paul, age 9)

"When I came in I didn't know how to express my feelings very well." (Jan, age 10)

"I learned how it is to be another person." (Susan, age 9)

"You can't be all tight inside. You have to relax." (Erik, age 9)

"You pretend like it is real, that it is really happening. Not that you just pretend, but really make other people see that it is really there." (Kim, age 10)

The comments above were made by children in a fifth grade class after they had participated in a series of theatre arts lessons. They were responding to a question about what they had learned. Obviously, they had learned a lot.

This introductory chapter essentially capsulizes the "why, what, and how" issues of teaching theatre arts in the elementary school. The "why" is addressed in the Background section, which describes the nature of theatre and the values its study brings to elementary school children. The "what" issue receives focus in the section on Theatre Elements and Concepts. Each of three essential elements is described and defined. The "how" issues are discussed in two sections: 1) the Creative Drama Process describes the format used for lessons in this book, which the teacher, in turn, can use to develop other lessons; 2) the Strategies and Management section provides suggestions for setting up a creative environment in which the children and teacher will feel successful. The final section of the chapter returns to the "what" — it is a scope and sequence chart showing the sequential development of concepts from kindergarten through grade six.

WHY STUDY THE THEATRE ARTS?

THE BACKGROUND

Theatre, or drama, is an integral part of the human experience. One has only to recall one's early childhood days, or watch young children at play, to realize that drama is a natural form of expression. One sees children playing house, cowboys, school, secret agents, characters from television — whoever and whatever captures their imagination. Such dramatic play is one of the most important ways children learn. It is a way to experience the world, to try on different roles, to walk in another's footsteps, to see "What it would be like *if* . . ."

Just as dramatic play is integral to each individual's experience, it is also integral to the history of the human species. In prehistoric times, aborigines would gather around the fire to act out the day's hunt, or evoke spirits to assist them in a battle, or petition the gods for rain. The Greeks are known not only for the Olympic games, but also for their plays. People would spend all day, several days in succession, watching play festivals. Throughout the ages, in every culture, one finds evidence of theatre. Today, we commemorate many kinds of events, from inaugurations to football games, with parades and pageantry. Theatre can be found in almost every community, whether it is done by a group of friends, or a community group, or a professional company. Theatre is one way people have found to grapple with, and reflect upon, the problems and the joys of the world.

Values and Goals

There are two major goals for studying theatre arts:

> *to help each child develop his or her potential,*
> *to help each child understand and appreciate the art of theatre.*

Although the two are separated for discussion purposes, the goals of each should constantly reinforce the other.

2

Child Development

Children grow in many ways—physically, mentally, socially, creatively, spiritually. The following remarks suggest ways that participation in the theatre arts helps the child grow and develop.

The theatre arts seek to help children develop an awareness of themselves as *physical beings*. The body and the voice comprise the instrument with which one creates and communicates. Self-confidence develops as children begin to recognize and appreciate their own capabilities, and their ability to communicate.

The theatre arts seek to help children become aware of themselves as *creative beings*. During the creative experience, one becomes so involved in the activity that ideas flow in rapid succession, imagination soars, and relationships are perceived. In drama, suddenly the movement, the words, the total expression are truthful and right. Even if the experience is momentary, one feels at once exhilarated and satisfied.

The theatre arts seek to help children envision themselves as *organizers of experience*. They learn to solve problems and to shape and control what is happening, by using their minds and bodies to give form to the art.

The theatre arts seek to help children appreciate themselves as *reflective beings*, responding thoughtfully to people, situations and the environment. Drama encourages attentive listening and observing, as they learn to discuss and analyze their own experiences and those of others.

The theatre arts seek to help children become aware of themselves as *social beings*. Drama takes place within the framework of a group. In order to create with others, children need to develop a sensitivity toward their classmates which allows mutual trust and respect to build, as they participate in the give and take of improvised drama. The content of drama helps them to empathize with and become more understanding of the feelings and actions of others.

The Art of Theatre

The goal is to help children understand and appreciate the art of drama, which is a story told by means of dialogue and action. There are two levels of understanding involved: an intuitive understanding and an intellectual understanding. Because children come to school fully steeped in play, they have already begun to grasp intuitively the essence of drama. Experience in the theatre arts which is totally involving to the individuals enhances this intuitive understanding. As they mature, children also like to understand intellectually what is happening. Theatre to them is a meaningful game in which knowing more about the rules makes the game more fun to play. This knowledge also gives them more freedom to manipulate the design dramatic structure for themselves. They learn to function as playwrights, actors, designers, audience, and as part of a cooperative unit.

Students function as playwrights. They learn about decisions playwrights have to make concerning

- characters' action and dialogue
- plot structure
- theme
- setting
- time

Students function as actors. They learn about decisions actors have to make concerning

- a character's physical attributes, objectives, feelings
- use of the body
- use of the voice

Students function as designers. They learn about decisions designers have to make concerning the use of line, shape, color, texture in

- set design
- costume design
- lighting design

Students function as audience members. They learn to
- become attentive observers and listeners
- appreciate theatrical events
- use appropriate audience etiquette
- evaluate and make aesthetic judgments

Students function as a cooperative unit. They learn to
- contribute ideas
- respect the contribution of others
- work as a team to solve problems

If a child consistently develops a character, knowing who, what, where, and why about the character, if he or she consistently creates plots with beginning, middle, climax, and end, if he or she can either watch or participate in a scene and state its strengths and weaknesses, both in acting and plot development, one can be reasonably certain the child has an intellectual understanding of theatre.

To summarize, the study of theatre arts is really the study of life. The child learns more about himself or herself, more about other people, through acting out and reflecting upon human experiences.

WHAT IS MEANT BY THEATRE ARTS IN THE ELEMENTARY SCHOOL?

THEATRE ELEMENTS AND CONCEPTS

The focus of studying theatre arts in the elementary grades is not to train actors, but rather to nurture each child's creative and expressive potential as he or she learns about the art of theatre.

There are three broad categories, which are called "essential elements" in this book:

1) *Acting: Expressive use of the body and voice;*
2) *Playmaking/playwriting: Collaborative improvisations;*
3) *Responding and constructing meaning: Development of aesthetic sensibilities.*

Each of these elements is an important component of what many people call "creative drama." Creative drama was defined some years ago by the Children's Theatre Association of America as "an improvisational, non-exhibitional, process-centered form of theatre in which participants are guided by a leader to imagine, enact, and reflect upon human experiences."* Put another way, the teacher helps the children to think, to imagine, and to clarify their ideas, so they can act them out, using their own words and movement to express what they want to communicate—not for an audience, but for themselves and their classmates.

Although the term "creative drama" is still used, some people have preferred to refer simply to "drama" for children and youth—or "theatre," or "improvisation." **Intentionality** may be a key difference. For example, it is the **intention** of this book to help teach children about the art of theatre, to help them develop knowledge and skills which are inherent in the art form. The theatre standards set forth in the document, *National Standards for Arts Education,* published in 1994, are very **intentional** about what

---

*"Terminology for Drama/Theatre With and For Children: A Redefinition." *Children's Theatre Review* 28 (Winter, 1978): 10–11

The American Alliance for Theatre & Education is now the name of the national professional association for the field of theatre for children and youth.

students should know and be able to do. The skills are not a by-product of other subject areas or child development. They are, rather, taught with the **intention** of helping students reach certain levels of achievement.

Essential Element One
Acting: Expressive Use of the Body and Voice

Each person uses an "instrument" to communicate and express ideas. This "instrument," quite simply, is limited to one's body and voice. In order to increase expressive skills, the instrument needs to be "tuned" and the player needs to understand the capabilities of the instrument. The following is a brief description of those components, or concepts, which lead to increased expressive skills. The italicized words are concepts for which there are specific activities suggested in Chapters Two, Three and Four.

Movement activities are very important. They serve to free the child's energy and emotions; they allow the child to become aware of the workings of the body and to control them; they increase the ability to communicate; they help to focus the child's imagination. Some of the movement activities in this book are rhythmic, which involves moving and expressing according to a particular rhythmic pattern. Other movement activities involve free exploration of movement elements, or using movement to depict human or non-human roles, or using movement to communicate abstract concepts, such as fire, wind, power, love.

The body acts and responds because of the senses. *Sensory awareness* activities attempt to sharpen perception and appreciation of how the senses help us to know and enjoy the world. *Sensory recall* activities help the children to remember the way things feel, look, sound, smell and taste, and to recreate those sensations even when they are present only in the imagination, not physically.

Expressive use of the body and voice involves movement, the senses, and feelings. Feelings, or emotions, are the core of being human, and the core of drama. Joy, sadness, fear, melancholy, boredom, contentment only begin a list of emotions that could continue for pages. Children need to recognize and begin to understand their emotions and to realize that feelings are part of what it means to be human. Activities in *emotional recall* help children understand that they are not alone in experiencing certain feelings, and help them empathize with others.

Body movement, the use of the senses, and emotional recall are necessary for pantomime. *Pantomime* is the use of movement and gesture to express ideas and feelings. It is communication through action, not words. Pantomime, sometimes referred to as "body language," is an important building block of speech. It precedes speech in development, but also extends and reinforces speech.

Practice in speaking helps children become fluent in verbal communication, as well as promoting clear articulation and voice control. Children use their *voices* as they learn to express themselves by what they say and how they say it. Pitch, volume, intensity, rate of speed are all part of vocal communication.

Essential Element Two
Playmaking/Playwriting: Collaborative Improvisations

When one gives form or stucture to an idea to be enacted, it is called "playmaking" or "playwriting." Playwriting generally refers to a formalized script, which is set forth in a particular way. Playmaking is a more informal approach. Playmaking is what children do when they decide who the characters are and what the characters will be doing, but they don't necessarily write it down. In this book, both playmaking and playwriting involve collaboration among the students. Together they plan and then enact their plan in an improvised dramatization based either on a piece of literature, or on an original story developed by the students.

Characterization involves more than just knowing who the characters are—more, for instance, than knowing that the character is a bank teller, a robber, or a policeman. It involves imagining the *physical attributes* of the character. Is the character big, small, muscular, frail? Does the character move with big, heavy, slow steps? Light, quick, bouncy steps? Is the character wearing a costume that might affect the movement, like a king's robe or an elegant ball gown or a space suit? Characterization also involves knowing the *objective* of the character. That is, what does the character want to do— to surprise someone, to hide, to scare, to persuade, to apologize, to tease . . .? Knowing the objective of a character often helps determine how the character moves. For example, if the objective of a scuba diver is to explore a sunken ship, the diver will move quite differently than if the objective is to rescue a fellow diver from a shark. *Attitude* is another aspect of characterization which affects what the character does and how he or she does it. For example, imagine that the objective is "to hide." If the character is frightened, he or she will show that emotion while trying to find a hiding place. If the character is mischievous, he or she will act quite differently while finding a hiding place. Another aspect of characterization is the way a character *speaks*. For example, in the story of "Hansel and Gretel," how would the witch's voice be different from Gretel's? How might the voice of a bully be different from the voice of someone who is very timid? How something is said reveals as much about a character as the actual words that are spoken.

There are several concepts which will help the children develop original stories, or *plots*. Understanding plot development, of course, is as necessary for composition and appreciation of literature as it is for theatre arts. The analysis of plot *structure* can be very complex, but the elementary level lessons in this book limit that analysis to "beginning, middle, climax and end." Most plots are centered around a *conflict* of some sort. Specific activities help the children understand the basic causes of conflict — person vs. person, person vs. environment, person vs. self. The plot structure and conflict usually reveal an underlying message of some sort, or *theme*. Recognizing themes in literature and choosing themes to write about or improvise around help students understand the enduring appeal of folk and classic dramatic literature. Where a story takes place, the *setting*, is also important to plot development. The possibilities for action in a supermarket are quite different than they would be in a cave, or on the moon, or at the beach. The *time* of a story can be important as well. Time can refer to a time in history — present day, the Civil War, the year 2086 A.D. — or a time of day, such as three o'clock in the morning. In the latter example, a doorbell ringing in the middle of the night would probably be reacted to in quite a different way than a doorbell in the middle of the afternoon.

All of the playmaking/playwriting activities involve improvisation, whether the children are playing the characters or whether they are using *puppets* to play the characters. Children enjoy puppets, and sometimes those children who are inhibited at first, find it easier to participate if they have a puppet to "hide behind." In Chapters Two and Three, there are instructions for making simple hand and shadow puppets. The making of the puppets, however, is only the first step. Bringing them alive through movement and voice is the most important part of using puppets in a theatre arts activity.

Essential Element Three
Responding and Constructing Meaning:
Development of Aesthetic Sensibilities

The intent of the first two essential elements is to guide students to express their understanding of the world by developing their "personal voice" through improvisations. They study the skills of the actor and the playwright by actively engaging in the creative processes each of these roles entails. In the third essential element, students apply the knowledge they have learned by responding to and analyzing the work of others. They observe, they listen, they reflect, they evaluate. They attempt to construct meaning for themselves and for society from the performance they have witnessed. By this means they are developing their aesthetic sensibilities. The role they are taking is that of the audience.

The term "audience" is used in two different contexts—the classroom and the theatre. When doing drama in the classroom, occasionally some children will watch, while others act out an idea or a scene. Those watching are the audience. It is as important to be a good audience member in the classroom as it is when attending a performance at a theatre. The response of the audience is necessary for the completion of the theatrical event.

Just as children become better appreciators of art by seeing great works of art, so children must see plays, preferably in a theatre, to understand better the art of theatre. Theatre arts concepts are reinforced as the children see actors use their bodies and voices to create characters, much like the work the children have been doing in their own class. There is an excitement, a sense of "magic," that occurs in the theatre, when the actors are right there with the audience, that is quite different from watching television or going to a movie. Students are encouraged to see as many live theatre performances as possible.

Theatre Conventions

There are certain theatre conventions which adults take for granted. Students, however, should know about them before attending a theatrical event. For instance, before a performance the lights in the lobby may blink off and on to tell the audience to take their seats because the performance will soon begin. Then, when the audience lights dim in the theatre and go out, the performance is about to begin. If a curtain is used in the performance, when it goes up, or opens, the performance has begun. (The curtain going down, or closing, indicates the end of an act or the performance.) Sometimes, at the end of a scene or an act, all the lights will be turned off—a moment called a "blackout." After a performance is over, the actors come back on stage, in bright light, to bow while the audience applauds—called a "curtain call." Then the house lights come on and people leave.

Audience Etiquette

When students know what to expect, they usually know how to behave. There is a specific lesson in Chapter Two dealing with audience etiquette. It is a good lesson for each grade to review before attending a performance. Proper behavior in the theatre is necessary for two reasons. Most obvious is the fact that one should be considerate of other members of the audience who want to see and hear what is happening on stage. Less obvious may be the actors' relationship with the audience, which is what separates live theatre from film and television. The theatre experience is only complete when there is an audience. The audience members actually help the actors when they listen attentively, laugh at appropriate times, or even gasp when something unexpected happens. Generally, the better and more attentive the audience is, the better the performance.

Similarities and differences in television, film, and live theatre

Drama was defined earlier as a story told by means of dialogue and action. That definition is accurate for film and television, as well as live theatre. In fact, the concepts described before with regard to the expressive use of body and voice, and creative drama are true for film and television, too. There are, however, a number of differences.

The most apparent difference, of course, is the actual presence of actors in a live theatre performance. Besides the special relationship between the actors and the audience, there are other differences, such as the setting, the acting, the time of action, special effects, camera angles, and the position of the audience. While there are specific lessons dealing with those differences in the following chapters, a brief overview follows here.

Because the camera is so mobile, the *setting* of the stories can be shown realistically and in great detail in films and television. (References to "theatre" will refer to live theatre, rather than movie theatres.) In the theatre, the setting is limited to what can be represented on the stage, by sets, set pieces (such as furniture), and lighting. Furthermore, on stage the set pieces must be placed so that the actors can move around easily and so that the audience can see their faces at all times; whereas for film, scenes can be shot showing the exact time of day, weather and other environmental conditions. In the theatre, audience members are required to use their imaginations to create the reality of the setting in their minds, based on the "clues" given by the sets and lights.

The *time* the action takes place can also be shown more realistically in films. For example, an actual winter snowstorm can be filmed, but only referred to or indicated on the stage. "Flashbacks," or scenes that are remembered by certain characters, can be shown immediately and realistically on film. In the theatre, flashbacks are possible, but may be more difficult for the audience to follow. Because the camera not only can move, but can start and stop, the illusion of time passing can be realistically portrayed. For example, a character may be fixing breakfast in a bathrobe in one scene, and, in less than an instant, the film can show her walking down the street with briefcase in hand. In the theatre, the costume and set changes would take actual performance time. With film, the actors can change clothes, adjust makeup and go to a different location before the camera starts rolling again. The film audience is not consciously aware of all the adjustments that have to be made. They simply accept the "fact" that the time of the story has changed.

There are some differences in *acting* for the theatre and for films, too. The basic difference has to do with the "size" of the action. Because the camera can move so close to the actor, a mere twitch of the eyebrow can be filmed and the audience will see it. Such a twitch would be lost in the theatre, because the audience is too far away to see such subtle action. Gestures and movements must be very realistic for film, or the character will not seem believable. Depending on the size of the theatre and the position of the audience, the stage actor chooses gestures carefully so they can be seen by all. The gestures must seem realistic to the audience, but if they were seen closely, they might be somewhat exaggerated. The stage actor must also move so that the audience can see at least part of her or his face most of the time. Rarely, for instance, would the actor stand with the back to the audience while talking to another character. The voice is used differently, too, depending upon whether one is acting for the stage or film. A character can whisper on film and the audience will understand every word, because the microphone is very close. On stage, such a whisper would be inaudible; the actor would have to use a "stage whisper," which is quite loud and includes exaggerating the consonants. The stage actor learns how to project his or her voice, so that it can be heard in the very back row and yet not seem to be shouting. The film actor, however, can and must speak in a normal voice.

Special effects are used for both theatre and film, but there are limitations to special effects in theatre—most of which have to do with danger, and the illusions which can be created with the camera. One readily accepts car chases, crashes, fires and fights as being "true" on film, because they appear so realistic. What the film audience doesn't see, of course, is all the very detailed planning that goes on to create these effects; nor do they see the special safety suits and the ring of people standing by to extinguish a fire, for example, immediately after the stunt. The audience isn't aware that the camera stops after the stunt and then starts again, usually on a different scene. Nor is the audience aware that the battleship they see in a film, may, in fact, be merely a twenty inch replica floating in a tub with a wave making machine. Obviously these kinds of effects are not possible in the theatre. Certainly there are special effects possible in the theatre, such as fog, explosions, storms, and many others, but the reality of stage effects depends a lot on the willingness of the audience to accept the illusion and imagine the details.

The eye of the camera really becomes the eye of the film audience. *Camera angles* allow the audience to see minute details and various points of view. One can see, for example, a character at a distance walking down the street, and then see the character in a close-up in which only the face fills the entire screen. The camera "chooses" what the audience will see, whether it is a crowd, two people, one person, or only hands gesturing.

The *position of the audience* is related to camera angles, with regard to films. The audience can "move around," because the camera moves around, even though the audience is seated in one place during the whole time. In the theatre, such seeming movement is not possible. The actors move, the audience doesn't. There are a number of audience seating arrangements in theatres. Sometimes the stage is in the middle, with the audience all around. Sometimes, the audience is seated on three sides of the stage. Sometimes, and most commonly, the audience is seated in front of the stage. In the latter, it seems as if the audience is looking through the fourth wall of whatever setting is on stage.

On an audience commitment continuum, television requires the least amount of commitment, because the viewer can switch channels at will. Some viewers even keep track of two programs at once, by switching channels frequently. It is possible to walk around, eat, stretch, and so on during the program. Films in movie theatres require more audience commitment. The viewer physically goes to the movie theatre and pays money to see the film. Talking during the film, while inconsiderate of the rest of the audience, will not affect the performances of the actors. In most cases, television and film dramas require very little imagination from the audience, because everything is presented so realistically. Live theatre requires the greatest amount of audience commitment. Not only does the audience physically go to the theatre and pay money to see the performance, but they are necessary participants in the performance. The theatre audience says, in effect, "Yes, I'm willing to believe the people are in front of a fireplace," even though it is obvious that they are looking at lights and cellophane flames. The theatre audience uses imagination and concentration to help the actors create the play. They respond, not by talking, but by laughing and applauding at appropriate times. The actors know the audience is there. Together, they create the theatre experience. Together, they create the magic of belief.

Aesthetic judgments

By participating in theatre art activities and attending live theatre performances, students learn how to evaluate and make informed aesthetic judgments. In other words, they learn to tell *why* they liked a particular play or performance, or why they did not like it. They learn how to analyze the behavior of various characters. They learn how to analyze plot, recognize conflicts, predict resolutions and make suggestions for alternative courses of action.

Obviously, different schools will attend different performances, and performances will vary from year to year. In order to provide a concrete model to analyze and evaluate, a play script has been included in this book, for each grade. The students can act out the play as simply or elaborately as they wish, or they can just read the play outloud and discuss it according to the lesson. The model can then be applied to whatever performances are attended. The focus for analysis in each grade is tied into the character and plot concepts they have been learning about in the first two essential elements. For example, in Chapter Two, the students are learning about the physical attributes of characterization and character objectives. When they analyze characters after seeing a play, they will focus on those same concepts.

Other Theatre Elements

The three essential elements described above are those without which there would be no theatre. Theatre needs

1) a playwright who develops an idea or story, which involves action;

2) actors, who perform the action;

3) the audience members, who watch and respond to the action.

There are, however, other elements which are important to the theatrical event: designing, directing, and researching are three. While these three do not receive primary focus in this curriculum, they are embedded in the lessons. For example, when students are dramatizing a story or an idea, they will arrange the classroom setting to indicate specific locales, they decide who will play each character, when each enters the scene, and so on—even though the concept for the lesson is not specifically labeled "designing" or "directing." A brief description of the designing, directing, and researching elements follows.

Designing: Envisioning and arranging the environment

When reading or listening to a story, or when making up an original story, one gets a picture in one's mind about what the various settings may be like, what kind of day (or night) it is, what the characters are wearing, the sounds that may be particular to a given place, and the mood of the piece. All of these are part of the environment of the story.

Designers for the theatre envision the environment and make choices about how they can communicate that environment to an audience in a way that will contribute to, or enhance, the meaning of the play. Their choices are visual—with regard to the set, costumes, and lights—and aural—with regard to sound effects and/or music.

In the primary grades children are encouraged to imagine the environment of stories they dramatize. They may even arrange furniture and other objects to suggest a particular setting. Or they may use fabric or accessories to suggest the costumes of certain characters.

In the intermediate grades, lessons involve envisioning settings and costumes for particular dramatizations, making models and/or arranging the playing space and costumes appropriately. Students are also encouraged to attend to the visual and aural aspects of plays they see and to analyze how those aspects add to, or detract from, the meaning of the play under scrutiny.

Directing: Planning classroom improvisations

Directors are those who collaborate with designers and actors to develop aesthetically unified production concepts for informal and formal theatre, film and television productions. Even children in the primary grades can collaboratively plan and rehearse improvisations and demonstrate various ways of staging classroom dramatizations. As they progress, children enjoy leading small groups in planning visual and aural elements. They develop social, group, and consensus skills as they plan and rehearse improvised and scripted scenes to be presented to an audience of their peers.

Researching: Finding information to support classroom dramatizations

In the theatre, there is frequently a person called a "dramaturg." The dramaturg is one who researches cultural and historical information to assist the actors, the playwright, the director and designers in making appropriate artistic choices. Young children who are dramatizing a story set in a different country, or in a different time period, can find visual materials in the library to help make their dramatizations more accurate. As their reading and library skills develop, they can find books, articles and videotapes which will greatly enhance their understanding of other times and places. Such understanding will enhance the decisions they make when, for example, they develop an improvisation about the Civil War, or the Bill of Rights, or when they dramatize a piece of literature from Africa or Mexico. Teachers using this curriculum are encouraged to help their students apply research to support their dramatizations whenever possible.

In working with the lessons, teachers will probably begin to pick and choose various activities which can be combined effectively for a particular class. The following discussion of the creative drama process is intended to help teachers plan their own lessons, in addition to using those in the book.

HOW DO THE THEATRE ARTS WORK
IN THE CLASSROOM?

CREATIVE DRAMA PROCESS

The lessons in Chapters Two, Three, and Four of this book follow a simple format, known as the creative drama process. Teachers will find the process familiar because it is similar to that used to teach almost all subjects. For example, in other subjects, material is generally presented in some way, then directions are given so the students can apply the concepts, and that application is followed up by some kind of evaluation of what they did. The parts of the creative drama process include: introduce, present, plan, act, and reflect/evaluate. The difference is primarily in the labeling of some of the parts. The function of each part is briefly described below. The application of the process is described in detail in the lessons themselves.

I. Introduce

The introduction provides the motivation for the material which is used as the basis for dramatization. The purpose is to engage the attention of the students and to help them to relate their own experiences to the material. Sometimes this is accomplished by asking the children questions about their own experiences, sometimes by combining discussion with action of some sort which will help them identify with the material.

II. Present

If the material for dramatization is a story, it is best presented by telling, not reading. Telling a story allows for eye contact with the students, and makes the story seem more real to them. Before telling the story, or poem, the teacher might want to ask them to listen for something particular. For example, "While you listen to this story, see if you can tell which character felt just as afraid as you have before." Or, "Listen to see how Juan solved his problem."

If the dramatization is based on students' original stories, the Introduction usually flows right into the Plan for action, which follows.

III. Plan

A. Plan based on a story or poem

After the story, the teacher and students make a plan for acting out a portion of the story. The teacher asks questions. The questions may focus on just one character—Pandora in "Pandora's Box," for instance. Depending on the objective of the lesson, questions may refer to such concepts as the attitude of the character or how the character talks. There should always be questions about how the character feels in a certain situation. For example, "How did Pandora feel after she opened the box? How would *you* have felt?" Feelings connect people to other people, causing empathy, whether the people are fictional or real.

Sometimes there are fights or physical conflicts in the story which teachers are understandably leary about acting out. One constant rule is "No Touching!" This rule presents an intriguing challenge to students when there is a scene with obvious physical contact. A few questions from the teacher will help. For example, "How can we make it seem as if the Evils are attacking Pandora without actually touching her?" Ask a couple of students to demonstrate their ideas.

The teacher often decides beforehand how many students will act at any given time. Usually all the students want to play the main characters, so it is a good idea to set up a situation where they can all have that experience. Perhaps all the children can try out a particular character simultaneously, or half the class can play at one time. For example, all could play Pandora just before and after she opens the box. As Pandora, they can all react to imaginary Evils that fly out of the box. Then, later, the roles may be divided among the students for the playing of a scene or the whole story.

The teacher also needs to decide what to do during the playing. There are three possibilities. One is to "*sidecoach*." That is, the teacher gives suggestions from the side, while the students pantomime. They listen and respond appropriately without stopping their action. (There are many side-coaching suggestions in this book.) A second possibility is to *play a role*, to help the children keep the action going. For example, the teacher could play the "captain," or a companion to the main character. Choose a role that has built-in authority to it, so questions can be asked which spur their action while they play. Needless to say, students love it when the teacher plays, too. (Examples for this kind of guidance are given in the lessons.) The third possibility is to stand on the side and simply be an *appreciative audience*.

B. Plan based on original ideas

Sometimes, the students will be working in groups to develop their own scenes. On these occasions, the teacher goes around to each group to help them, if necessary. They need to decide *who* they are, *where* they are, and *what* they are doing. They also need to decide how the scene begins and how it will end. (Specific directions are given in the lessons.) After they have their ideas, they should try playing the scene.

Sometimes, the whole class will be working on one idea. For example, they are all deepsea divers. The teacher asks questions to help them visualize the scene and the action: Why are you making this particular dive? What might you find? What dangers must you be aware of? What equipment do you need? How will you communicate with your diving partner? In this particular situation, the teacher might choose to be the captain of the diving boat who gives them instructions, signals them about approaching danger, tells them when to return to the boat, and so on.

IV. Act

After planning, the students are ready to put the plan into action. They should all get into their places and be very quiet. When they are quiet, the teacher gives the signal to begin. "Curtain" is a word used by many to signal the beginning and ending of the action.

V. Reflect/Evaluate

After the action, the children are generally eager to talk about their experience. The purpose for such follow-up discussion is twofold: to help the children make connections between the art of drama and life; and to help them recognize and appreciate the aesthetics of drama by observing closely, listening attentively, and making judgments.

The direction of the discussion varies depending on the content of the lesson and sometimes on the age of the children. Sometimes the material lends itself to *reflective questions*, such as "What did you have to do to be successful in the game we just played?" Or, "Discuss other situations in which a person needs to observe what is going on very closely." Or, "How were events in this story similar to events in your own life?"

Sometimes the objective of the lesson is best reinforced by *evaluative questions*. For example, if the objective was to pantomime very clearly, the teacher might ask, "How could you tell that this diver found a very heavy treasure chest?" Or, "What did Pandora do that let you know she was curious?" The students may also have suggestions about how they could make the scene better. Questions to that effect are appropriate. For example, "How could we improve the scene between the shark and the divers to make it seem more exciting?" As the children's experiences in drama activities increase, their evaluative comments will show a more detailed and deeper understanding of the art form.

VI. Plan and Replay

Repeat the process, focusing on another character, or another part of the story, or replaying the first scene to strengthen it. This cycle can be repeated as many times as the teacher and class wish.

Each lesson ends with a brief discussion and reinforcement of the objective.

STRATEGIES AND MANAGEMENT

The key to success in theatre arts activities lies in two areas: *concentration* and *imagination*. The extent to which children concentrate and imagine determines the effectiveness of a particular activity. In many ways, the two are intertwined. Using the imagination involves getting an image, or picture, in one's mind. In order to get that picture, one needs to concentrate, to focus on a particular idea. That kind of focus is necessary, or the child will not know what to do. His or her actions will be vague and may also be disruptive to the rest of the group. Fortunately, there are strategies and management considerations which can greatly assist in achieving success. Topics to be considered include selection of material, space, time, atmosphere, warm-ups, control, visualization, questions, grouping, cool-downs, and sharing with an audience.

Selection of material

The lessons in this book have been effective with many classes. However, you, the classroom teacher, know your students best. And if you don't think a particular lesson would interest your class—don't use it! There is a wealth of material to draw from, however, and almost any lesson can be successfully adapted to different materials.

If the lessons written for your grade seem either too simple or too advanced for your particular class, feel free to use lessons from other grades. Repetition is no problem. In fact, look at the kinds of characters and games children play on their own—they enjoy playing the same thing over and over! Furthermore, in drama, they continue to learn each time they play something.

Space

Some activities can be done without any changes in the usual classroom arrangement. However, some may require more space for the students to work. It may be that you can move furniture to one side to create an open space. Or, perhaps, there is a different room in your building which you can use. Sometimes lunchroom tables and chairs can be moved aside. Or there may be a stage, or a multi-purpose room. One of the hardest spaces to work in is the gymnasium. First, the acoustics are usually such that it is difficult to talk and to hear; second, it is a place where the children are accustomed to making a lot of noise, so discipline can be a problem; third, it is usually too big and the students find it difficult to stay within certain boundaries which are necessary for communication and control.

Time

Your concern with time involves the length of a single drama lessons, and the time of day you do it. There is no set length—some activities may take ten minutes, some may take thirty minutes, or even longer. You may want to combine some of the shorter activities. For example, you could use one rhythmic movement activity and one sensory awareness activity during the same session.

The time of day in which creative drama happens is more important. Students need to be alert and concentrating in order to do creative work. Lessons that are done when students are tired and irritable will only be frustrating to them and to you. Or, if they are already "higher than kites," you will have a difficult time helping them concentrate. (A movement activity in that instance, however, might help release energy and provide focus. See the description of "warm-ups" in this chapter.) The point is to choose a time when the students are most apt to produce creative and concentrated work.

Atmosphere

The atmosphere in the classroom needs to be very supportive and encouraging for the children. You are trying to bring out their most imaginative and creative ideas. They need to trust you and their classmates to be receptive to their ideas. In fact, there are really no "right" or "wrong" answers to questions—as long as they are thoughtful and honestly intended. If you find that some children give "silly" answers, they are either not concentrating or they are trying to get attention, and you need to deal with that either by asking them to rethink their response, or ignoring them. A warning must be added here however: What may seem "silly" to you, may not seem so to the student at all. When you respond seriously, respecting what they

23

have to offer, the students will soon learn to produce their best. You will also find the students modeling your behavior—appreciating what others do and the fact that each person has unique things to offer. "Put-downs" and sarcastic remarks from the children are unacceptable in a creative climate. Drama can be a big confidence builder, and frequently children who have trouble in other subjects will feel better about themselves when they participate in drama.

Warm-ups

Recognizing that elementary students have an abundance of energy, you may want to begin each drama session with a warm-up. A warm-up is usually a movement activity that releases their energy, works their imagination, and prepares them to concentrate. The rhythmic movement and interpretive movement activities in this book can be used as warm-ups. (Remember, repetition is perfectly fine.)

Control

Each person has his or her own tolerance level for noise. There will be some noise during drama activities—during the planning and acting stages, especially. However, there is a difference between acceptable and unacceptable noise. Acceptable noise is when the students are really involved in the task at hand and ideas are flowing rapidly. Unacceptable noise is when they are "goofing off." Even acceptable noise may rise beyond your tolerance limits and the children will need to be reminded to lower the decibels.

A "control instrument" can be enormously effective for getting the students' attention. A drum, a tambourine, a cymbal, a triangle are all possibilities—better than using your voice to shout above their noise. The students will quickly learn to "freeze" when you strike the instrument, ready to listen for directions. The first lesson for each grade, called *Getting Started*, suggests introducing such a control device. The important thing is to use it consistently, and insist that they respond to it before continuing.

The role you play can also help with control, as was suggested earlier in the discussion about planning the action. For example, you, as the "king of the forest," could very logically demand that all your subjects be quiet and listen to the royal commands. Because you do it in character, the students will respond appropriately.

Sidecoaching can also help with control in that students must listen to you while they are acting, incorporating suggestions you offer. Sidecoaching helps them focus their attention.

Another perfectly acceptable strategy to use when the children's behavior is unacceptable is simply to call a halt to the action. Discuss the problem and ask for suggestions and recommitment. Then try the activity again. If the earlier behavior continues, discontinue the drama for that day.

Visualization

Never let the students act unless they have a clear idea of what they are going to do, or you will invite confusion and chaos. One technique is to ask them to close their eyes and imagine themselves going through a particular action—you may even want to sidecoach while their eyes are closed. Sometimes the lessons suggest the use of music. If so, play the music and ask them to imagine the action while it is playing. Another technique is to ask them to raise a finger when they have a clear idea of what they plan to do, or sit down, or give some other observable signal.

Questions

The questioning technique may be the most important consideration of all. The right question at the right time will yield the most thoughtful responses from the students. Questions which are probing generally begin with "why," "how," "where," "what," and "when." These are in contrast to superficial questions which elicit "yes" or "no" responses. The rule of thumb is never to ask a question which might elicit a "no" response, when you *want* to hear a "yes" response. For example, "Do you all want to act out the deep sea divers?" You can rest assured that someone will say "No," whether it is meant or not!

Grouping

Students need to learn how to work in groups and how to share with one another. Working in a group is a skill that develops gradually. It is usually best to begin with dividing them into pairs, and then work up to groups of three, four and even five.

They also need to learn to work with classmates who are not their "best friends." There are numerous ways of dividing them into working groups. One, of course, is to count off, with all the "one's" working together, the "two's," and so on. Another is to group them by the first letter of their names—all those whose names begin with A, B or C work together. Or group them by shirt colors, or by seat positions, or by those who have a younger brother, an older sister. The possibilities are vast.

Cool-downs

If and when you find the students highly excited after a drama lesson, use a "cool-down" activity to help them relax and prepare them for the next classroom activity. You might play some relaxing music and have them sit down, or lie down and "dream" to the music. You might have them imagine they are melting ice cream cones, or water evaporating, or a cloud moving slowing in the sky, or a raindrop sinking into the earth, or a puppet with no one holding the strings, or a cat sleeping in the sun. The children may even come up with some relaxing images themselves, if you ask.

Sharing with an audience

After students have had many experiences creating drama, some or all of them may wish to share a particular activity with groups outside their own classroom. They may want to share with another class on their own grade level, or older students may want to share with a younger class. When a class has particularly enjoyed dramatizing a certain story—either from a piece of literature or from an original idea—they may want to refine it and strengthen it by rehearsing many times. They may want to videotape rehearsals, so they can see themselves and evaluate what they are doing. Knowing they are going to perform for an audience often provides great incentive to concentrate and prepare thoroughly.

While it is possible for children to use a prepared script, usually the characterization and action turn out to be very stilted and non-creative at the elementary age. If they do work from a script, the script should be approached much like a story is approached. In other words, the script can be read once or twice, the characters discussed, and then portions of the plot can be improvised by the children, before they put the whole thing together. They use their own words, rather than strictly adhering to the script. The script provides the plot structure, just as a story does.

The project can be as simple or elaborate as the teacher and class wish. The entire class may want to be involved in the project in some way. Some might want to gather props together, some may want to experiment with simple lighting, some may want to create simple costumes, some may want to work on sound effects. Such preparations are excellent for building group cooperation skills.

SCOPE AND SEQUENCE

The following pages show the scope and sequence of the concepts as they develop from kindergarten through grade six. Although this volume deals only with grades four through six, teachers may wish to see how the concepts have progressed from the primary grades. The arrows on the chart indicate that a particular concept is continued in the next grade.

THEATRE ARTS
Scope and Sequence—Elementary Grades

Essential Elements	Kindergarten	Grade One	Grade Two	Grade Three
Acting: Expressive use of the body and voice	Develop body awareness and spatial perception using · *movement* ————————————————→ · *pantomime* ————————————————→ · *voice* ————————————————————→ 　　　　　　　　　 · *sensory awareness* —————————→			· *sensory recall* · *emotional recall*
Playmaking/ Playwriting: Collaborative improvisations	Dramatize literary selections using · *pantomime* ————————————————————→	· *puppetry*	· *shadow play* ——————→ · *dialogue* ————————→	
Responding and Constructing Meaning: Development of aesthetic sensibilities				View theatrical events emphasizing · *player-audience relationship* · *audience etiquette*

THEATRE ARTS
Scope and Sequence—Elementary Grades

Grade Four	Grade Five	Grade Six
Develop body awareness and spatial perception using · *movement* ⟶ · *pantomime* ⟶ · *voice* ⟶ · *sensory awareness and recall* ⟶ · *emotional recall*	· *emotional recall in character* ⟶	

Dramatize literary selections using
· *pantomime* ⟶
· *plot structure*
 	
· *characterization* emphasizing
  · *physical attributes*
  · *character objectives*
  · *dialogue*
 	
· *puppetry* ⟶
· *shadow play*
	Dramatize original stories using
	
	· *conflict*
	
	· *scenarios*
	· *characterization* emphasizing
	  · *attitude revealed in behavior*
		⟶
		· *setting*
		· *time*
		⟶
		· *characterization* emphasizing
		  · *speech revealing character*

View theatrical events emphasizing · *player-audience relationship* · *audience etiquette* · *analysis of physical attributes and character objectives* · *recognition of dramatic conflicts* · *prediction of plot resolution* ⟶ Compare television, film and live theatre emphasizing · *setting* · *acting*	· *analysis of character's attitude revealed in behavior* · *recognition of kind of conflict* ⟶ · *evaluation and aesthetic judgments* ⟶ · *time of action* · *special effects*	· *analysis of how speech reveals character* ⟶ ⟶ · *camera angles* · *position of audience*

Chapter II:
GRADE FOUR

Fourth graders who have been participating in the theatre arts curriculum have had experiences in *movement, sensory awareness, emotional recall, pantomime, imitation of sounds and creation of simple dialogue*. Those expressive skills are applied and reinforced in the fourth grade. The more abstract concept of *interpretive movement* will be added this year. And there will be greater emphasis on creating *original dialogue*.

In creative drama, in addition to using pantomime and puppetry, children will use *improvisation* to learn about *plot structure*, and they will begin to learn about *characterization*, by focusing on the *physical attributes* and the *objective* of a character. They will also engage in writing dialogue for characters.

Lessons are included which will assist in the children's aesthetic growth. When they *view a theatre performance* they will have the opportunity to demonstrate their understanding of *audience etiquette* and the *player-audience relationship*. They will also learn how to observe some of the concepts they worked on in the playmaking/playwriting lessons, such as the *physical attributes* and *objectives of characters* in a play. Their experiences will also help them recognize *dramatic conflicts*. A play script is included as a *model for analysis*.

The fourth grade lessons also include activities which will help the children recognize *similarities and differences among television, film, and live theatre*, with particular emphasis on the *setting* and the *acting*.

In the event that a class has not had prior experience in classroom drama, the Cross Reference Guide included here provides a ready access to concepts and page numbers. Classes may benefit from activities described in the third grade before they work on the activities for the fourth grade. In any case, the teacher may wish to review earlier lessons. (The third grade activities are in Volume One.)

On the other hand, a given class may demonstrate considerable skill in a certain concept and benefit from deepening their understanding by participating in activities from Grade Five. Children enjoy repeating theatre arts activities, so "borrowing" from another grade level is perfectly acceptable. Repeating activities within the grade level is also acceptable, and, in fact, desirable, because students become more proficient with repetition. Refer to the Scope and Sequence, pages 28–29, to see when concepts are introduced.

The following on-going personal and interpersonal behaviors may be set up in a chart form. Students should evaluate themselves periodically on how well they are doing. The student's self-assessment can be compared with the teacher's assessment of the behaviors.

1. *I follow class direction.*
2. *I cooperate with others.*
3. *I show respect for others by being a good listener.*
4. *I respond to the ideas of others.*
5. *I respect the space of other students.*
6. *I observe classroom and safety rules.*
7. *I concentrate on assigned tasks.*
8. *I demonstrate appropriate audience etiquette.*
9. *I show respect for others' feelings.*

THEATRE ARTS
Cross Reference Guide

Essential Elements	Grade Three	Page No.	Grade Four	Page No.	Grade Five	Page No.
Acting: Expressive use of the body and voice	Develop body awareness and spatial perception using					
	• *movement*	184–190	• *movement*	37–45	• *movement*	140–148
	• *pantomime*	195–199	• *pantomime*	50–53	• *pantomime*	155–158
	• *voice*	204–206	• *voice*	56–58	• *voice*	162–165
	• *sensory recall*	191–194	• *sensory recall*	46–49	•• *sensory recall*	149–154
	• *emotional recall*	200–203	• *emotional recall*	54–55	• *emotional recall in character*	159–161
Playmaking/ Playwriting: Collaborative improvisations	Dramatize literary selections using • *pantomime and dialogue* • *shadow play*	207–228 229–242	• *pantomime and dialogue* • *shadow play* • *puppetry*	59–64 97–108 97–108	Dramatize original stories using • *pantomime and dialogue* • *puppetry*	166–168 193–196
			• *plot structure*	65–75	• *conflict*	169–179
			• *characterization* emphasizing • *physical attributes* • *character objectives* • *dialogue*	76–96 76–83 84–89 90–96	• *attitude revealed in behavior*	180–192
Responding and Constructing Meaning: Development of aesthetic sensibilities	View theatrical events emphasizing • *player-audience relationship* • *audience etiquette*	243–248 243–248	• *player-audience relationship* • *audience etiquette* • *analysis of physical attributes and character objectives* • *recognition of dramatic conflicts* • *prediction of plot resolution*	109–112 109–112 113–130 113–130 113–130	• *analysis of character's attitude revealed in behavior* • *recognition of kind of conflict* • *prediction of plot resolution* • *evaluation and aesthetic judgments*	197–210 197–210 197–210 197–210
			Compare television, film and live theatre emphasizing • *setting* • *acting*	 131–132	• *time of action* • *special effects*	211–212 211–212

A NOTE BEFORE BEGINNING: The sentences which are in italic are stated as if the teacher is talking directly to the children. They are either directions, questions, or sidecoaching comments. Sidecoaching means that you are observing the children and making comments while they are acting, in order to spark their imaginations, suggest new ideas, or encourage their good work.

The italicized sentences are intended only as suggestions. Each teacher has an individual style, and should tailor remarks and questions to that style, as well as to the needs of the particular class.

GETTING STARTED

Drama Objectives: Develop an initial understanding of drama, through discussion and action; recognize importance of imagination

Related Objectives:
    Language Arts: Use nonverbal communication
    Physical Education: Develop coordination, reaction, and balance

Materials: A control device, such as a drum, or tambourine

Introduce: Write the word "drama" on the board, scrambling the letters. For example,

> *ramad*

Tell the class that the word is the name of something they are going to be doing in class. They need tools to do it and they have all of the tools they need with them right now. See if they can unscramble the letters.

What tools are needed to do drama? Accept all answers, but the basic tools to emphasize are

> *the voice,*
> *the body,*
> *the mind.*

Each tool is very important. Ask why they think the mind is important. Stress the importance of *imagination.*

Plan: Tell the students that today they are going to exercise their imaginations:

> *Find your own place in space, where you can work without bumping into anyone else.*
> *At your feet you will see an imaginary length of rope.*
> *When I give the signal to start, you are to pick up the rope and begin to use it in some way. Think of as many things to do with the rope as you can.*

Act: Use the drum or the tambourine to give the signal to begin.
   After two minutes, give the same signal to stop.

> *How many thought of over five things to do with the rope?*

   Find out some of their ideas by having volunteers demonstrate one idea each.

Plan: Ask them to find a partner. They are still using an imaginary rope. This time it is a thick rope for a game of Tug of War. Ask each pair to hold their rope, determining how thick it is and trying to feel it in their hands.
   Review the game. One person is on each side of an imaginary line. They are both holding on to the rope. The object is for each person to pull on the rope so that the opposing person is pulled across the line.
   Since this rope is imaginary, ask them what they will have to do to make it seem as if this is a real Tug of War. Talk about give and take—when one person pulls hard the other has to show that he or she is being pulled. Then the other person pulls hard and the opponent shows how much he or she is being pulled, and so on. You might ask two volunteers to demonstrate. Ask those watching what they are doing that makes it seem real and what else could be done.

Act: Each pair establishes their own imaginary line. All pairs will play simultaneously. Again, use the drum or tambourine to start the action. After they have played for fifteen seconds or so, you might need to tell them that you are going to count silently to ten. At that point you will sound the drum and the person in control of the rope will pull the opponent across the line. There will still be some who said they were both in control of the rope. If so, pronounce the game a draw.

Reflect: Ask how many were able to imagine they were really having a tug of war. *What did they do to make it seem real? What was hard about it?*
   Discuss imagination:

   Why is imagination important in drama?
   How is it important in almost all of life?
   Why would a scientist who is trying to find a cure for cancer need to use imagination?

Assessment: In this lesson, and in other early lessons, you may find that their verbal descriptions are more vivid than their actual playing. That is because they may be still feeling a bit shy—not sure whether they can trust each other or you yet—and because their pantomime skills have not caught up with their imaginations. Note what they are able to do now and encourage them to use their imaginations. You should see continuous progress in pantomime as they have more experiences in drama.

ACTING:
EXPRESSIVE USE OF BODY AND VOICE

Concept: Develop body awareness and spatial perception though *movement*

HEAVY AND LIGHT

Drama Objective: Use energy to create the illusion of being very heavy and very light

Related Objectives:
Language Arts: Employ active listening in a variety of situations
Physical Education: Participate in activities related to muscular strength, endurance, flexibility; develop coordination and balance

Materials: A drum or tambourine to accompany the movement

Introduce: Tell the class to imagine they are jogging around the playground, only they are to do it in place. Direct attention to how they use their arms as well as their legs when they jog.

Act: Sidecoach:

Continue jogging, but imagine you have lead weights on your feet and legs. It is very difficult to move.
Now you have weights on your arms, as well.
Now there is one around your waist. Feel the weight as you continue to jog.
Suddenly the weight around your waist is removed.
Next the weights on your arms are gone.
Then the weights on your legs and feet are gone.

*Not only are the weights gone, but somehow you are now only a
    fraction of your normal weight — almost feather light.
You almost bound in the air, you are so light.
Float down to the ground, and relax.*

Reflect: Discuss the feelings of being heavy and light. This activity, inci-
dentally, is a good one to use when the children are tense and need to relax.

Assessment: Rate them on how well they followed directions and accomplished the objective.

EYES AHEAD

Drama Objective: Observe and follow a rhythmic pattern

Related Objectives:

Language Arts: Employ active listening in a variety of situations

Physical Education: Develop coordination and balance; participate in rhythmic activities

Introduce: Tell them you are going to see how well they can work together in a group. Divide the class into groups of five or six. Each group makes a line, so that each person sees only the back of the person directly in front of him or her at all times.

Plan and Act: The first person in each row is the leader. The leader does a movement for the group to follow that involves *moving only the arms and hands.* The leader should move slowly so others can follow. After a few moments, give a signal to stop.

The first person goes to the back of the line and the second person becomes the leader. This time the leader uses *hands, arms, feet and legs, but does not move forward.*

Each time there is a new leader, give different directions:

Use your whole body, but move in slow motion.

Use your whole body and move forward, being sure your line doesn't interfere with any other line.

Move from side to side.

Stay in place, but move up and down.

Reflect: Ask them what was easy and hard about the activity. Who had the responsibility for making sure the team moved exactly together? The answer, of course, is "Everybody!"

Assessment: In addition to the objective, note which children relish the leadership role and which are more reluctant. The latter may need help with building confidence and peer approval. The former may need help cooperating in group settings so that all have a chance to contribute.

FALLING SAFELY

Drama Objective: Fall down safely

Related Objectives:
    Language Arts: Follow multi-step directions
    Physical Education: Develop coordination and balance

Introduce: Children love to fall down. Frequently, when they act out stories, one of them will incorporate falling. The following are two falls that will be safe, if they practice the step-by-step sequence. Direct them to practice slowly, several times, while you call out the sequence.

The important point is to avoid falling on any bony parts of the body. Do not let the knees, hips, elbows, wrists, shoulders, spine, or head hit the floor. Fall in as relaxed a manner as possible while protecting the bones.

Plan: Back fall:

1. Step back on right foot
2. Lift left leg
3. Hands above head
4. Sit on right heel and roll on fleshy musculature next to spine. Don't let hands hit the floor.

This fall may be done with either the right or left foot back. Lifting the leg tucks the coccyx so the person does not hit his or her "tail bone" when falling. Have students learn the fall by simply **sitting** on their own heel. This is a very controlled way to learn a move that may later be embellished to **look** out of control.

Sidefall:

1. Lift right hand above head
2. Point knees to the left
3. Isolate buttocks to the right
4. Make body look like a closed parenthesis:)
5. Fall to the right, making sure not to lead with the hip.

Fall like a rocker on a rocking chair, and fall onto the fleshy parts of the body: calf, hamstring, buttock, muscles next to spine. Don't try to stop the natural flow of the fall.

After they become proficient in the falls, add variations, such as the following:

· Fall in slow motion
· Fall in doubletime
· Fall as if being hit in the stomach
· Trip over an imaginary object

Students will have other suggestions to add.

Reflect: Talk about difficulties they may have in learning the falls. Like anything else, practice is necessary! Discuss why it is important for actors to learn how to fall safely.

Assessment: This activity should be practiced on several days—it can be a warm-up before you start other lessons. At some point, each student should successfully demonstrate both falls in the prescribed sequence.

SHAKE IT UP!

Drama Objective: Use movement to stimulate the imagination

Related Objectives:

Language arts: Employ active listening in a variety of situations

Physical Education: Participate in activities related to muscular strength and endurance, flexibility, and cardiovascular endurance; develop coordination and balance

Introduce: Ask the students what their bodies do when they are very, very cold. It shivers and shakes. That is what they will do today—shake.

Act: Sidecoach:

Begin by shaking your hands.
How many different places can you shake them?
> *in front*
> *behind*
> *overhead*
> *one high, one low*
Add another part of the body.
Add more parts until you are shaking all over.
Shake as fast as you can.
While you are shaking, think of something you have seen that shakes. For instance, a cement drill, clothes dryer, cold dog, gelatin.
Become the shaking thing you have seen in your imagination.

*Now shake slowly. Are you still the same thing or something differ-
ent?*
Shake slowly down to the floor. Gradually stop shaking. Relax.

Reflect: Talk about some of the "shaking" things they became.

Assessment: Before talking about some of their "shaking" things, ask
them to write what they were on a piece of paper. That way you can find
out which children are engaging their imaginations and which will need
practice and encouragement.

BIG BEACH BALL

Drama Objective: Relax the body by using images

Related Objectives:
   Language Arts: Employ active listening in a variety of situations
   Physical Education: Participate in activities related to flexibility, develop coordination and balance

Introduce: Tell students that one method a lot of people use when they want to relax is imagery. That is, they use their imaginations and relax as if they were the picture they have in their minds. Today they are going to practice using the image of a beach ball.

Act:

> *Imagine that you are a big, round, beach ball, being bounced back and forth.*
> *You sail through the air and bounce very gently when you land.*
> *Bounce back and forth several times.*
> *Suddenly you realize you are losing air.*
> *Gradually slow down until finally you can't bounce any more.*
> *You become flatter and flatter, until all of the air is gone.*
> *Relax.*

Reflect: Ask them whether they were able to accomplish the objective of relaxing. Ask them to mention other images that might be very relaxing. See Appendix A, page 379 for other ideas.

Assessment: Note those children who need more work in learning how to relax. Ask them to think about it and tell you, another day, what image they might find relaxing. When doing this lesson another time, ask each person to think of his or her own image and use it to relax. Ask about their images later.

GROUP OBJECTS

Drama Objective: Create the shape and movement of objects, in small groups

Related Objectives:
  Language Arts: Use nonverbal communication; participate in group problem-solving activities

Materials: Index cards with the name of an object on each

Introduce: In a previous lesson, they each became a beach ball, bouncing lightly and gently back and forth. In this lesson, they will become various objects, but they will create the objects in groups.

Try out one or two group objects. First, divide them into groups of four or five. Each group is to create the shape of a huge beach ball and show how it moves. Everyone in the group is to be part of the object. You may want to use the same sidecoaching as you did in the Big Beach Ball lesson, on page 44. Point out the different ways of moving and working together used by some of the groups.

Have them try out another image—that of a campfire. Don't allow too much planning time. They should make decisions together as quickly as possible.

Plan: Give each group an index card with the name of an object on it. Tell them you will give them only two minutes to plan how they will form the object and make it move.

   Possible objects include: parachute, airplane, robot, lawn mower, sprinkler, car.

Act: Each group shows the rest of the class what they have created. Those watching should try to determine what the object is.

Reflect: Ask them what was hardest about solving the problem they were given.

Assessment: Rate them on how successful they were accomplishing the objective and how well they seemed to work in their groups.

Concept: Develop body awareness and spatial perception through *sensory awareness and sensory recall*

LISTEN AND IMAGINE

Drama Objective: Use the sense of hearing to stimulate the imagination

Related Objectives:
Language Arts: Employ active listening in a variety of situations; use a variety of words to express ideas.

Introduce: Tell the students to close their eyes and listen to the sounds they hear *outside* the classroom. Each person should focus on one of the sounds and listen closely to it.

Who might be making the sound? Why?
Is the person doing something or going somewhere?
Think up a little story about the sound.

Act: After a couple of minutes, tell them to open their eyes and share their story with the person sitting next to them.

Reflect: Talk about how our imaginations get ideas through the senses. This time it was through the sense of hearing. How could the sense of taste stimulate your imagination? Sight? Touch?

Assessment: Did each student share his or her story with a partner?

THE BEACH

Drama Objective: Use the senses to pantomime beach activities

Related Objectives:

Language Arts: Employ active listening in a variety of situations; use a variety of words to express feelings and ideas; use adjectives correctly

Physical Education: Develop coordination and balance

Introduce: Ask the class to find a comfortable position to sit in on the floor and to close their eyes. They are to imagine they are sitting on a log somewhere at their favorite beach. While they are imagining, sidecoach by asking questions such as the following:

> *What is the day like? Feel the warmth of the sun.*
> *What sounds do you hear?*
> *Put your hands on the ground—what are you touching?*
> *What do you see around you?*
> *What one thing would you like to do at the beach?*

Act:

> *Open your eyes, trying to keep the image of the beach. Begin to do the one thing you would most like to do there.*

There will be a variety of responses. Some may just want to lie down in the sun, while some may want to go swimming, or build sand castles, or play with a frisbee.

Reflect: After they have had a few moments to play, ask them what images seemed most real to them. What sounds did they hear? What beach smells did they recall?

Assessment: Ask them to choose the sense that seemed to be strongest in helping them recall the beach. They are to write a paragraph describing what they see at the beach, or feel, or hear. They should use a variety of adjectives so that the reader can "see," or "feel," or "hear," too.

THE ATTIC

Drama Objective: Use the senses to pantomime exploring an attic

Related Objectives:
  Language Arts: Employ active listening in a variety of situations; use nonverbal communication; use a variety of words to express feelings and ideas
  Science: Use skills in acquiring data through the senses

Warm-up: Tell the class that in a few minutes they are going to do something that requires concentration and keen use of the senses, so they are to practice sharpening their senses for a bit.

The sense of smell is first.

> *Close your eyes and see whether you can smell chalk, or paste or anything that might let you know you are in a classroom, just by the smell.*

Next, the sense of hearing.

> *With eyes closed, what sounds do you hear?*
> *Imagine someone is walking down the hall. Listen to the footsteps.*

Now, the sense of touch.

> *Touch something in your pocket or on your desk. Be aware of how it feels.*
> *Put it down and **imagine** you are touching it. Let your fingers remember what it felt like.*

And, the sense of sight.

> *Recall your bedroom at home, the furniture, the colors, what the floor is like.*
> *Recall what your room looks like when it is dark and all you see are big shadowy shapes.*

Introduce: Ask if they have ever been in an attic. How would they describe an attic to someone who had never heard of one before? Try to bring out descriptions that touch on each of the senses. For example, an attic might have a musty smell, be dark and full of cobwebs, have creaky floors and low ceilings, and be full of boxes and trunks.

Plan: There is something exciting about exploring an attic, because you never know what you might find up there.

> *Imagine that there is a big, old vacant house and you have decided to explore it.*
> *You discover it has an attic. How will you get into the attic?*
> *Try to get such a clear picture of the attic in your mind that you can actually **feel** the cobwebs in your face, **smell** the musty air, **hear** the creaking boards, **see** the boxes and trunks.*

Act: *At my signal, begin exploring the attic to see what you might find.* After they have played a couple of minutes, suggest:

> *As you look around, you find something very unusual.*
> *Look at it carefully.*
> *Where could it have come from?*
> *What will you do with it?*

Reflect: After they have played out the action, many will want to share what they found in the attic. They could either tell about it or pantomime what they found for the rest to guess. Ask what they heard or touched that made the attic seem real to them.

Assessment: Other places to explore which are rich in sensory detail might include a cave, an old abandoned house, or a thick forest. You may want to give them a writing assignment in which they list a certain number of sensory details they might find in a cave, for example. Working with a partner might prove interesting and helpful.

Concept: Develop body awareness and spatial perception through *pantomime*

REACHING FOR A REASON

Drama Objective: Pantomime activities suggested by a particular movement

Related Objectives:
 Language Arts: Employ active listening in a variety of situations; use nonverbal communication
 Physical Education: Develop coordination and balance

Introduce:

Stand up and reach as high as you can.
Stretch as far to each side as you can.
Stretch as far down as you can.
Now let's give you a purpose for reaching:
Straighten a crooked picture which is very high on the wall.
You see some flies. Get a fly swatter and reach way out to swat them.

Plan and Act: Ask them to think of other reasons they might be stretching and reaching.

 As ideas are suggested, the whole class follows through with the pantomime. Or, you might ask them to keep their ideas a secret and have five or six at a time show their ideas to the class.

Reflect and Evaluate: The class tries to determine exactly what each one is doing. Ask them what details of the pantomime were especially clear.

Assessment: Check to see whether those students who were having difficulty engaging their imaginations when the drama lessons first started are now coming up with ideas quite readily.

SPORTS

Drama Objective: Pantomime outdoor sports

Related Objectives:

Language Arts: Employ active listening in a variety of situations; participate in group problem-solving activities

Physical Education: Develop coordination and balance; participate in modified games

---

Introduce and Plan: Divide the class into groups of five or six. Each group is to choose one outdoor sport to pantomime. They should think of the equipment they will need and how they will pantomime the sport so that the class will be able to know what it is. Give them a minute to plan.

Act: When the groups show their sports to the rest of the class, let them play it for awhile, even if the class knows what they are doing right away. The class should look for specific actions which are appropriate to playing that sport.

Reflect and Evaluate: Talk about details of pantomime that were very realistic. Keeping their eyes on the ball, the energy used in swinging the bat, or passing the ball, are examples of the kinds of things to emphasize.

Assessment: Rate them on the clarity of their pantomime.

DEEP SEA DIVING

Drama Objective: Pantomime deep sea divers

Related Objectives:

    Language Arts: Employ active listening in a variety of situations;
    use nonverbal communication;
    use a variety of words to express feelings and ideas
    Physical Education: Develop coordination and balance

Materials: You may wish to use background music when they are diving, such as "Neptune," from *The Planets Suite*, by Holst.

Warm-up: First, guide the class in a warm-up, using the rhythmic movement activity called **Heavy and Light**, on page 37.

Introduce: Ask if they know of any people who put weights on to do a particular activity. Give them some clues if they don't suggest deep sea divers or scuba divers. Then ask them questions such as the following:

> *Why do divers use weights?*
> *What other equipment do they use?*
> *Why do they always dive with a partner, or a "buddy"?*
> *What are some reasons they might go diving to the bottom of the sea?*

Ideas may range from finding a sunken ship to looking for specimens for scientific research.

Plan: Designate one part of the room as the boat which will take them out to sea. On that boat they will find the diving gear they need.

Each finds a buddy, and they go to the boat and help each other put on the gear.

Act: You can play the role of the head of the expedition who will stay on the boat once they dive off. Tell them not to put on their headgear, or helmets, until you tell them to, because after that they will not be able to talk at all. Ask them how they will communicate with their buddies underwater. The answer, of course, is through pantomime.

Decide what their diving mission is, according to one of the suggestions they made earlier. As the head of the expedition, you can set the tone for he seriousness of their mission and the potential dangers. Tell them they have been chosen to participate in this expedition because they are internationally known expert divers, and this is a particularly important mission. Ask them, in character, what their particular expertise is — underwater photography, for example. Each one should have a specific goal for the dive, whether it is to take pictures, find clues, gather unusual specimens or something else. When they descend, you will be the only person who can communicate with them, through a specially designed speaker in their helmets. Take a moment before the dive to "test" the speaker system with them. Then they jump off the boat with their buddies. (Some will probably know that they jump off the boat backwards.)

After they have played for awhile, you might communicate with them, telling them about potential danger:

My radar has picked up a dangerous object in your vicinity.
I don't know what it is. Be very careful.

After they have "conquered" the enemy, tell them your gauges show that the air supply is low, and it is time to ascend. Warn them to come up *very* slowly, so they don't get the "bends."

Reflect and Evaluate: When all are back to the boat, they remove their gear and share tales of their adventure.

Ask them how they communicated with their buddies.

How could their pantomime have been improved?

Assessment: Rate them on the quality of their pantomime and their concentration. Were they able to refrain from talking while underwater?

Students may want to think of other underwater adventures. For example, they may find clues to the lost city of Atlantis or King Neptune's Kingdom.

Concept: Develop body awareness and spatial perception through *emotional recall*

REMEMBER A TIME WHEN . . .

Drama Objective: Use emotional recall to act out specific emotional states

Related Objectives:
  Language Arts: Use a variety of words to express feelings and ideas; participate in group problem-solving activities

---

Introduce: Ask the class how they feel right now. Answers will probably vary from "happy" to "bored." Ask them to name some other feelings they have had in the past and list them on the board.

Focus on one of the feelings, such as "mad," and ask them to recall a situation in which they were really mad.

  How does your body feel when you are mad?
  What kind of expression might you have on your face when you are mad?

Plan: Divide the class into small groups and assign each group a particular emotion from the list on the board. It is all right if more than one group has the same emotion. Each group is to think of a situation in which one or more of them are feeling that emotion.

Act: The groups act out their situations for the rest of the class. The class will try to determine what the feeling is.

Reflect and Evaluate: Ask the class what specific actions let them know the feeling the group was trying to communicate. They may also want to suggest ways the scene could be stronger.

Assessment: Ask them to write about a time they remember being particularly happy (or sad, whatever emotion you wish to use). They should describe their feelings and their actions.

54

IT DEPENDS

Drama Objective: Show how actions change when circumstances change

Related Objectives:
    Language Arts: Employ active listening in a variety of situations; draw conclusions

Introduce: Ask the students to think of three different things they do when they wake up in the morning.

Acts: They will repeat the same action, but the way they do it will change, depending on the situation.

1. *It is a bright, sunny day. You are feeling great and there is going to be a party at school!*
2. *It is March, and you are getting tired of school. The day is gloomy and rainy. You expect to get a test back on which you know you did poorly.*
3. *Your dog was killed the day before and you wake up remembering and missing the dog.*
4. (In pairs) *You are angry because a younger sister or brother is being a pest and has hidden the toothpaste. You may use words.*

Reflect: Ask them how their actions were different in the various situations. Talk about pace and energy changes.

Assessment: Note whether there were appropriate changes in action in the different situations.

Concept: *Voice*

THE LOST KITTEN

Drama Objective: Use persuasive arguments in a given situation

Related Objectives:

   Language Arts: Employ active listening in a variety of situations;

   recognize a speaker's purpose for a presentation;

   use a brief set of reasons to persuade a peer or adult

Introduce: They work in groups of four. Two are the parents, and two are the children. This is the situation:

> *The two children are walking home from school on a rainy day, when they hear a little kitten meowing. They investigate, and in the bushes they find a poor bedraggled kitten, soaking wet and crying pitifully. The kitten has no identification collar. They take the kitten home and try to persuade their parents to let them keep the kitten. Previously their parents have never allowed them to have a pet for various reasons.*

Plan: Everyone imagines he or she is one of the parents for a moment. Ask them what arguments they might have for not keeping the pet. Do the same in the role of the children.

Act: They play out the scene, beginning with the finding of the kitten. While the two children are doing that, the parents should be at home doing whatever they might typically be doing.

After they have played for awhile, tell them they have one minute to end the scene. Will they be allowed to keep the kitten?

Reflect: Afterward discuss the various arguments they came up with.

Assessment: Ask students to think of other situations in which they have had to be persuasive. In groups, they can act out a situation for the rest of the class. The class can suggest other ideas they might have added to help the arguments.

THE PHONE CALL

Drama Objective: Describe how vocal tone and pitch reflect feelings

Related Objectives:
 Language Arts: Employ active listening in a variety of situations; use a variety of words to express feelings and ideas

---

Introduce: Each one is to imagine telephoning a best friend. They have something very important to tell the friend. Sometime during the conversation, they are to have a big argument about something and hang up. Maybe they'll call the friend back, maybe not.

Plan and Act: Give them a minute to think about the call and what it is they are going to tell their friends. (The friend is imagined). Remind them to think about what their friend is saying on the other end of the phone.

Reflect: Afterward ask them how their voices changed when they began to argue.

Assessment: Ask them how they can tell when someone in their family is mad, focusing the discussion on vocal quality.

LEAVE A MESSAGE

Drama Objective: Speak clearly and distinctly
Related Objectives:
    Language Arts: Adapt content and formality of oral
    language to fit purpose
    Music: Develop the voice for clear diction
Materials: Tape recorder and blank tape

Introduce: Ask whether they have ever called someone on the telephone and heard a recorded message. Point out that sometimes people have to be away and they don't want to miss important calls, so they use the recording device.

Plan: They are to imagine that they have a recorder on their telephone at home. They are going to go somewhere after school and want to let their mothers know. They call up and give the following information:

Tell who you are,
what time it is,
where you will be,
how you can be reached,
when you are coming home.

Act: Record about six children a day and listen to the recordings to evaluate. The class will become bored if too many record on one day.

Evaluate: Evaluate according to the clarity of the message.

Assessment: Rate them on accomplishment of the objective. Those who did not speak distinctly enough should re-record until every word is understood.

PLAYMAKING/PLAYWRITRING: COLLABORATIVE IMPROVISATIONS

Concept: Dramatize literary selections using *pantomime* and/or *dialogue*

TUG OF WAR

Drama Objective: Pantomime the action of the characters in the story

Related Objectives:

Language Arts: Use problem solving in a group; use nonverbal communication; understand feelings and emotions of characters; identify an implied main idea; select from an oral presentation the information needed; understand words in context; present stories for entertainment; become acquainted with a variety of selections, characters, and themes of our literary heritage

Physical Education: Develop coordination, reaction and balance

---

Warm-up: Use the tug of war activity from the Getting Started lesson, on page 35.

Introduce: A tug of war is about a certain kind of power—who is the strongest, who has the most physical strength. Ask students if they can think of other kinds of power.

Tell students to think about kinds of power while they listen to today's folk tale from West Africa.

Present: *TUG OF WAR*

Adapted from a West African tale

Now Turtle had a mighty fine opinion of himself. He didn't care that he was small, he still thought he was the equal of the largest animals in the forest. He boasted about his "good friends," Elephant and Hippopotamus. He had the audacity to say that he was just as powerful as they were.

"If the truth be known," confided Turtle to Parrot, "I have more brains in my toes than they have in both their heads combined."

Parrot was shocked at Turtle's words and told all the animals what Turtle had said. Soon the word spread to Elephant and Hippopotamus.

Elephant just laughed and said, "Let him talk. I can't be bothered with someone of so little consequence."

Hippopotamus, likewise, laughed and said, "Turtle? Turtle? That little runt? Give me a break!"

When Turtle heard that Elephant and Hippopotamus were making fun of him, he stretched out his head, held it high, and said with righteous indignation, "Indeed? How interesting. We'll just have to see about this, won't we?" And Turtle, head still high, set off to visit Elephant.

Now everyone knows that elephants are big. But when we are talking about this elephant, we are talking about BIG! As in gigantic, colossal, humungous! Why his trunk alone was eight miles long. His ears could be sails for a clipper ship. When Turtle came upon him, he was lying down.

"Hello, friend Elephant," said Turtle, with confidence.

Elephant flapped an ear and the wind almost turned Turtle over.
"Who is calling me 'Friend'?" he glowered.

"It is I, Turtle. I have come a long distance to visit you, my friend."

Elephant stood up slowly, blocking the sun for miles. "Let's get this straight," said Elephant in his powerful voice. "Not only are you not my friend, I have heard that you call yourself my 'equal.' The only thing 'equal' about that is that it is 'equally' untrue."

"I beg to differ," said Turtle pompously, "And I propose to prove it to you."

"What?" sputtered Elephant, not believing his ears. "You propose to prove you are my equal?"

"Well," said Turtle, "that may not be quite true. It is possible that I am, in fact, more than your equal—that I am greater than you."

Now this idea seemed so ludicrous to Elephant that he couldn't be angry anymore. He just bellowed with laughter and said, "All right, Turtle, you're on. Where is your proof?"

Turtle picked up the end of a very long, strong vine. "Let us have a tug of war," he said. "I will give you this end and then I will travel until it is stretched out and we will begin tugging. We won't stop, even if it is time to eat or sleep, until one of us wins or the vine breaks."

Elephant shook his head with laughter, "Yes Sir, Mr. Turtle. Just shake the vine when you are ready."

Turtle went off with his end of the vine to look for Hippopotamus. Now, was Hippopotamus big? Yes, he was BIG! He was so big that when he went into the water to bathe, he caused a tidal wave! Nonetheless, Turtle went up to him.

"Hello there, friend Hippopotamus."

"Watch who you are calling 'Friend,'" grumphed Hippopotamus.

"If we are not already, we shall soon become great friends," responded Turtle, not to be put off by the cheerless Hippopotamus.

"The way I hear it, you have been saying bad things about me," accused Hippopotamus. "Like you think you are smarter than I am."

"Well maybe I am and maybe I'm not," said Turtle. "Why not put it to a test?"

"What do you mean?" asked Hippopotamus suspiciously.

"Let's you and I have a tug of war," said Turtle. "I have your end of the vine right here. If one of us pulls the other over, that one shall be called greater. If the vine breaks, we shall be considered equals."

Hippopotamus thought Turtle had taken leave of his senses. But, at last, he consented in order to get rid of him.

Off Turtle went, saying he would shake the vine and that would be the signal to begin.

Turtle went to the middle of the vine and shook it vigorously, so that it quivered to both ends, signaling Elephant and Hippopotamus. Then Turtle stood back and laughed as the vine became taut.

Turtle was very hungry after all the walking he had done. So he went home and made himself a delicious lunch and followed that with a nap.

When he awoke, several hours had passed. He decided he had better check the vine. There it was, trembling because it was stretching so hard. First it would move one way, then it would slowly move the other way. Neither one was winning. Turtle decided the time had come—he took out his knife and cut the vine in the middle. WHAMO! went Elephant as he fell backward into the forest. KABLAMO! went Hippopotamus as he fell backward into the water.

Turtle took one end of the broken vine over to Elephant who was sitting on the ground unable to walk.

"Elephant, how are you? What is wrong with your leg?" asked Turtle.

"I must say, Turtle, I underestimated you. I don't know how it is possible, but I have to admit we are equals. I need to rest my leg for awhile, but perhaps you could come by for dinner, friend Turtle."

"I'd like that, friend Elephant." And Turtle smiled as he went to get the other broken end of the vine to take to Hippopotamus.

When Turtle arrived at the water, he saw Hippopotamus rubbing his head and groaning.

"You aren't looking so well," said Turtle.

"That's how I'm feeling too," said Hippopotamus. "When the vine broke I banged my head on a rock in the water. I had no idea you were so strong, Turtle. I am sorry if I was rude to you before. I am pleased to call you 'Friend.'"

Turtle stayed and had tea with friend Hippopotamus, until it was time to join friend Elephant for dinner.

And now, when the animals hold a council meeting, you will see three chairs in the honored position. One for Elephant, one for Hippopotamus, and one for Turtle. Because, of course, Turtle had proven they were equals. Hadn't he?

Plan: Discuss the kinds of power revealed in the story.

Ask them to describe the size of the three animals. How did the elephant and hippopotamus react when the turtle asserted he was their equal? How would they describe the personality of the turtle?

To get a sense of the enormous size of the elephant and the hippo, divide the class into four groups. Two groups will create the elephant, two the hippo. Everyone in the group is to be part of the animal. The animal needs to be able to move, and show how it is tugging on the vine. They may want to sketch out how each person will function on the chalkboard or a piece of paper.

Act: Two of the groups play the tug of war scene first, while the others watch to see whether they really look like they are straining with all their might. One person from the audience can pantomime snipping the vine, with the animals reacting accordingly.

Evaluate: Talk about what the first players did well and make suggestions about how it might be improved. A discussion about how each member of a group needs to contribute to the goal may be in order.

Then the other two groups play, incorporating the suggestions. Discuss the second playing.

Plan: Talk about the encounter between the turtle and the elephant, and the turtle and the hippopotamus. Choose one person to be the turtle, or two or three could create the turtle and still be a good deal smaller than the other animals. Choose groups to play the elephant and the hippo. They will need to decide who will be the voice for each animal and how that voice will sound.

Act: Act out the story. This would be a good story to videotape.

Reflect and Evaluate: Review the video tape. Discuss how effective they considered their pantomime to be. How well did they work together?

Assessment: Do they seem to understand the necessity of cooperation in group work? How effectively did they pantomime the story?

Concept: Dramatize literary selections using *improvisation* which leads to an understanding of *plot structure*

THE BIRDS OF SUMMER

Drama Objectives: Describe plot structure in terms of beginning, middle, climax and end; use improvisation to enact the climax of a story

Related Objectives:
Language Arts: Understand feelings and emotions of characters; select from an oral presentation the information needed; present stories for entertainment; become acquainted with a variety of selections, characters, and themes of our literary heritage; respond to various forms of literature; describe the time and setting of a story; draw conclusions
Social Studies: Explain how groups influence individual behavior

---

Introduce: Stories and plays are generally about a character who has a problem. Sometimes the problem is so large that it concerns a whole group of people. For example, in some parts of the world people don't have enough food to eat—hunger is a serious problem. Ask the students to name other problems that affect whole groups of people.

Ask them to listen for the problem the people have in the story they are about to hear and to remember the sequence of events that happen as they try to solve the problem.

Present: *THE BIRDS OF SUMMER*

Gretchen Will Mayo

Some Native American legends say there was a time in which animals and humans lived, worked, and talked together. To the Ojibwas and other Algonkians, humans were one kind of "people" and animals were other kinds of "people." In an Ojibwa story about the Big Dipper, it is sometimes hard to guess which is which.

The Ojibwas tell us it is Fisher we see in the group of stars now called the Big Dipper. The Fisher is a lesser-known animal rather like a large mink. It is a cunning hunter and fierce fighter. The handle of the Big Dipper, the Ojibwas said, is Fisher's long, bushy tail.

It was the now-swept time long ago when winter seemed never to end. All the people searched the land for some sign that the cold was melting, for summer's turn had arrived. But summer did not come.

As one day blew over the next, the anxious people wondered what to do and called a meeting. Huddled by the lodge fire, Fox, Muskrat, Beaver, and all the brothers of the tribe sat silently. They called upon the spirit of the animal whose name they had been given to help them find a solution. It was finally a cunning hunter named Fisher who spoke first. "Summer has not come because the birds of summer haven't returned," said Fisher, who had traveled many distant hills.

"What could have happened?" the people wondered. They talked about how the birds left each year as the trees turned golden.

"Never have the birds failed to return," said the most ancient of the elders.

While the people talked, Fisher was thinking. "I think I know who might be holding back the birds of summer," Fisher said shortly. "I have a selfish cousin who wants all good things for himself. He has been named Cruel-Face. If he has captured the birds of summer, he will keep them."

With angry cries the people asked Fisher what they could do.

"This Cruel-Face has the will of a grizzly bear," Fisher answered. "But the bowl he fills for himself spills into the hands of his followers. To keep their comforts, his people jump to every command of this man-without-a-heart."

Fisher looked slowly around the campfire at the faces of Beaver, Caribou, Fox and the others. "Prepare for a journey of ten sleeps," he said. " We must go to Cruel-Face to bring back the birds of summer."

The people agreed and parted to gather their things. In the morning Fisher led his people out of camp and across the wind-swept fields.

They traveled through groves of barren trees. They walked along snow-blanketed game trails. They struggled through snow drifts and over frozen rivers. On the eighth day, cold still swept the ragged path. On every side, the world stretched grey and lifeless. Fisher told them to make camp for the night and to look into the campfire for visions of a warm and sunny day. But some of the travelers mumbled about turning back.

The next morning, as they walked, the air began to feel warmer. The snow melted into the path and streams gurgled. By evening the travelers had removed their heavy robes. They came upon a wide, clear lake and laid down their packs in the sweet-smelling grass along the shore. It felt like spring.

When the people wondered at this change, Fisher pointed to the light of campfires across the lake. "That is the village of Cruel-Face. Warm breezes blow here because the birds of summer have never left this place," he said. "I will find Cruel-Face but you must help."

The Fisher worked out a plan. Muskrat and Beaver were to start first before dawn. It was their job to make holes in the villagers' canoes and weaken their paddles. "When light begins to break," he said to Caribou, "you must swim into the lake. Fox will make barking noises to signal Caribou's crossing," he continued. "The rest of you must set up a commotion that all the world will hear." Fisher thought for a moment, then he added, "There is one more thing. If the birds of summer come along, don't wait for me. Follow them!"

"We won't go without you," cried Caribou, "no matter what happens."

But Fisher silenced Caribou. "No, my friend, whatever happens, we must release the birds of summer. Their spirits cry out to travel their own path."

"We will see that nothing stops them!" Caribou said, and everyone agreed.

When dawn came, Fox's barking awakened Cruel-Face's people. Creeping from their lodges to see what the noise was about, they saw Caribou jumping into the lake. The eager villagers raced to their canoes with their bows and arrows. Caribou swam farther into the deep waters until only his shining antlers could be seen from the shore.

Fisher, hiding in the brush, watched the villagers hurrying off. Then he stole to the lodge of their chief.

He found Cruel-Face seated before a small fire in the center of his earthen floor. A collection of arrow shafts was at his side. All around him, filling the lodge from floor to ceiling, were stacks and stacks of birchbark boxes.

The bullish chief hunched toward the fire, using a long stick to jab again and again into a small heating pot resting on glowing logs. The pot held warm sturgeon glue which Cruel-Face was using to join feathers to arrow shafts.

Fisher saw that Cruel-Face was too busy making his arrows to notice him. Fisher peered through the smokey air and he listened. Then he crept toward the boxes.

Cruel-Face suddenly was on him like a snarling wolf. But Fisher was quick. Snatching the glue stick from Cruel-Face's grasp, Fisher swished the dripping stick round, swabbing the mouth of the chief with a thick stroke of warm glue.

The astonished chief's hands shot to his face, where they stuck like a leech sticks to bare skin. He leaped up to cry out, but no cry came. His mouth was glued tight. Cruel-Face hopped around the lodge. Feathers flew. Boxes crushed. Sticks scattered.

The agile Fisher wasted no time. He dashed among the boxes, opening one, poking a hole in another. It was just as he had suspected. From the first box flew the thrushes and the warblers. From the second came finches and sparrows. Then came jays and wrens, swallows, woodpeckers, and bluebirds.

As his cousin thrashed about the lodge. Fisher opened every box. A rainbow cloud of birds rose from the lodge of the selfish chief. Like smoke it drifted out and over the lake where the people of Cruel-Face in their leaky canoes looked up.

"Look!" cried a warrior.

"Listen!" called others. "The birds of summer are getting away!" They began to whip their canoes around toward the village. Their paddles, damaged by Muskrat and Beaver, broke against the urgent strokes of the villagers. The canoes took on water and sank. Soon the people of Cruel-Face were swimming for shore.

As the birds of summer flew across the lake and over the forest, Fox, Caribou, Muskrat, Beaver, and all of Fisher's friends followed in great haste. Behind them a winter wind was already swirling around the lodges.

As for Fisher, he was still dodging the thrashings of the angry chief, but one small box remained to be opened. Using an arrow shaft, Fisher poked a hole in the box and out darted a flurry of hummingbirds. They flashed and shimmered around the head of Cruel-Face while Fisher dashed out the lodge.

As a rabbit runs before the fox, Fisher ran from the chief to join his friends. He ran through the village, past the lodges, and smack into the raging mob of cold, wet villagers emerging from the lake.

Like an animal cornered, Fisher crouched, looking for an escape. Then he sprang for a tall tree. Climbing furiously, Fisher heard the panting of the angry villagers behind him. The tree shook. Branches snapped. Beyond him stretched only the sky.

"Brave Fisher!" whispered the stars. "Brave Fisher, you are our brother." Their voices called like the song of a hundred birds. Fisher thrust out his arms. Then, tearing from the grasp of the people, rising over treetops and hills, Fisher joined the friendly stars in the winter sky.

Beaver, Caribou, Fox, and the rest of the travelers returned to their village with the birds of summer. Before them, all the way, flowers bloomed and sleeping buds unfolded. But fear froze their hearts when the people thought about what might have happened to Fisher. After only one night, they set upon the path again to find their friend who had not returned.

The moon wasted from bright fullness to a thin sliver while Fisher's people searched for him. One night the people had gathered around the campfire when one small boy pointed to the sky. "I see Fisher there among the stars!" he said.

The people looked. Then they looked again. "Brave Fisher has escaped to the sky country!" they murmured excitedly one to the other. Then they hurried to tell the story of Fisher and the birds of summer to all the people of the village.

"We will keep those birds of summer for ourselves from this day on," some of the villagers cried when they heard the story. "We can make sure the warm winds of summer always blow across our land."

But others looked up at the sky and asked, "What would Fisher say about this?"

"Fisher would say the birds of summer should be free to be themselves," said Fox, and many agreed.

That is why things are as they are. For half of the year the people walk lightly in warm breezes. They smell the fragrance of a thousand flowers and work to the song of the meadowlark. But when the traveling moon appears in the heavens, the birds of summer take wing. Cold winds blow. The sun sinks lower in the sky and snow sweeps the path. Then the people search the winter sky for Fisher and make the long nights pass more quickly sharing stories about their brave friend and the birds of summer.

Plan: First, discuss the story in terms of plot. You may want to chart the various parts on the chalkboard.

> *Usually, the **beginning** of any story states the problem. What was the basic problem? What might have happened if the problem had not been solved?*
>
> *The way a story **ends** relates to the problem in some way. How did this story end, in terms of the problem?*
>
> *The **middle** of the story tells how the characters go about trying to solve the problem. List the sequence of events in this story.*
>
> *Before the end of the story, there is usually an exciting part where the problem might have a chance of being solved. That part is called the climax. What was the **climax** of this story?*

Discuss the climax scene in greater detail. There are really three things happening simultaneously: 1) Fisher fights with Cruel-Face and releases the birds; 2) the villagers see the birds getting away and try to get to shore; 3) the animals who came with Fisher watch. If this story were to be a movie, it could be edited so we could see some of the fight, some of the struggle with the villagers in their canoes, back to the fight, and so on. To do all of those things at once on the stage, however, would be chaotic—we wouldn't know where to look and the story would be lost. The necessary part of the climax, of course, is the confrontation between Fisher and Cruel-Face. Focus on that by asking questions such as the following:

> *What was Cruel-Face doing when Fisher crept up to his lodge? Describe the process of making the arrows. Right where you are, show Cruel-Face busy making his arrows (Give them a couple of minutes to try on the character.)*
>
> *What was going through Fisher's mind while he watched Cruel-Face? How did he enter? How do you suppose he was feeling? (Ask one or two to demonstrate how Fisher would creep in.)*

At this point you might want to re-read the portion of the story from "Cruel-Face suddenly was on him like a snarling wolf," to "A rainbow cloud of birds rose from the lodge of the selfish chief." Afterward, ask them to list every action, in sequence, and write it on the chalkboard.

In pairs they are to plan the fight scene, from Fisher watching Cruel-Face making his arrows though to Fisher running out of the lodge after the last box has been opened. The one rule which they must not violate is that they must never touch one another. They make it **seem as if** they are fighting, but they **never touch**. If any pair should touch, they are to be seated immediately.

Act: Several pairs may volunteer to show their scene to the rest of the class. The class can imagine they are friends of the Fisher, watching through small chinks in the walls.

Evaluate and Plan: Talk about the scenes in terms of building suspense, wondering whether Fisher would be able to accomplish his goal or not. What parts of the scene seemed real as they watched? How could it be even better?

The scene actually continues after Fisher rushes out the door. Ask what happens. Plan for some to be the angry villagers, some to be Fisher's friends, watching, and some the stars who whisper "Brave Fisher!" — welcoming him "like the song of a hundred birds." Again, the villagers are not to actually touch Fisher. They could actually yell once as he comes out and freeze in angry positions while he climbs up to make his escape. Each group (villagers, friends, stars) needs to plan what they will do and say.

Act: Play the entire climax.

Evaluate: Ask what they liked better about the playing this time. Why is timing crucial in the climactic scene? How do they want the audience to feel when they watch the scene?

Assessment: Did they either show or talk about the climax in a way that revealed knowledge of how the problem of the characters relates to the climax of the story? Were they able to make plans and carefully implement them while they improvised?

APPLICATION OF PLOT

Drama Objective: Improvise original stories which include the four parts of a plot

Related Objectives:
  Language Arts: Use a variety of words to express feelings and ideas; make organized oral presentations; present stories for entertainment; predict probable future outcomes; draw conclusions

Introduce: Review the parts of a plot as discussed in the previous lesson.

Plan: Divide the class into small groups of three or four. Give each group a beginning and indicate the problem. They are to decide on a middle, a climax, and an ending. They may add as many characters to their scene as they have in their group. The following are suggestions for scenes, but feel free to construct your own.

1. You open the closet door and all the clothes are gone.
2. Your father told you not to swim too far from shore.
3. You are hiking up a steep mountain path and one of you stumbles and injures a leg.
4. You are playing baseball and the ball hits an old lady and knocks her down.
5. You take your new bicycle to school against the advice of your parents.
6. You take something very valuable to school to show the class, and lose it.
7. You call your dog for dinner and he doesn't come.
8. You told on somebody and now no one will play with you.

Allow a few minutes for planning and trying out the scenes. Ask them to outline the plot, using the headings of beginning, middle, climax and end.

Act and Evaluate: The scenes can be acted for the class audience. After each scene, ask the audience to identify the beginning, middle, climax and end. This may take two days to complete.

Assessment: The scenes and the discussion following the scenes can be assessed according to the drama objective. One way to insure that all the children are able to identify the parts of the plot, instead of just those who participate in class discussion, is to ask them to write their responses to two or three of the scenes.

Concept: Dramatize literary selections emphasizing the *physical attributes of characterization*

A BUSHEL OF THANKS

Drama Objective: Use posture, gestures, and movements which show the physical characteristics of the people portrayed

Related Objectives:
   Language Arts: Select from an oral presentation the information needed, understand feelings and emotions of characters; use a variety of words to express feelings and ideas; identify an implied main idea; recall facts and details that support the main idea; predict probable future outcomes; draw conclusions; become acquainted with a variety of selections, characters and themes of our literary heritage

---

Introduce: Talk about the concept of appreciation
   What is the purpose of saying "Thank you"?
   If you did something nice for someone and he or she didn't say anything, what would you think? How would you feel?

Tell them to keep that in mind as they listen to the story. The story is an old folk tale from the Latin American country of Chile.

You may want to stop reading the story after "Is this a 'happily ever after' story? Not yet. There is more." Ask them to give their ideas about what happens next.

Present: *A BUSHEL OF THANKS*

Adapted from a Chilean folktale

His name was Juan Hollinao—a poor, old man who lived in a shabby shack. He worked hard, but just barely made enough to live on. Some days there was not a scrap to eat. However, when he did have food, he was ready to share with anyone. He was known for his generosity and kindness.

Most people thought he lived alone. And he did, except for Little Mouse. Little Mouse couldn't have picked a better home, because Juan always left some food out for her. "After all," he would say, "mice have to eat, too."

One day Juan looked in his cupboard for a crust of bread he knew was there. It was gone. Little Mouse had eaten all but a few crumbs. He looked at Little Mouse with sad eyes, "I always leave something for you, Little Mouse. You should remember that I must eat too. Try not to be so greedy."

Little Mouse hung her head. Juan was right,she had been greedy. She knew very well that most people would have thrown her out long ago. Juan had always been kind to her. She thought about how she might repay him properly for his generosity. She disappeared for a few days.

One day she hurried in the house, excited about what she had heard and about her wonderful plan. "Juan, there is a king, far away from here, who is so rich he uses bushel baskets to measure his gold! The best part is that he has an unmarried daughter. She is a little older than most princesses and she would be a perfect wife for you!"

Juan started to laugh, but Little Mouse stopped him. "Juan, you must listen to me and do as I say. It is very simple. Go to the king and ask if you might borrow a bushel basket to measure your gold."

Now Juan really laughed. "I don't know where your head is, Little Mouse, but I don't need a bushel basket to measure imaginary gold. I can use an imaginary bushel basket for that!" And he laughed some more.

"Very well. I'll go to the king myself! Goodby!" She was determined to reward Juan for his kindness. Off she went.

When she arrived at the gate of the palace, she went behind a rock and changed herself into a page boy. The mouse page was dressed so handsomely that people assumed he belonged to a very wealthy person.

In fact, that is exactly what the guard thought when the mouse page asked to speak to the king, and he ushered the page right in.

"Your Majesty, I have a request. My master, Juan Hollinao, asks if you would please lend him a bushel basket."

"A bushel basket?" inquired the king. "Whatever for?"

"To measure his gold, Your Highness."

"Really?" The king stroked his head. "Your master must be a very rich man. Perhaps richer than I?"

"I don't know about that, Your Majesty. All I know is that he is in need of a strong bushel basket to measure his gold."

"Very well, you may take the bushel basket to him. However, I want to meet this rich man. Tell him he must return the basket to me himself. If he doesn't, he will never have cause to count gold again."

"Thank you, Your Majesty. He will return it himself."

Shortly before reaching Juan's house, the mouse page changed back to a mouse. And, in fact, it was comical to watch her struggling to drag the basket the rest of the way. Juan looked out the window and went out to give Little Mouse a hand.

"Now what on earth am I to do with this basket, Little Mouse?"

"Not a thing. Not a thing. Just return it to the king. If you don't, he will relieve you of your head."

"But look at me—I can hardly go before the king in these ragged clothes! This is really going too far, Little Mouse."

"Don't worry. Don't worry. You'll be fine. Besides, you really have no choice, if you value your life."

Off the two of them went. Along the way they had to cross a rope bridge over a deep steam. Juan was afraid.

Little Mouse took him by the hand to help him across. The bridge bounced and swayed. Juan was holding his breath. In the middle of the bridge, Little Mouse ran between Juan's feet. Juan lost his balance and plunged into the cold water.

Little Mouse jumped in and helped Juan out. What a sorry sight Juan was— ragged clothes torn even more, and soaking wet. "I can't go to the king like this!" cried Juan.

Little Mouse had to agree. "Stay here and dry off. I'll be right back."

Little Mouse ran directly to the palace, changing back to the handsome page before entering the gates.

"Oh, Your Majesty," cried the mouse page, "I have dreadful news. My master was on his way here when his horses bolted while crossing a stream. His carriage tipped over and he is soaking wet. He won't be able to come today."

"Nonsense," said the king, "I am most eager to meet your master. I'll send him some clothes and my horses and carriage." And so he did.

Putting on those fine clothes did something for Juan. He stood up straight and tall. Indeed, he looked twenty years younger, and certainly he looked like a wealthy nobleman.

He arrived at the palace in the king's fine carriage, where the king received him as if he were royalty. All manner of festivities were prepared. Juan, of course, was perplexed about how Little Mouse had managed all this. But, he was also pleased, and enjoyed every minute.

When the king's daughter saw Juan, she blushed. Would this noble gentleman make her his bride? She had been taking care of the palace since her mother died and had had no time for suitors. But this attractive person was so different!

The king was thinking along those lines as well. He could hardly ask for a finer son-in-law than one who measured his gold in bushel baskets!

"Juan, you may marry my daughter. After the wedding, I'll lend you my carriage and servants to help you prepare your palace. My daughter and I will follow."

Lucky Juan! Poor Juan! His heart was in his throat. He tried to tell the king the truth, but every time he started to speak, the mouse page distracted him or told him to "Hush up." There was a flurry of activity and before he knew it he had married the princess.

Juan and the mouse page were put in the carriage. "Oh," wailed Juan, "What will they say when they see where I live? What will I do?"

"Juan, so far things are fine, right?" asked the mouse page.

"Yes, but . . ."

"Then you have no reason to think they will change. Have a little patience, man!" admonished the mouse page.

Juan said nothing for the whole trip. He sat with downcast eyes, knowing he was a doomed man. When they drew close to his hut, he looked up. What a wonder! In place of his shabby shack was a beautiful palace! Juan looked at the mouse page, but the page was gone. Little Mouse was in his place, "This is for you because you have been so good and kind. The palace has everything you and your princess could ever want. May you have much happiness."

Is this a "happily ever after" story? Not yet. There is more.

A long time went by and it is true that Juan and the princess were very happy. Juan became accustomed to all his riches. If the truth be known, he was very busy and forgot about his friend, Little Mouse.

One day, Little Mouse died. The princess, seeing only an old dead mouse, had her thrown on the garbage heap behind the palace.

That same day, Juan happened to pass by. He recognized Little Mouse at once. Tears sprang to his eyes as he gently took her in his hands. "Little Mouse, my friend, you are the one responsible for all my wealth and joy. How could I have forgotten you," he wept. "I deserve to be punished for neglecting you. One thing is true, Little Mouse, you will have the finest funeral in all of Chile."

Juan made arrangements for a casket of the finest gold, encrusted with jewels. He sent for flowers from many countries. The palace looked like a garden.

Juan sat by the golden casket for hours, asking Little Mouse to forgive him. Then, amazingly, Little Mouse opened her eyes. "Juan, I am not really dead. I was so disappointed when you forgot all about me and what I did for you. Being thrown on a garbage heap is . . . well, it's humiliating. I just had to find out if you would remember."

Juan apologized profusely and he meant every word. "I know I can't undo what was done, but at least you can now come and live in my room."

"No," said Little Mouse. "My work is done. You did remember — even though you forgot for awhile—and you thanked me. Some people don't remember to give thanks." That said, Little Mouse closed her eyes and died.

Plan: Ask them what they thought about the ending of the story. Why was Juan so sad when Little Mouse appeared to be dead?

In some ways Juan was lucky. He had the opportunity to thank his friend, as well as to apologize to her, before she died. Sometimes people don't get around to that until it is too late.

The drama lesson today focuses on the "physical attributes of characters." Ask them what they think that means.

Talk about Little Mouse first—who, by the way, can be male or female. Obviously she was a rather unusual mouse, since she could talk, move a bushel basket and change herself into a human being.

> *What did she look like in her mouse form?*
> *How did she move?*
> *Take a moment to transform yourself into Little Mouse, looking through cupboards for something to eat.*
> *Now jump way ahead in the story and let us see how Little Mouse struggled with the bushel basket.*
> *Now we'll go back a bit in the story to when Little Mouse changes into a page. Before you change, think about it a moment. Is the transformation slow or fast? How does the page feel in his handsome clothes? How will his posture show that he is the page of a nobleman, so the guard will let him in? When I give the signal, change into the page, walking into the king's castle.*

Next, talk about Juan. His physical transformations aren't as radical as those of Little Mouse, but they are perceptible changes, nonetheless. Try to lead them away from the stereotype of shaky, feebleness for "old age," since he obviously wasn't *that* old. His life had been hard, however, and that can often take its toll on one's appearance. You can have them all trying out the various transformations while you are discussing them, or you can have them try them out after the entire discussion.

> *In the first part of the story Juan is described as a poor, old man, who worked very hard. What picture does that conjure up in your mind? Think about his posture and the way he moves.*
> *What do you think his attitude toward life was before the mouse came up with the plan to go to the king?*

When he "accidentally" fell into the water, how did he feel? How would that affect his posture and movement?

Then he puts on the clothes sent to him by the king. How was he described in the story when that happened? What picture of him do you have in your mind now? Why did the clothes make such a difference? How do you think his voice might have changed, as well as his posture?

There is probably one more change in Juan's appearance that happens later on in the story. This change doesn't have to do with clothes, but is caused by something that happened. What might that be? (When he discovers Little Mouse on the garbage heap and mourns her.) *How did he feel? How did that affect him physically?*

In pairs, let them choose one of the transformation scenes: 1) Little Mouse changing to the page and going to the king (either the first or second visit); 2) Juan falling in the water and then changing when putting on king's clothes—with mouse page assisting; 3) the last scene when Juan discovers Little Mouse on the garbage heap, through to the end. They are to plan the scene and rehearse it.

Act: Volunteers may show their scenes to the class. The class is to pay close attention to the physical characteristics of the characters.

Evaluate: Discuss the transformations they saw.

Assessment: Ask them to write a paragraph about either Juan or Little Mouse, describing in detail how they changed. They can be graded on their performance, during the planning part of the lesson and the scene work, on their discussion, and on their paragraphs.

Concept: Dramatize literary selections emphasizing the *objectives of the characters*

THE WIND AND THE SUN

Drama Objective: Communicate the characters' objectives

Related Objectives:

Language Arts: Employ active listening in a variety of situations; select from an oral presentation the information needed; use a brief set of reasons to persuade a peer or an adult; understand feelings and emotions of characters; use a variety of words to express feelings and ideas; make organized oral presentations; present stories for entertainment, respond to various forms of literature; become acquainted with a variety of selections, characters, and themes of our literary heritage

Social Studies: Support individual's rights to have differing opinions

---

Introduce: Divide the class into groups of five or six. Present the following riddle. In their groups they are to decide on an answer for the riddle, and develop some movements which will show what the answer is without telling it outloud.

> *What flies forever*
> *And rests never? (Answer: the wind.)*

Each group shows their answer to the rest of the class. Afterward, ask them which answer most closely fits the riddle. They will probably arrive at the correct response. If not, tell them.

> *Suppose that two people are arguing about which of them is the stronger.*
> *How might they prove who is stronger?*

They might fight; they might have a contest to see who could lift the heaviest weights.

Tell them there is an old fable in which two characters were arguing about who was stronger. One character was the wind and one was the sun.

Present: *THE WIND AND THE SUN*

Adapted from an Aesop's fable

Wind and Sun had an argument one day, about which was the stronger.

"I am the stronger," boasted Wind, puffing out his cheeks and blowing so hard that every leaf on the trees shook. "You sit up there, Sun, and do nothing but shine—that is, when I don't blow the clouds across the sky. When *that* happens, you can't even be seen! Of course I'm the stronger."

"Don't be too sure," answered Sun calmly, filling the air with his warm radiance. "I'll tell you what. We'll have a contest, shall we?"

"Certainly," said Wind. "Then everyone will know, once and for all, who is the stronger. What shall the contest be?"

"See that fellow over there?" said Sun, gazing across the countryside toward a winding, white road. Along it walked a traveller with a cloak about his shoulders.

"I see him," said Wind.

"Well then, let's see which of us can get his cloak off first."

"With all my heart!" agreed Wind. "That's easy. I'll have his cloak off his back in no time."

So saying, he began to blow. "Phoo-oo-oo!" The traveller on the road took no notice. But Wind had scarcely begun. He blew harder, and then harder still, until the water of the lakes turned to great waves, and the trees were bent almost double, and the birds in the air were dashed hither and thither with the force of the gale. But the traveller, instead of taking his cloak off, only held it closer around him; and the harder Wind blew, the tighter he clutched it. It was no good. Even when Wind roared like a thousand demons, and blew so as to snap the branches from the stoutest oaks, he could not get the traveller's cloak off his back. At last Wind was tired out and could blow no more.

It was Sun's turn. By now the sky was all covered over with dark storm-clouds, but as soon as Wind stopped blowing they gently drifted apart, and Sun shone warmly down over the green fields. Warmer and warmer grew the air under his pleasant beams, and soon the traveller unbuttoned his cloak and let it hang loosely about him. Thanks to Sun's kindly heat he was soon glad to take it off altogether and carry it over his arm.

"There!" said Sun. "Which of us got it off—tell me that."

Wind only growled and said nothing. But he knew he was beaten. Sun was the stronger after all.

GENTLENESS DOES MORE THAN VIOLENCE.

Plan: The story opens before the contest has been decided on, with the wind and the sun arguing about who is stronger.

> *How might you show that argument?*
> *What might the wind and sun be doing when they argue?*

One possibility is to have the sun and wind alternately show what they can do—perhaps getting madder each time until the contest is set.

Divide the class into groups to have them work out the opening argument. Some can be the wind and the sun, some can show the effects of the wind and the sun's action. Ask them to think about what kind of voices the wind and sun might have. They are to end the opening argument by deciding to have a contest.

Act: Each group acts out the opening argument.

Evaluate: Discuss their work, talking about the best ideas from each. Then choose ideas from each which would make the best opening.

Plan: Plan the contest.

> *What is the objective, or purpose, of the wind? The sun?*
> *Both have the same objective: to prove who is the stronger.*
> *How does the wind feel when the man begins to tighten his cloak?*
> * What does he do?*
> *What is the sun doing in the meantime?*
> *What other characters might be in the play to help indicate the*
> * strength of the wind?*
> *How do you want to end the play?*

Cast the parts.

86

Act: Some students may want to make the sound effects of the wind, while others act it out.

Evaluate: Ask what parts of the play were believable. Were the objectives of the wind and sun clear? What could be done to strengthen the play?

Assessment: Note how well the actions, as well as the words, communicated the objectives of the characters.

APPLICATION OF CHARACTER OBJECTIVES

Drama Objective: Recognize that a character always has an objective

Related Objectives:
    Language Arts: Identify the multiple causes of a given event or a character action; use a variety of words to express feeling and ideas; make organized oral presentations; understand the feelings and emotions of characters

Introduce: Ask:

> *Why does a bird listen to the ground?*
> *Why does a dog bark?*
> *Why do you knock on a door?*
> *Why do you raise your hand in class?*
> *Everything we do, we do for a reason or a purpose. Another word for purpose is* **objective**.
> *Imagine that you go into your room and close the door. What might be your reason—your objective? Maybe your objective is to be alone, because you are angry; maybe it is to get away from your younger brother; maybe it is to hide a birthday present.*
> *Imagine you are baking a cake; what might be your objective? Your objective is the reason why you do something.*

Plan: A playwright has to decide what the objective is for each of the characters. In a play, the main characters have trouble achieving their objectives. The trouble is the conflict of the play, which makes the plot interesting.

Divide the class into pairs of threes. Give each group a card with a character and action on it and a blank for the objective. The group decides what the objective is.

For example:

Character	Action	Objective
Mother	calls her son	

There are a number of possible objectives: to run an errand; to clean up his room; to eat dinner; to answer the phone. The group decides on one of the objectives to act out.

A list of characters and actions follows. You may wish to add others, or, after the class works with the idea for awhile, they could make up their own lists.

Character	Action	Objective
1. Boy or girl	throws a rope out from a boat	
2. Cat	stalks a mouse	
3. Boy or girl	listens to a record	
4. Young child	rides a bike	
5. Boy or girl	skates	
6. Boy or girl	washes a car	
7. Boy or girl	looks in a drawer	
8. Boy or girl	hides	
9. Boy or girl	walks on tiptoe	
10. Boy or girl	paints a picture	
11. Dog	whines and whimpers	
12. Grandparent	reads outloud	

Act: Each group should have several turns. Those who are watching are to try to determine both the action and the objective being played.

Evaluate: Those watching try to determine the objective of the character's action. Was the objective clear? If not, how could they clarify it?

Assessment: Ask them to write down the objectives of some of the characters after they see a scene.

Assign them to watch a television program and determine what the objective is for each of the main characters.

Concept: Dramatize literary selections emphasizing *original dialogue*

THE STONE IN THE ROAD

Drama Objective: Improvise and write dialogue for the story

Related Objectives:
  Language Arts: Use a variety of words to express feelings
  and ideas; adapt content and formality of oral language to
  fit purpose; understand the feelings of characters; become
  acquainted with a variety of selections, characters, and
  themes of our literary heritage; use fundamentals of
  grammar, punctuation, and spelling

Introduce: Discuss a hypothetical situation with the class, such as the following:

> *Suppose you wanted to be really nice to your family, so you cooked
> all the meals, cleaned up the dishes, cleaned the house, and
> brought your family whatever they wanted when they wanted it.
> You did this not for one day, but everyday for weeks.*
> *Your family was delighted, and soon they didn't even offer to help,
> they just let you do everything. In fact, if you were at all slow when
> they called you to do something, they got angry. How would that
> make you feel, when you were trying to please them?*

Tell them that that situation isn't too different from something that happened in a particular story.

As they listen, they should try to get a picture in their minds of what the various characters are doing and what they look like.

Present: *THE STONE IN THE ROAD*

Adapted from an old tale by Winifred Ward

There was once a Duke who lived in a fine house on the edge of a little village. He was kind and generous to the village folk, and many a time he helped them when they were in trouble.

If the wind blew the roof off a man's barn, the Duke would send his servants to help him build another. If there was illness and distress in the town, he could be counted on to help unfortunate families. When crops were poor, the villagers could be sure that he would not let them go hungry.

As the years passed, however, the Duke realized that people relied too much on his generosity. They were becoming more and more lazy, and instead of being grateful, they were envious and discontented. He resolved, therefore, to test them to find out whether there were not at least a few villagers who would exert themselves for the good of others. He hoped in this way to make the people see themselves as they really were.

One morning very early he went out to the highway and pushed a large stone into the very middle of the road. He had to tug and pull with all his might, but he would allow no one to help him. Just before he pushed it into place, he took from under his cloak a bag of gold, and dropping it to the ground, he covered it with the stone. Then he went behind a nearby hedge to watch what might happen.

Before long a farmer came along, driving some sheep to market. He could scarcely believe his eyes when he saw the big stone blocking the way.

"Run ahead, lad," he said to his son, "and see if it is really a stone." For it was only beginning to be light, and he thought it might be something that had fallen out of an ox-cart.

It *is* a stone, father," said the boy after he had explored. "How ever could it have come there?"

"Well, one thing is sure," replied the farmer. "*We'll* not try to move it. Let the Duke's servants get it out of the way." And with the help of the boy, he drove the sheep around the stone, grumbling all the while about the trouble it caused him.

Before long, two country women came along, carrying baskets of eggs to sell. They were so busy talking about the price they hoped to get for their eggs and wishing that it would be enough to pay for the cloth for a new dress that when they saw the stone they did not at first appear to be surprised. Indeed, one of them sat on it to pull up the heel of her shoe, and discovering that she was somewhat tired, she decided to sit until she was rested. Only then did it occur to the second woman that she had never seen a stone here before.

"Why, a carriage could never get around this thing," she said. "I wonder that the Duke leaves it here!"

But her companion, resting on its broad surface, was dreaming of the fine clothes she would have if she were rich like the Duke's lady. She could not know that well within her reach was a tidy sum of money that would buy more dresses than she could wear in a lifetime.

Hour after hour a procession of people passed along the busy highway, some scolding about the stone, others enjoying the novelty of it, but none offering to move it out of the road. There were laborers, well-to-do merchants, soldiers; some proud ladies who were turned back because there was not room for their carriage to pass; a scholar, so deep in his reading that he stumbled over the stone; a peddler, a minstrel, a beggar.

The Duke had all but given up hope when, about dusk, he heard a gay whistle in the distance. It came from the miller's son, who was trudging along the road with a heavy sack of meal over his shoulder. Suddenly the whistling stopped.

"A stone in the middle of the road!" he said to himself. "That's a queer place for a stone as big as that! Someone will fall over it!" And in less time than it takes to tell about it, he had put his sack of meal on the ground and shoved the stone off the road. As he went back to get the meal, he saw the bag of gold.

"Somebody has lost this," he thought. But no sooner had he picked it up than the Duke stepped out from his hiding-place.

"Read what is written on the bag, my boy," he said.

"For him who moves the stone," read the astonished lad. "Then—?"

"It is for you," said the Duke kindly. "I am glad to find that there is one person in our village who is willing to go to some trouble out of thoughtfulness for others."

"Oh, thank you, thank you, sir!" cried the boy. "It was a little thing to do! You are very kind!" And off he sped to tell his mother of his wonderful good fortune.

Plan: There are number of characters mentioned in the story, plus many others that could be added. The focus for this lesson will be on the dialogue of the characters—the words they say and the way they say them. First, however, it will be helpful to imagine what the characters are like—what they look like, how they move, what kind of personalities they have, why they are traveling on that road, and so on.

Try out some of the characters by showing how they would move:

> the proud ladies,
> the scholar,
> the beggar,
> the soldiers.

Ask them what other interesting characters might come down the road and react in different ways to the stone, but not move it. For example, maybe a mother and her children see the stone and decide to eat their lunch on it. Or an artist comes by and decides to paint it.

The story gave a little sampling of what some of the characters might have said, but they could say quite a bit more. Do not go over the dialogue used in the story, or the students may not be able to think of anything else.

Divide the class into groups of three or four. The task of each group is to encounter the stone in some way, playing certain kinds of characters. They are to decide what the characters will say and how they will say it. They should decide on a name for each of their characters. After they have rehearsed the scene once or twice, they should write the dialogue down, using the correct form.

For example:

> Matilda: What on earth is that?
> Hortense: We must be on the wrong road!

Act: Establish where the stone is. Maybe a large table could be used as the stone. Each group enters, one at a time to encounter the stone. They should not hold the paper with the dialogue they wrote. It is all right if they do not use the exact words they wrote down. They can continue to improvise.

While one group is playing, the others should listen to the dialogue of the characters.

Evaluate: Discuss what they did, emphasizing dialogue that was appropriate for the characters and the situation. They may have suggestions to make the dialogue more interesting or appropriate for the specific characters. Ask what a playwright has to think about when he or she writes dialogue for characters.

Assessment: Rate them on the improvisation of the scene, as well as the written dialogue.

APPLICATION OF CHARACTER DIALOGUE

Drama Objective: Improvise and write dialogue

Related Objectives:

> **Language Arts:** Use a variety of words to express feelings and ideas; adapt content and formality of oral language to fit purpose; understand the feelings of characters; use fundamentals of grammar, punctuation, and spelling

Introduce: Favorite children's rhymes and stories can take on very amusing twists when imagination is applied. For example, in *The True Story of the Three Little Pigs* by A. Wolf (as told to Jon Scieszka), we learn that the wolf only wanted to borrow a cup of sugar when he went to the pig's house. It happened that he had a terrible cold and, although he tried mightily to prevent it, he sneezed so hard that he blew down the little pig's house!

Today, the students will have a chance to use their imaginations to write dialogue for a scene that never made it into print before. This lesson assumes some familiarity with little children's stories. If they are lacking in this area, either have them look up the story or rhyme in the library, or adapt the lesson so it uses characters and stories familiar to them.

Plan: Students, working in pairs, should do the following:

1. Select a title—either from those suggested below, or one of their own invention. It is all right if more than one group selects the same title. Seeing how different imaginations work is interesting.
2. Talk about the characters' objectives and personalities.
3. Improvise the action and dialogue.
4. Write the dialogue for the characters.

In some cases, they may prefer to write before they act the scene.

Possible titles:

How the Spider Won Miss Muffet's Friendship

The Wolf and Red Riding Hood's Grandma Announce Their Marriage

Goldilocks is Sued for Damages by Papa Bear

Little Bo Peep Admits She Needs Glasses

Humpty Dumpty Reveals His Real Identity—He is Not an Egg

Why Little Jack Horner Had to Sit in the Corner

What Hansel and Gretel Do With the Dead Witch

Cow Jumping Over the Moon Is the First Astronaut

Why the Troll Was So Ornery He Wanted to Eat Goats

Cinderella and the Prince Make a Shoe Commerical

Act: Each pair describes where and when their scene takes place. They have the option of reading the dialogue as they wrote it, or improvising the scene. Their acting is likely to be more stilted if they read the lines.

Evaluate: Talk about parts of dialogue that are interesting, and ideas that show potential if they work on them further.

Assessment: Rate them on how well they accomplished the objective.

Concept: Dramatize literary selections using *shadow play and puppetry*

THE STRANGE VISITOR

Drama Objective: Construct shadow puppets and act out the story

Related Objectives:

Language Arts: Select from oral presentation the information needed; use a variety of words to express feelings and ideas; relate experience with appropriate vocabulary; follow multi-step directions; describe time and setting of story; make organized oral presentations; present stories for entertainment; respond to various forms of literature; understand feelings and emotions of characters; adapt content and form of oral language to fit purpose and audience

Art: Discover, explore, and examine art elements including line, color, shape, texture, value, form, and space; express individual ideas, thoughts, and feelings in simple media including drawing, painting, constructing and modeling three-dimensional forms

Music: Move to express mood and meaning of music

Materials: Lightweight cardboard;
Scissors, masking tape, heavy thread or fine wire, paper fasteners, hole punch;
Rods, made from dowels, skewer sticks, straws, hangers, etc; A large, heavy cardboard box, such as an appliance box; A white sheet, or other white material, as wrinkle-free as possible; Two lamps, 100 or 150 watts;
Translucent materials such as colored cellophane, 1/16 inch sheet plastic which can be painted, or gauze;
Music with an eerie sound, such as "Adagio," from *Music for Strings, Percussion and Celesta*, by Bartok.

Introduce: Play the music. Ask the children what kind of mood the music creates. Among the answers will be the word "mysterious," or a similar word. Ask the children to move their hands in a mysterious way to the music. Then tell them to get up slowly and move their whole bodies to the mysterious music.

Tell them you know a story that is just as mysterious as the music. It is about an old woman who is sitting by a spinning wheel, spinning. Describe, or ask the children to describe, how a spinning wheel works.

Present: *THE STRANGE VISITOR*

Adapted from an English fairy tale

A woman, alone, sat spinning one night.
    She sat, and she spun.
    So alone.

A gust of wind; the door opened.
No one there?
Mmmm.

In came a pair of broad, broad feet
And sat themselves down by the fireside.

A woman, so lonely, sat spinning that night.
    She sat, and she spun.
    Was she alone?

In came a pair of long, long legs.
Sat themselves down on the broad, broad feet.

The woman, so lonely, sat spinning that night.
    She sat, and she spun.
    Was she alone?

In came a body, so round that it whirled.
Sat itself down on the long, long legs.

The woman, so lonely, sat spinning that night.
    She sat, and she spun.
    All alone?

In came a pair of long, waving arms.
Sat themselves down on the body.

The woman, so lonely, sat spinning that night.
    She sat, and she spun.
    All alone?

In came a head; it wobbled and lurched.
On top of the long waving arms it perched.

The woman, so lonely, stopped spinning that night.
She looked at the creature.
Her voice choked with fright.

"How did you get such broad feet?"
    (The creature responded, and I repeat,)
    "From much walking, from much walking."

"How did you get such long, long legs?"
    "From wandering the earth
    To see what it's worth."

"How did you get such a round, round body?"
    "From chasing in circles,
    Unending circles."

"How did you get such long, waving arms?"
    "From swinging the sickle,
    The axe and the sickle."

"How did you get such a wobbly head?"
    "It's held by a thread
    Waiting to be fed."

"But, what did you come for?"
    "Come for?
        YOU!"

brad together

overlap separate arms and legs

CONSTRUCT:

Shadow puppets are really silhouettes. Sometimes they are made entirely of lightweight cardboard, which will make the figures appear all black when they are placed behind the screen. Sometimes parts of the figures are cut out and colored cellophane is taped in, which will show up when behind the screen.

For this story, you may want to have all the figures solid, except for the fire in the fireplace, where the flames could be red and yellow. If you think the parts of the body would be more ominous with color added, that is also a possibility.

The puppets should be in proportion to each other, of course. A general rule of thumb is to make them about 12″ for easy manipulation and viewing by the audience.

Tape hinge and straw

THE OLD WOMAN:

She should be hinged at the hips, so she can move forward and backward when she is spinning.

1. Make the hinge by overlapping the two parts of the body. Punch a hole in both parts and loosely insert a paper fastener (brad), so the parts can move easily.

2. Attach a rod to the middle of the figure. If you use a straw for the rod, fasten it with a masking tape hinge. If you use a different rod, tape a paper clip to one end. Attach it to the figure with a brad, or by "sewing" thin wire on the figure and inserting the paper clip.

BODY PARTS:

Each part will need a rod attached. The feet are two figures, which move separately, but both can be operated by one puppeteer. The same is true for the legs and arms. For the head, cut out facial features to make them show up.

Use separate rods for all body parts.

SCENERY:

You will need a spinning wheel, a chair, and a fireplace. The "door" is offstage. The scenery is stationary and can be attached to the inside frame of the stage, by hanging it with thread from the top and making a flap that can be taped down to the floor of the stage.

fold
flap
to box floor

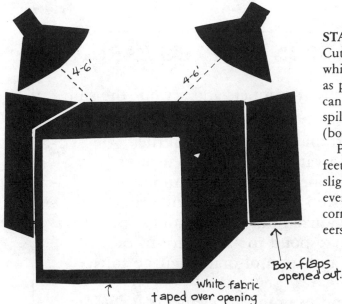

4-6'

4-6'

Box flaps
opened out.

↑
White fabric
taped over opening

STAGE:
Cut a rectangle in a large, heavy box. Fasten the white material to the inside of the opening as tightly as possible. Leave the sides on the box, so the box can be placed on a table and so that the light will not spill out the sides. Decorate the front of the stage (box), if you wish.

Place two 100 or 150 watt lamps about four to six feet behind the screen on each side. Focus the lamps slightly downward, to distribute the light fairly evenly across the screen. If the lights are positioned correctly, there will be no shadows from the puppeteers themselves.

Act: Each puppet moves as indicated by the story and when it talks. The puppets should generally be very close to the screen for everything they do. When the individual body parts speak, they should move in some way. Each part might take a "step" toward the back of the stage when it speaks, momentarily disassociated from the rest of the body until the head completes it again. Moving backward will make it appear larger. At the end, "Come for? YOU!" the body could "lunge" toward the old woman and then both of them could fly all the way backward until they disappear. Experiment with the effects until the class finds one it likes.

This particular story is an excellent one for choral reading. Several children might want to practice it until they achieve the mood they want.

The Bartok music also adds a lot to this story.

Evaluate: Talk about how the puppets, scenery, voices and music helped create the mood. Is there any way the story could be even more scary?

Assessment: Cooperation skills are important to the success of production. If they were able to create the mood of the story by putting all the elements together, they are making good progress in learning how to work together.

WHY MOSQUITOES BUZZ IN PEOPLE'S EARS

Drama Objective: Construct body puppets and act out the story

Related Objectives:

Language Arts: Select from oral presentation the information needed; use a variety of words to express feelings and ideas; relate experience with appropriate vocabulary; follow multi-step directions; describe time and setting of story; make organized oral presentations; present stories for entertainment; respond to various forms of literature; adapt content and form of oral language to fit purpose and audience

Art: Discover, explore, and examine art elements including line, color, shape, texture, value, form, and space; express individual ideas, thoughts, and feelings in simple media including drawing, painting, constructing and modeling three-dimensional forms

Materials: Paper plates, boxes, cardboard
Butcher paper, shopping bags, fabric remnants or old pillowcases;
Newspaper, stuffed old stockings, strips of crepe paper;
Stapler, masking tape, scissors;
Felt tip markers, crayons, colored paper scraps;
String, rubberbands

Introduce: There is nothing more annoying than a mosquito! This West African legend explains how the mosquito came to be such a nuisance.

Present: *WHY MOSQUITOES BUZZ IN PEOPLE'S EARS*

Adapted from a West African folktale by Monica Michell

One lazy afternoon, Mosquito saw Iguana napping in the sun. "Wake up, Iguana," said Mosquito. "I have a joke to tell you."

"Go away, don't bother me!" grumbled Iguana. "I am trying to sleep, and besides, I have already heard all your silly jokes."

Mosquito would not go away. He kept pestering Iguana. Finally, Iguana stuck two sticks in his ears and lumbered off through the tall grass.

Python saw Iguana coming. "Good day, Iguana," called the snake. Iguana did not answer, he did not even nod his head. "Oh no!" thought Python. "Iguana must be angry with me. I fear he is plotting some mischief against me. I'd better find a place to hide." Python looked about nervously and slithered into a nearby rabbit hole.

When Rabbit saw the big snake coming into her burrow, she was terrified. She hopped out the back way and scurried into the rain forest as fast as she could scamper.

Monkey was sitting in a tall tree eating a banana. He saw Rabbit running for her life and figured that some dangerous beast was chasing her. Monkey dropped his banana and began leaping about and screeching a warning to the other animals in the forest. In his excitement, Monkey happened to step on an old, rotten tree limb. It broke and fell with a crash on Mother Owl's nest, killing one of her owlets.

"Oh, my poor precious baby," wept Mother Owl. All the rest of that day and all through the night Mother Owl sat in her tree and cried. Her sorrow was unbearable.

Now everyone knows that it is Mother Owl's job to wake the sun each morning. But, after crying all night, Mother Owl could not manage even one small hoot. So, the sun slept on and darkness lingered.

The animals began to fear that the sun would never shine again. They decided to call on the Great Spirit for help. "Oh, Great Spirit, help us please! The sun won't come up and we can't see!"

All of a sudden, lightning crackled in the sky and thunder shook the earth. The animals waited in suspense. Then, the Great Spirit appeared before the assembled animals and roared, "What seems to be the problem?"

"Mother Owl won't wake the sun," the animals chorused.

"Mother Owl," said the Great spirit sternly, "Why haven't you hooted to wake the sun?"

"I have been crying all night and half the day," sobbed Mother Owl. "Monkey killed one of my precious owlets."

"I didn't mean to," said Monkey nervously. "I saw Rabbit running for her life and tried to help spread the alarm."

"Please don't blame me," whispered the trembling Rabbit. "Python chased me out of my own home."

"It wasn't my fault," hissed Python. "I was only trying to hide from Iguana."

The Great Spirit glared at Iguana. "Well, Iguana, what do you have to say for yourself?"

Iguana just blinked. Then he remembered the sticks in his ears and quickly pulled them out. "Excuse me, Sir. Would you mind repeating the question?" asked the Iguana politely.

"What mischief are you plotting against Python?" demanded the Great Spirit. "Why did you not say 'Good day' to him?"

"I am not plotting any mischief against my friend, Python," answered the bewildered Iguana. "And, I did not greet him because I did not hear him. I put these sticks in my ears because Mosquito was pestering me with his ridiculous jokes."

The Great Spirit looked at each animal one by one. "Hmmmmmm," he said. "Let me see if I've got this straight. Mother Owl's baby was killed by Monkey who was alarmed by Rabbit who was startled by Python who was frightened by Iguana who was buzzed at and bothered by that pesky Mosquito."

"That's right!" shouted all the animals.

"So it seems," said the Great Spirit ominously, "that Mosquito is the culprit! Bring him here to me. Mosquito shall be punished!"

Then the Great Spirit turned to Mother Owl and said kindly, "When you return to your nest, you will find that I have restored your precious baby back to life."

Mother Owl was overjoyed! She hooted her thanks and she hooted her joy and the sun came up at last!

But the animals never did find Mosquito, for he had hidden deep in the forest. So Mosquito never got the punishment he deserved. To this day, Mosquito has a guilty conscience. That is why he goes about whining and buzzing in people's ears: "Mmmzzzmm! Is everyone still angry at me?"

CONSTRUCT

In West Africa, the village storytellers sometimes use elaborate masks and costumes to act out their stories. The special kind of costume described here is called a body puppet. The body puppet is almost as big as the person wearing it, and is worn, like a costume, hanging from a string around the neck.

There are a number of characters in the story. Others can be added, or several children can play monkeys, pythons and rabbits.

1. Each child decides what character to play and decides how it should look.

2. Use a paper plate, a box or a cardboard cutout to make the puppet's head. Use paper scraps, crayons or felt markers to design the puppet's face.

3. Make the body out of butcher paper, shopping bags, fabric remnants or old pillowcases. Color or paint the puppet's body to suit the character.

4. Create legs, arms and wings out of rolled up newspaper, stuffed stockings or strips of crepe paper.

5. Securely attach the puppet's head, arms, wings and legs to the puppet's body with staples and masking tape.

6. Attach a string to the puppet's head and hang it around the neck so that the puppet hangs in front of the puppeteer. The puppet's head should cover the puppeteer's chest.

7. If you want, you can attach the puppet's arms and legs or wings to the puppeteer's own arms and legs with rubberbands or string, so that the puppet can walk, dance, wave or fly.

Act: The children should practice acting out the story without wearing the body puppets first, paying attention to the way the characters move and what their voices might sound like. They should stay with the basic plot but feel free to improvise action and dialogue as they go along. After they have gone through the story once or twice, they can do it with the costumes. This might be fun to perform for another class!

Evaluate: Talk about how the various characters moved and if the movements were fairly typical of each animal. They may have suggestions to improve the performance.

Assessment: Rate them on the performance, as well as the evaluative discussion.

RESPONDING AND CONSTRUCTING MEANING: DEVELOPMENT OF AESTHETIC SENSIBILITIES

Concept: View theatrical events emphasizing *player-audience relationship* and *audience etiquette*

APPLAUD!

Drama Objective: Understand that a good audience is necessary for the actors to do their best

Related Objectives:
Language Arts: Employ active listening in a variety of situations; present stories for entertainment
Social Studies: Express how groups influence individual behavior; describe psychological, sociological, and cultural factors affecting human behavior

---

Introduce: *How many of you have been to a play?*
What is the difference between going to a play and going to a movie?

If none have been to a play, ask:

> *How many have ever been to a circus, an ice skating show, or a magic show?*
> *How is going to those performances different from seeing the same thing on television?*

The major point is that the actors are right there in the same theatre as the audience. That is what makes going to the theatre different from going to a movie or watching television. The actors know the audience is there and they want to do the very best they can to entertain the audience. The actors actually know when the audience is interested in the play and likes what they are doing. Ask the children how they think the actors know that. They know it in two ways: one, the audience is quiet and listening; two, the audience laughs at funny things that happen and they clap after the show ends.

The actors, of course, are playing characters other than themselves. They are telling a story to the audience, in the form of a play. They know they aren't *really* the characters they are pretending to be, but they are doing what the characters would do in the play. It is important for the audience to help the actors by imagining that the story is really happening and that the characters are real. Both the actors and the audience need to use their imaginations, if the theatrical experience is to be a good one.

Plan and Act: Over a period of several days, give the children the experience of being both the performer and the audience. Ask them to tell a joke to the rest of the class. The audience is to imagine it is the funniest joke they have ever heard. They respond by laughing and clapping enthusiastically. You can even go so far as to have a joke told a second time by some of the children, while the audience whispers and gives no response at the end. Ask them how the audience made them feel each time.

Another way to reinforce the actor/audience relationship is to replay some of the activities done previously or plan new ones. The class is directed to show how a good audience would respond.

Reflect: Ask them to discuss appropriate and inappropriate audience behavior, and why audience response is important to the performance.

Assessment: Their discussion should reveal their understanding of the objective.

110

AUDIENCE ETIQUETTE

Drama Objective: Describe and use appropriate audience etiquette

Related Objectives:
Language Arts: Employ active listening in a variety of situations
Social Studies: Express how groups influence individual behavior; describe psychological, sociological, and cultural factors affecting human behavior

Introduce: First, discuss the meaning of the word "etiquette" in other situations they are familiar with, such as table manners, or being a guest in someone else's home.

There are certain things one does when going to the theatre, too, in order to be a good audience. See if they can think of some possibilities and list them on the board. Try to elicit other ideas from them by asking "What if . . ." questions to fit the rules of etiquette below. For example, "What if some people arrive late and have a hard time finding a seat. How would that affect the rest of the audience?"

Audience Etiquette

1. Arrive promptly for the scheduled performance.
2. Take care of bathroom business and drinks of water before taking your seat.
3. Be considerate of others around you. While waiting for the performance to begin, talk quietly and keep your hands, arms, and feet to yourself.
4. Just before the performance begins, usually the lights are dimmed and sometimes it is totally dark for a few seconds. Show your knowledge of this theatrical technique by sitting calmly when the lights go out.

5. Do not talk to your friends during the performance.
6. Save eating and drinking until after the performance.
7. Show respect for the actors by giving them your full attention during the performance. Show your appreciation for their work by applauding.
8. When the performance is over, wait patiently for your turn to exit.

Plan and Act: Practice entering the room and the rules of etiquette before attending a performance. Even though you may not be able to darken the room totally, turn off one bank of lights at a time to signify the dimming of the lights. Then turn on the lights for the "stage."

Some of the children may want to replay an earlier story they have done or perform one of their puppet shows. Whether they are actors or audience, the children should pretend they are at a real theatre.

Evaluate: Ask them to grade the class on their theatre etiquette in class. After they attend a performance, ask them to talk about the etiquette of the audience. What was appropriate? What was inappropriate or rude?

Assessment: Grade them on their audience behavior.

Concept: View theatrical events emphasizing awareness of the following: *physical attributes and objectives of characters; dramatic conflicts; prediction of plot resolution.*

NOTE: Viewing theatrical events means going to a theatre, or seeing a performance by a touring group who comes to the school. Most theatre companies will provide study guides to help prepare the children for a performance, and to further their understanding through follow-up activities.

The following lesson is based on a play, *Jack and the Northwest Wind*, included here. The lesson serves as a model of how to analyze certain aspects of a play. The play can either be performed by the students for their own benefit, or simply read out loud.

JACK AND THE NORTHWEST WIND

Drama Objectives: Analyze the physical attributes and objectives of the characters; recognize dramatic conflicts; predict the resolution of the plot

Related Objectives:
Language Arts: Employ active listening in a variety of situations; select from an oral presentation the information needed; identify an implied main idea; recall facts and details that support the main idea; identify the multiple causes of a given event or a character's actions; draw conclusions; respond to various forms of literature

---

Introduce: This play is based on a folk story that has been told and retold for generations in the mountains of North Carolina. The characters are more like cartoons than real people. Tell the children to try to get pictures in their mind of what the characters look like and what they are doing as they read the play.

Present: *JACK AND THE NORTHWEST WIND*

based on the play adaptation by Tom Behm

Characters

Narrator	Wind
Mother	Bully 1
Jack	Bully 2
Old Man	Father

The play takes place in four different locations: Jack's house; on the road; at the Old Man's house; at the house of the bullies.

NARRATOR: (Jack and his mother are huddled in scraps of rags they are using for blankets.)
Jack and his mother lived in the mountains, and they were awful poor. They just didn't have a thing. One winter it turned real cold and set in to snowin'.
(Jack and Mom shiver.)
The Northwest Wind commenced to blow!
(The wind waves his or her arms and blows. Mother and Jack shiver and hop about as wind blows.)

MOTHER:
Jack! I'm nearly frozen! Get some boards and the hammer and patch up the cracks in the walls a little!

JACK:
I'd be glad to but I lost the hammer last summer when I threw it at a skunk!

MOTHER:
Well, use a stone to nail the boards up!

JACK:
I used up all the nails making frog gig!

MOTHER: (Wind blows louder than ever.)
Jack, something has to be done or we'll freeze.

JACK: (he has a bright idea.)
I should go and tell the Northwest Wind to just stop blowing.

MOTHER: (Laughing)
That's the silliest thing I ever heard! But, why don't you! *(She exits laughing.)*

NARRATOR:
Early the next morning Jack took off directly into the wind to tell the Northwest Wind to stop blowing. He walked and walked. And the wind blew louder and louder.

OLD MAN: (enters)
Hello, Jack! (Jack is surprised.)
What you up to this *cold* winter day?

JACK:
I've started out to stop that Nortwest Wind. We're just about to freeze to death back home.

OLD MAN:
Why, Jack, you can't stop the Northwest Wind from a blowin'.

JACK:
I'll stop it all right—just as soon as I find the hole where it comes out at!

OLD MAN: (Laughs)
That might be an awful long way off, Jack. You just better come and have a warm supper at my place.

NARRATOR:
Jack was mighty hungry, so he went. And the old Man seated Jack before a long table. He took a tablecloth from a chest and said,

OLD MAN:
SPREAD, TABLECLOTH, SPREAD!

NARRATOR:
The table was suddenly filled with food—chicken, roast beef, potatoes, salads, pudding.

JACK: (Big reaction)
That's more food than I have ever seen!

(He eats wildly, improvises eating a chicken leg, carving a roast beef, and eating pudding.)

OLD MAN:
Jack, you ought to go on back home tonight and look after your mother. If you do that I'll give you this magic tablecloth.

JACK:
That would be a mighty nice thing to have.

OLD MAN:
Then it's yours.
(He mimes folding the tablecloth and gives it to Jack.)
Now, Jack, you be sure and not stop at the next house back down the road. There's some awful rowdy kids live there and if you hang around'em much, they're liable to steal your magic tablecloth.

JACK:
I'll be careful. Thanks for everything.
(They shake hands and then Jack circles the stage, walking home.)

NARRATOR:
As he approached the house down the road the rowdy kids came out to talk to him.

BULLY 1:
It's dark and the road is dangerous at night, you better spend the night here.

JACK:
No, I have to be gettin' home.
(Kids grab Jack by his arms and set him down.)

BULLY 2:
A man got robbed on this road just last night. You better stay.
(The two kids confer in stage whispers.)

NARRATOR:
Jack was afraid of losing his tablecloth, so he decided to stay.

BULLY 1: (Reaches for cloth)
What's that silly lookin' tablecloth?

JACK:
Oh, it's nothing — just a present for my mother.

BULLY 2: (Laughs)
What a stupid present — an ugly tablecloth — how dumb!

BULLY 1: (Speaking sarcastically and pulling on the tablecloth)
Sure wish womeone would bring me a tablecloth! (Laughs)

JACK:
Well, it may not look like much but watch this. SPREAD, TABLECLOTH, SPREAD!

NARRATOR:
And all manner of good vittles appeared and the kids ate . . . and ate . . . and ate!

NARRATOR:
Jack was mighty tired and soon he fell asleep.
That night the kids switched tablecloths and put one without any magic power for Jack to take home.
(Kids exit and bring back a phony cloth and spread it out.)
The next morning Jack took his tablecloth and headed home.
And the wind started blowing again!

MOTHER: (Enters)
Oh, Jack, you never stopped that wind. It's still a-blowin'.

JACK:
No, I never got to the place where it came out, but a man gave me a present to bring back home.

MOTHER:
What did he give you?

JACK:
A magic tablecloth that fills with tasty food!
(Holds up the cloth.)

MOTHER:
You try it out—I sure would like to see that!
(Sits down.)

JACK:
SPREAD, TABLECLOTH, SPREAD!
(Mother laughs and Jack is dumbfounded.)

NARRATOR:
But of course nothing happened. So Jack's mother took it and cut it up to make
him a shirt.
(She exits.)
Jack stayed home about a week. But soon that Northwest Wind got to blowin'.
So Jack left home again to try and stop it. Only this time he was careful to cross
behind the Old Man's house.
(Jack takes big sneaking steps, but the old man enters and walks in step behind
him. Jack is satisfied that the Old Man is not around and turns, sees him and
jumps and yells.)

OLD MAN:
Hello, Jack! Where you started to again this cold day? Going to stop the
Northwest Wind?
(He chuckles.)

JACK:
I sure am. And you're not going to fool me again. That old tablecloth wouldn't
do a thing you said it would.

OLD MAN:
Did you stop at the house where I told you not to?

JACK: (Hesitates)
Well . . . . .

OLD MAN:
Oh, I thought so. They got your tablecloth! You just come home with me now
and I'll sec if I haven't got something else to give you.

NARRATOR:
So Jack went.

OLD MAN: (Takes mimed chicken from box.)
Here is a chicken to take home. Now all you have to do is hold your hand under it and say, COME, GOLD! COME, and that hen will lay you golden eggs.

JACK:
A golden egg! Wow! Thank you!
(Takes the hen carefully.)

OLD MAN:
Jack, you recollect now and not stop at that place where those devilish kids live.
(Exits)

JACK: (Walking backwards)
I promise I won't stop there. Thank you.

NARRATOR:
But the kids spotted him and ran out to see what the old man had given him.

BULLY 1:
What's that ol' chicken under your arm, Jack?

BULLY 2:(Being silly)
What does it do, Jack, lay a golden egg?
(Laughs)

JACK:
How did you know?

BULLY 1:
No chicken can lay golden eggs!

BULLY 2:
Whoever heard of a chicken that lays gold eggs except in stories!
(Laughs a lot.)

JACK:
Sure can! Look. COME, GOLD! COME!
(They see the mimed egg pop out into Jack's hand.)

BULLY 2:
Why, Jack, you've just got to spend the night with us!
(Pulls Jack.)

BULLY 1:
You sure ought to show that trick to Daddy when he comes home.
(Pulls Jack.)

NARRATOR:
And they talked so fast (Kids talk gibbersih in Jack's ear and hum a lullaby as they play imaginary violins) that before Jack knew what happened, he fell sound asleep. And you know what happened, don't you?
(Bully 1 gets another hen.)
That's right, that chicken can't lay golden eggs—it can't even lay real ones—it's a rooster!
(Both kids exit laughing.)
The next morning Jack took the hen and hurried home. Naturally the wind was blowing'!

MOTHER: (Good-natured laughter.)
Well, Jack, I see you're back, and the wind's a blowin' right on.

JACK:
I never found the place where it came out, but I met that man and he gave me a chicken that lays golden eggs. Look—COME, GOLD! COME!

NARRATOR:
But there wasn't a single egg and Jack's mother killed the old rooster and served it for supper.
(She exits with rooster.)
Jack stayed around a few weeks. And soon the Northwest Wind started blowin' the hardest yet.
So Jack decided to try one more time. But again he decided to sneak past the old man's house.
(Jack sneaks backwards and the Old Man enters opposite and taps him on the shoulder. Jack responds with a big reaction of fright.)

OLD MAN:
Hello, Jack! What in the world are you doing back here?

JACK:
That chicken you gave me wouldn't do a thing you said. We cooked it and ate it.
(Turns to walk away.)

OLD MAN:
Did you stop at that house again?(Jack hesitates)
I thought so! They've got your hen! That's what happened sure. If you go home this time, I'll give you a club.
(Cross to box, opens the lid and mimes removing a club.)

JACK:
Now what do I want with a silly ol' club—you ol' mutt!
(Sits down.)

OLD MAN:
This is a magic club, Jack. Suppose you want to have it beat you up some firewood. You just point it at a tree and say. PLAYAWAY, CLUB! PLAYAWAY! KNOCK DOWN SOME WOOD!

NARRATOR:
And before his eyes that club knocked down a big tree, knocked it right down off the hill, plump into the yard, knocked it into firewood, and broke some of it up into kindlin'.

OLD MAN:
Here, Club.
(Imaginary club flies back into his hand.)

JACK:
That's the very thing I've been wanting.

OLD MAN:
Now you be sure and not stop at that house this time.
(Hands Jack the club.)

JACK:
I promise. Thank you.

BULLY 1: (Enters as Jack circles the stage on his way home.)
What you got this time, Jack?

JACK: (Smug)
Got a magic club! It can chop a tree into firewood!

BULLY 2: (Whines)
Oh Jack. We got no wood in. If you'd just knock some in for us, we'll be awful obliged.

JACK:
Well, all right. PLAYAWAY, CLUB! PLAYAWAY! KNOCK DOWN SOME WOOD.
(Pantomime throwing the club.)

BULLY 2:
Look at that! it knocked down a big . . .

JACK: (They pantomime watching it fall onto the stage.)
TIMBER!

BULLY 1: (All jump from the shock of the tree landing.)
WOOW!! Right down into the yard!

BULLY 2:
It's busted into firewood!

JACK:
Here, Club!
(They watch as it bounces into Jack's arms.)

BULLY 1:
Just wait 'til Daddy comes home now, Jack, and let him see what that club can do.
(Jack protests.)

BOTH:
Please, Jack, Please, please, please, please!

JACK: (Thinks a moment)
Well, I guess there's no harm in that. I'll wait right here.
(Kids sit and pantomime yawns and being tired.)

NARRATOR: And Jack fell fast asleep.
When the kids' father came home they told him about the magic club Jack was holding.
(Father enters and the kids whisper in his ear and gesture wildly.)

FATHER:
It's too dark now to knock up any more wood. Couldn't you kids try it out just a little on one of the big logs by the fireplace?

BULLY 2:
Sure. I'll just slip it out of Jack's hand and say, PLAYAWAY, CLUB! PLAY-AWAY! BREAK ONE LOG THERE ON THE PILE.

NARRATOR:
The club started in on that log, banged so loud that it woke Jack up! Jack saw what was going on and jumped up and ran out the door and hollered back:

JACK:
PLAYAWAY, CLUB! PLAYAWAY! KNOCK DOWN THE WHOLE HOUSE! BEAT EVERYBODY IN IT, IF THEY DON'T HAND OVER MY TABLE-CLOTH AND HEN, QUICK!
(Much jumping and yelling from the kids and father as the imaginary club beats them.)

BULLY 1:
Jack! Jack! Stop that club quick, or it will kill us!

BULLY 1:
Here's the hen.
(After they hand the items to Jack they all exit with Father chasing the kids.)

JACK:
Good! Stop, Club! Time to go home.

NARRATOR:
And the Northwest Wind started blowin' again. About daylight Jack got home.

MOTHER:
Jack, that wind's a-blowin' right on.

JACK:
Never mind that. Watch. SPREAD, TABLECLOTH, SPREAD!

NARRATOR:
And sure enough the magic tablecloth spread this time and it was filled with food!
(Mother eats.)

JACK:
Watch this. COME, GOLD, COME!

MOTHER:
That hen is layin' golden eggs!
(She started picking up eggs, but Jack stops her.)

JACK:
Wait a minute. PLAYAWAY, CLUB! PLAYAWAY!

MOTHER:
Look at the club makin' firewood! The pile is taller than the house!

JACK:
With the gold we can get a hammer and some nails and fix up the house fine.
(Jack and Mother raise their hands triumphantly and freeze.)

NARRATOR:
So, Jack never had to try to start out again to stop the Northwest Wind from blowin' in their house!

The following are questions about the characters. Some of the answers are found directly in the script. Others rely on the students' imaginations, as they picture what a particular character might be like.

Mother:

What is her objective?
How does she feel about her son, Jack?
What does she do that shows she cares about him?
What does she think each time he brings something "magic" home?
What does she look like? What kind of clothes is she wearing?

Jack:

What is his objective?
Use three different adjectives to describe him.
What does he think of the Old Man?
How does he feel about the Bullies?
Did he know what would happen with the bullies when he received the club, or was he just lucky? How will your decision affect the way he acts during that scene?
What is Jack's attitude toward his mother?
What does he look like? What is he wearing?

Old Man: (This character could just as easily be Old Woman.)

What is his objective?
Why does he keep helping Jack?
Who is he? How does he happen to have all these magic objects?
What does he look like? What is he wearing?
How does he walk?
What does his voice sound like?

Bullies:

What is their objective?
Use three adjectives to describe them.
What do they look like? What are they wearing?
How do they show they are bullies by the way they walk?
What do their voices sound like?
What do they think of Jack?
How do they move when the club starts beating on them? What do they say?

Father:

What is his objective?
Does he know his sons have taken Jack's tablecloth and hen? Is he surprised when they give the items back to Jack?
What does he think when he sees the club working?
How does he react when the club starts beating him?

Wind:

How can the wind use sound and movement to create an exaggerated, cartoon-like effect?
What would be a good number of actors to create the wind together?

Narrator:

What is the function of the narrator? Why is that role important?

Questions about the dramatic conflict:

What is the main conflict?(Jack wants his house to be warm and he is foiled both by his own wits and by the bullies.)
Each problem that arises makes the conflict stronger. List the various problems, or crises, in the correct sequence.
What is the climax of the play? (The climactic scene is when Jack directs the club to tear down the house unless the bullies return the cloth and hen.)

Questions about the resolution of the plot:

> *How was the basic conflict resolved?*
> *When did you get the first clue about what might happen at the end?*
> *What could have happened to change the ending?*

Staging Considerations: If the class is going to act out the play, they should keep the audience in mind when they answer the following questions.

> *What parts of the play require careful pantomime?*
> *How can Jack use the stage so it seems as if he is walking from place to place?*
> *How can the acting area be used so that one part is Jack's home, one the Old Man's home and one the bullies' home?*
> *There are a couple of comic parts when Jack is trying to avoid the Old Man. Read the stage directions and practice the timing.*
> *When acting the play, be sure to keep the action and the conversation moving quickly. There should be no pauses between speeches except when some action is taking place, and often that action is being done while the Narrator is speaking.*

Evaluating and making aesthetic judgments: since a theatrical event is a thing to be seen and not just read, one must see a performance in order to judge it. If class members have actually performed *Jack and the Northwest Wind*, they can evaluate it. If not, talk about a television show or movie most of them have seen. Questions such as the following can be tailored to most shows:

> 1. *What did you think about it?*
> 2. *Were the characters believable within the context of the plot? Were their objectives clear? Did the actors move and speak like the characters should?*

127

3. *Did the conflict and tension build through the play until the climax was reached?*
4. *How did the costumes help you know what the characters were like?*
5. *How did the scenery help you know where the action was taking place?*
6. *What might be done differently to improve the play?*

Assessment: There are a number of assessment possibilities, depending on whether you use this lesson just for analysis or for acting. You might want students to respond to the questions about dramatic conflict and character objectives in writing.

Before the play: Most theatre companies provide a study guide for teachers to use with the children both before and after the play. Such a guide can help prepare the children for seeing the play. The better prepared they are, the more they are likely to enjoy the performance. They will anticipate what is about to happen, and know something about the plot and characters.

If the play is based on a story or book, you may want to read the story, or excerpts from the story, to the children. They will understand the play better if they know the basic plot beforehand.

You might want the children to act out a few of the more exciting scenes before they see the play. You could also ask the children to recall and enact times when they were afraid, or sad, or joyous, just like the characters in the story. They will find it interesting to compare what they did with what the actors do in the play.

If there are any concepts or words you think they might not understand, these should be reviewed beforehand.

If the play is set during a particular historical period, you might want to bring in some pictures of the period. Discuss the types of clothes people wore, what kind of transportation they used, what kind of homes they lived in.

After the Play: Providing a variety of ways for children to respond to seeing the play is important to reinforce their learning. If you were given a study guide, you may find follow-up suggestions that will appeal to your class. The following is a list of activities which many teachers have found useful. Obviously these are "generic" suggestions, and you would want to tailor them to fit the particular play the chidren saw.

1. **Draw:**
   a. *Draw your favorite character, or the most exciting scene.*
   b. *Draw the set.*
2. **Dramatize:**
   a. *Show how each of the characters walked.*
   b. *Choose one scene from the play to act out. Why was that scene selected?*
   c. *Act out a scene from another story which shows courage, feeling afraid, reaching a goal — whatever is appropriate to the play that was seen.*
3. **Discuss:**
   a. *What was the most exciting part of the play? How did you feel during that part?*
   b. *Who was your favorite character? What did you like about him or her?*
   c. *How was the play the same, or different, from the story or book it was based on? (If appropriate.)*
   d. *How did you have to use your imaginations when watching the play?*
   e. *What was the main conflict? How was the conflict resolved?*
   f. *What could have happened to change the ending?*
   g. *How did the designers of the scenery, costumes, props and lights use their imaginations?*

Assessment: Give them opportunities to respond to at least one part in each of the sections — draw, dramatize, discuss (in writing). Their responses will illustrate their understanding.

Concept: Recognize similarities and differences among television, film and live theatre, emphasizing *the setting and the acting*

ACTING FOR A CAMERA

Drama Objective: Recognize that acting in live theatre is different from acting in films or on television

Related Objectives:
    Language Arts: Employ active listening in a variety of situations; adapt content and form of oral language to fit the purpose and audience; present stories for entertainment

    Materials: If at all possible, use a videotape recorder, or a movie camera.

Introduce: Use *Jack and the Northwest Wind* as the basis for discussion.

Imagine you are seeing Jack and the Northwest Wind on television. How might it be different from seeing the play in a theatre?

Bring out the fact that the mobility of the camera would allow shots on location, such as a real house, a real road and so on. People watching television or films don't have to use their imaginations as much to believe that things are really happening in a certain place.

How is acting on television or film different from in the theatre?

Think of sitting in a theatre. How close are the actors to you? There is usually quite a lot of distance between the actors and the audience.

Now think of sitting in a movie house. The **screen** may be some distance away, but how close do the actors seem?

In the theatre, actors often need to use bigger movements and gestures, and they even need to talk louder, so that the audience will see what they are doing and hear what they are saying. They also need to make sure they are at least partially facing the audience.

In the movies actors can use small, very natural movements and the camera will see that for us. The actors can even whisper if necessary, and the sound equipment will pick it up. And the camera can move around from the back to the front of the actor if that is the desired effect.

Plan and Act: Use the first scene between Jack and the Old Man for the following activity. Ask two children to act out the scene for the rest of the class, making sure that the audience can see everything they do and hear everything they say. Use a video camera to tape the scene, if possible.

Then ask them to replay the scene, making all their movements and gestures as normal as possible, and not worrying about whether everyone in the class can hear them. Tape the scene, using close-up shots when desired.

Evaluate: Compare the way the scene was acted the first time to the second time. It is possible that the second time was still too exaggerated to seem natural on camera. They may have suggestions for toning the acting down. If you are working without a camera, talk about the kind of camera shots they imagined.

Assessment: Ask them to apply their knowledge by giving them the following description and having them write how it might be done if it was being 1) acted on a stage in a theatre and 2) videotaped or filmed. If you wish, they can work in pairs.

> The attic was dark and dismal. Tiny creatures were hiding in corners and hanging from rafters, waiting to see what would happen. The stairs creaked as Erik and Theresa crept up. Both were afraid but they knew the answer they were seeking was in the attic.
> "Listen," whispered Erik.
> They heard the moaning they had heard earlier. It was closer now.
> They had one more step to climb. They looked at each other.
> Theresa said, "Now."
> They stepped into the attic and found the answer.

Chapter III
GRADE FIVE

Fifth graders, who have been participating in this theatre arts curriculum, have had experiences in *movement, sensory awareness, emotional recall, pantomime, and original dialogue.* Those expressive skills are applied and reinforced in the fifth grade.

Up to this point, the majority of the playmaking/playwriting lessons have centered around literary selections. In the fifth grade, students will dramatize their own *original stories.* They will continue to learn about plot structure, improvising and writing scenarios with special emphasis on the *nature of conflict.* They will go deeper into characterization by focusing on how a character's *attitude* is revealed in behavior.

Lessons in aesthetic growth apply the concepts the students have been working on in other lessons. For example, when they *view a theatre performance* they will be able to demonstrate their understanding of *conflict* and *character attitude.* They learn how to *evaluate* and make *informed judgments* about a theatrical event. A play script is included as a *model for analysis.*

If the students have not attended a live theatre performance before, they may benefit from the lessons on audience etiquette and the player-audience relationship in Chapter Two. In fact, a review of those points would be helpful for all students.

In Grade Five, *similarities and differences among television, film, and live theatre* continue to be explored. This year the two aspects discussed are the *time of action* and *special effects.*

A multi-faceted unit, called "Swapping Scenarios," culminates the year's work, providing opportunities for students to enter into the roles of *playwright, critic* and *actor.*

Responsibilities and skills in *group problem solving* are important features of the fifth grade work in drama. Students are given numerous opportunities to evaluate the work of their group and their own participation in the group.

In the event that a class has not had prior experience in classroom drama, the Cross Reference Guide included here provides a ready access to concepts and page numbers. Classes may benefit from activities described in the fourth grade before they work on the activities for the fifth grade. In any case, the teacher may wish to review some of the earlier lessons.

On the other hand, a given class may demonstrate considerable skill in a certain concept and benefit from deepening their understanding by participating in activities from Grade Six. Students enjoy repeating theatre arts activities, so "borrowing" from another grade level is perfectly acceptable. Repeating activities within the grade level is also acceptable, and, in fact, desirable, because students become more proficient with repetition. Refer to the Scope and Sequence, pages 28–29, to see when concepts are introduced.

The following on-going personal and interpersonal behaviors may be set up in a chart form. Students should evaluate themselves periodically on how well they are doing. The student's self-assessment can be compared with the teacher's assessment of the behaviors.

1. *I follow class directions.*
2. *I cooperate with others.*
3. *I show respect for others by listening to and watching their presentations.*
4. *I listen and respond to the ideas of others.*
5. *I contribute ideas.*
6. *I respect the space of others.*
7. *I observe classroom and safety rules.*
8. *I concentrate on assigned tasks.*
9. *I demonstrate appropriate audience etiquette.*
10. *I show respect of others' feelings by carefully phrasing evaluative comments.*
11. *I respond appropriately to constructive criticism.*

THEATRE ARTS
Cross Reference Guide

Essential Elements	Grade Four	Page No.	Grade Five	Page No.	Grade Six	Page No.
Acting: Expressive use of the body and voice	Develop body awareness and spatial perception using					
	• movement	37–45	• movement	140–148	• movement	228–236
	• pantomime	50–53	• pantomime	155–158	• pantomime	243–244
	• voice	56–58	• voice	162–165	• voice	249–258
	• sensory recall	46–49	• sensory recall	149–154	• sensory recall	237–242
	• emotional recall	54–55	• emotional recall in character	159–161	• emotional recall in character	245–248
Playmaking/ Playwriting: Collaborative improvisations	Dramatize literary selections using		Dramatize original stories using		Dramatize original stories using	
	• pantomime and dialogue	59–64	• pantomime and dialogue	166–168	• pantomime and dialogue	259–262
	• shadow play	97–108				
	• puppetry	97–108	• puppetry	193–196		
	• plot structure	65–75	• conflict	169–177	• setting • time	263–270
	• characterization emphasizing	76–96				
	• physical attributes	76–83	• attitude revealed in behavior	180–192	• speech revealing character	271–283
	• character objectives	84–89				
	• dialogue	90–96				
Responding and Constructing Meaning: Development of aesthetic sensibilities	View theatrical events emphasizing					
	• player-audience relationship	109–112				
	• audience etiquette	109–112				
	• analysis of physical attributes and character objectives	113–130	• analysis of character's attitude revealed in behavior	197–210	• analysis of how speech reveals character	284–298
	• recognition of dramatic conflicts	113–130	• recognition of kind of conflict	197–210	• recognition of kind of conflict	284–298
	• prediction of plot resolution	113–130	• prediction of plot resolution	197–210	• prediction of plot resolution	284–298
			• evaluation and aesthetic judgments	197–210	• evaluation and aesthetic judgments	284–298
	Compare television, film and live theatre emphasizing					
	• setting		• time of action	211–212	• camera angles	299–301
	• acting	131–132	• special effects	211–212	• position of audience	299–301

A NOTE BEFORE BEGINNING: The sentences which are in italic are stated as if the teacher is talking directly to the children. They are either directions, questions, or sidecoaching comments. Sidecoaching means that you are observing the children and making comments while they are acting, in order to spark their imaginations, suggest new ideas, or encourage their good work.

The italicized sentences are intended only as suggestions. Each teacher has an individual style, and should tailor remarks and questions to that style, as well as the needs of the particular class.

GETTING STARTED

Drama Objectives: Develop an initial understanding of drama, through discussion and action; match and coordinate movement with that of partner

Related Objectives:
   Language Arts: Use nonverbal communication
   Physical Education: Develop coordination, reaction, and balance
   Music: Move to express mood and meaning of the music

Materials: A piece of slow, flowing music, to encourage slow movements, such as "Seagulls" from *Music for Rest and Relaxation*

Introduce:

Think of your favorite television program.
What is one reason you like it so well?

Ideas might be listed on the chalkboard. Although the reasons will differ, they will probably fall into categories, such as lots of action, interesting story, interesting characters. Tell them that all their ideas are part of a subject they are going to be studying in class. The subject is drama.

What are the people called who play the various characters on television? (Actors)

An actor has tools to use, just as a carpenter has tools.
What tools do you think actors use?

Bring out the idea that the basic tool of the actor is him or herself—the *body, mind, and voice.* Actors need to keep their bodies in good condition, just as carpenters must see that their tools are always ready to work. Actors often do this by using exercises or games. Tell them that in class they will be doing some of the same things actors do, in order to sharpen their minds, bodies and voices. The following activity is an example.

Plan: The students should all stand where they can see you. Play the music. Tell them that you are looking into a mirror, and they are all the mirrors. What will they do when you raise your right hand? (They will raise their left hands, like a mirror image.) Make very slow, continuous movements. The object is for the mirror image to copy your movements exactly as you do them and, as much as possible, at the same time you do them. They will get the idea after a short time.

Act: Divide the groups into pairs. One is the person looking into the mirror, the other is the mirror image. They may make any movements they wish as long as they are slow. Tell them you will walk around and when you look at them it should be difficult to know which person is the mirror and which is moving. Reverse the roles.

Reflect and Evaluate:
> *What was easy (difficult) to do?*
> *When were you unable to follow your partner's movement exactly?*
> *Explain how this is a lesson on concentration and cooperation. How are those two tools of the actor?*

Assessment: Note their varying levels of concentration. You should see continuous progress in duration and intensity as they have more experiences in drama.

To extend this lesson, suggest descriptive words for the movement. For example, move powerfully, joyfully, gracefully, heavily. Students can suggest words, as well.

ACTING:
EXPRESSIVE USE OF BODY AND VOICE

Concept: Develop body awareness and spatial perception through *movement*

MIRROR DELAY AND RELAY

Drama Objective: Synchronize movement

Related Objective:
   Physical Education: Develop flexibility, coordination and reaction

---

Introduce: You may want to begin with the basic mirror exercise on page 139. Then increase the difficulty by directing the partners to do delayed mirrors. That is, the partner who is the mirror image waits for two or four beats before beginning the movement. The movement is continuous, but delayed just a bit. When they have mastered the delayed mirrors, they will be ready for the relay.

Plan: Ask the class to form a circle (If you are going to play with them, join the circle. If not, stay outside the circle.) Each person looks to the left and remembers who that person is. Then they scatter throughout the room and find a place to stand, making sure they can see the person they were to remember. They do not have to be close.

Act: Choose one person to start the movement. The person looking at the leader begins a delayed mirror—soon the whole class will be involved. After awhile tell the leader to make one last movement and freeze in position.

Reflect: Ask for their reactions to the activity. Were there any pleasant surprises or unexpected problems? What is the result if one person does not follow the movement exactly?

Assessment: Rate them on how well they accomplished the objective. This activity can be repeated on different days. They ought to improve each time.

CONCENTRATE!

Drama Objective: Exchange movement patterns with a partner

Related Objectives:
   Language Arts: Use nonverbal communication
   Physical Education: Develop coordination, reaction, and balance
   Music: Move to express mood and meaning of the music, including steady beat and body sounds

Materials: A control device, such as a drum, or tambourine

Introduce: This activity includes several phases. Proceed only as far as the children are able to maintain their concentration. Each time they do the activity, they should be able to go farther with it.

They work in pairs. Direct them to listen while you clap a steady four beat rhythm. (Or use a drum.) They echo what you clapped.

Plan and Act:

1. Tell them that while you clap, each pair is to decide on some kind of movement which will keep time to the beat. (This is a good time to introduce the control device you have selected. When you strike it, they are to freeze immediately and listen for directions. For example, they will be busy planning their movements. When you want to begin the action, get their attention with the control device.) They both move together to the beat. Clap the four beat phrase several times, pausing between each phrase. The pairs repeat their movement phrase each time.

141

2. Tell them that you will clap the same rhythm, but each person is to do a different movement. The partners face each other, but each does his or her own movement to the rhythm. Repeat several times.
3. The next time, each person is to do what his or her partner did the last time.
4. Finally, draw their attention to the fact that you paused at the end of every four beats. This time, each person starts out with his or her own motion for four beats. When you begin the next set of four beats, they do their partner's motion. At the next set, they change back to their own motion. They change at each new set of four beats. This takes real concentration!

Reflect: Ask them at what point it became difficult for them to concentrate. What does a person have to do when concentrating? Paying close attention and being alert for signals help, along with tuning out other distractions. What can they do when they notice their minds wandering? Refocus that attention on the task to be accomplished!

Assessment: Note which phase of the lesson the majority were comfortable with and the next time begin with that phase and continue on.

CAUTIOUSLY

Drama Objective: Create an action based on a particular movement quality

Related Objectives:
Language Arts: Use nonverbal communication
Physical Education: Develop coordination, reaction, and balance

Introduce: Tell the class they are going to find out what parts of the body can be moved without moving the rest of the body.

Plan and Act: Begin at the bottom, with the feet. As parts are named, the whole class moves that part for a moment. After many parts are moved, ask them to try to move everything at once.

Now add something else to the movement—an attitude, such as the following:

> *Move your eyes **cautiously**.*
> *Move your head and eyes cautiously.*
> *Move your arms and head and eyes cautiously.*
> *Move around the room in that cautious way.*
> *What might you be doing? Keep moving cautiously and an idea will occur to you.*

As ideas occur, listen to them. There will probably be a great variety. Have them repeat the movement with their particular idea in mind. For example, someone might have the idea of moving a package with a bomb in it. He or she moves it carefully and cautiously, then throws it or detonates it, or whatever the student decides. Another person might have the image of walking a tight rope in a circus. They could decide what they are carrying to help them balance, and what tricks they might be doing on the tightrope.

Reflect: Ask them to share their experiences. Draw their attention to how many different ideas they came up with based on just one word—a tribute to the human imagination!

Assessment: Note any students who were not able to come up with an action. Some children have not exercised their imaginations in a long time. The imagination seems to atrophy just as muscles do from lack of use. Another possibility is that some just don't trust their ideas are "right" yet. Your continual positive reinforcement toward a variety of ideas will help.

WHO ARE YOU?

Drama Objective: Create the action of a character, stimulated by movement

Related Objectives:
    Language Arts: Employ active listening in a variety of situations; use nonverbal communication; use a variety of words to express feelings and ideas; experience and relate to the feelings and emotions of characters

Materials: Drum or tambourine

Introduce: Beat a slow, quiet beat on the drum. Tell the class to listen to the beat of the drum and move the way the beat tells them. The class moves to the beat and stops when the beat stops.

Plan:

Who or what might move like that?
What might the character be doing?

Act:

Move to the beat again, becoming the character you have in mind and doing what the character would do.

Use the same slow beat, but after a couple of minutes beat with very loud, sharp bangs.

Reflect: Afterward ask what characters they were and what happened when the drum sounds changed.

Assessment: Find out if everyone in the class came up with an idea, instead of just those who always share their ideas in a discussion, by asking each student to write at least two sentences—one sentence telling who the character was and the other telling what happened when the drum sounds changed.

FIRE

Drama Objective: Use levels of space to create movement of two different characters

Related Objectives:

Language Arts: Employ active listening in a variety of situations; follow the logical organization of an oral presentation; select from presentations the information needed; use a variety of words to express ideas; understand the feelings and emotions of characters

Physical Education: Develop coordination, reaction, and balance; participate in rhythmic activities that develop self-expression, creativity, and endurance

Music: Move to express mood and meaning of the music

Materials: Drum and tambourine

For the warm-up, use a lively piece of music, such as "Movin'," by Hap Palmer; For the forest fire, a good choice is "The Infernal Dance," from Stravinsky's *Firebird Suite.* For the regeneration, the "Finale," from the *Firebird Suite,* helps create the mood.

Warm-Up: This movement warm-up explores the three levels of space: low (down on the floor), middle (standing, but not reaching up), and high (reaching and leaping as high as possible).

Ask the class to find places on the floor where they won't be touching anyone else. Play a piece of lively music. Every time you hit the drum, they are to change positions, but stay in the low level of space. They should be able to make five or six changes without repeating positions. Do the same thing with the middle level.

With the high level, it will be easier for them to explore the space with continuous movement, rather than stop and start changes of positions.

Then, ask them to make movements in each level of space, varying from high, to low, to middle, as they wish.

Introduce:

How many of you have ever been around a campfire?
What is special about a campfire?
Let's create a campfire right here. Gather some wood.

They build the fire, and "light" it.

Watch the fire. Describe the way the flames move.
Each of you add one piece of wood, watch that piece, and use your
*   hands to imitate the fire as it burns your piece of wood.*
Campfires are nice, but other fires may not be so nice.
What could happen if someone dropped a match in the forest?

Plan:

How does that kind of fire move differently from the campfire?
How does it start out? How does it progress?
What does the fire want to do? (To survive it must devour and
*   destroy.)*

Ask each one to find a place on the floor and to imagine being a twig, or a clump of dry grass or something that would easily ignite. At a signal in the music, which is easily identifiable in the "Infernal Dance," each one imagines that a match has been dropped, and they ignite.

Act: As they play, sidecoach, using some of the descriptive words they used earlier in describing the fire.

As the fire rages, suggest to them that they suddenly come to a river.

You become panicky. You try to cross, but you can't.
You look around desperately for something else to burn, but every-
*   thing is gone.*
Slowly, you die down.

Fade the music out, but continue to sidecoach, suggesting the devastation of the forest:

Weeks go by, months go by, even years go by, and nothing is appar-
*   ent but charred earth.*

At this point, play the "Finale" softly.

> *Underground, something is happening.*
> *Life is beginning to stir slowly.*
> *Imagine you are a seed of some sort which is beginning to grow*
> *underground.*
> *Slowly push through the earth and out into the world again.*

Reflect and Evaluate: Afterward, ask them about the feelings they experienced, both as fire and as the plant. Ask how the movements were similar and different.

Replay: You may wish to replay the fire part, adding characters of animals reacting to the fire. Whether the animals escape or not is up to them. If you do this, *be sure* they understand that those playing the fire must make it *seem* as if the fire is touching the animals, but it *must not literally touch*. A few volunteers could demonstrate how this could be done.

Reflect: Afterward, a discussion of fire and its consequences would be appropriate.

Assessment: How well did they incorporate the three levels of space in their movement? How well did they concentrate on interpreting the characters, as opposed to moving randomly with no apparent purpose?

Concept: Develop body awareness and spatial perception through *sensory awareness and sensory recall in character*

BLIND WALK

Drama Objectives: Heighten the senses of hearing and touch; take leadership responsibility seriously; trust a partner

Related Objectives:
Language Arts: Use nonverbal communication
Physical Education: Develop coordination, reaction, and balance
Science: Use skills in acquiring data through the senses

Materials: You may want to use blindfolds for this activity

Introduce: Tell the class they are going to experience what it might be like to be without sight.

Plan: They work in pairs; one is designated as "A" and one is "B." The "A's" will be blindfolded, or close their eyes, and be guided around the room by the "B's." "A" should hold onto the arm of "B." "B's" must be very careful with their non-sighted partners. Discuss responsibilities of the sighted person.

Act: They explore the room. "B's" guide "A's" to touch various surfaces, to see if they can identify them. Allow a couple of minutes for exploration. Then they reverse roles.

After several experiences, you may want to make the activity more difficult. Put some obstacles around the room, like chairs, or wastebaskets. This time the guides do not touch their non-sighted partners at all. They just walk beside them and tell them how many steps to take, when to turn, when to stop and so on. They should move very slowly.

Reflect: Discuss what they experience when they had their sense of sight taken away.

149

Assessment: This is generally quite an exhilarating activity and the discussion is lively afterward. Some may have difficulty trusting their partners enough not to peek at first, but those who are able to stay "blind" will learn a lot about themselves and their senses. Replay this activity after a month or so and see if the trust level has increased for some of them.

WORD CHAIN

Drama Objective: Listen and respond at the appropriate time

Related Objectives:

    Language Arts: Employ active listening in a variety of situations; follow the logical organization of an oral presentation; adapt content or oral language to fit purpose; present stories; use the fundamentals of grammar

Materials: An index card, or piece of paper, for each student. Each card has two words on it. The second word on one card must always be the first word on another card.

For example:

First card:	bull	Second card:	forest
	forest		hole
Third card:	hole	Fourth card:	smoke
	smoke		(and so on)

Introduce and Plan: The first time the game is played, you may want to prepare the cards; other times, the students might prepare cards in groups. Explanation of the game follows. You may want to use only half the class at one time.

Distribute the cards at random.

Act: You start the story. For example:

    Once upon a time, there was a bully whose name, appropriately enough, was Bull.

A student in the class will have a card on which the first word is "Bull." That student takes up the story, beginning with the word "Bull." If the second word is "forest," the student must end his or her part of the story with the word "forest." For example:

> *Bull decided he would go out looking for trouble one day. He found himself cutting through a dark forest.*

Another student will have a card with the word "forest" on it, and will continue the story with that word, ending with the second word on the card.

And so it continues, with the last person concluding the story. It is permissible to add a few incidental words before the first word. For example, "In the forest . . ."

Reflect: Discuss what was easy and hard about the game. Ask what they had to do to make it work.

Assessment: How well were they able to accomplish the objective without your intervening?

MOUTH WATERING!

Drama Objectives: Recall the taste of a favorite food and pantomime eating it; react to partner's pantomime

Related Objectives:
   Language Arts: Use nonverbal communication; use a variety of words to express feelings and ideas

Introduce: Divide the class into pairs. Designate who is "A" and who is "B." The "A's" are to think of their favorite food to eat—something that makes their mouths water just to think of it.

Plan and Act: They are to pantomime eating it in front of their partners. The "B's" are to imagine that "A's" food is something they absolutely can't stand. "A" can't understand how "B" could possibly dislike this delicious food. Maybe "A" will try to get "B" to taste a bit of it. They may talk as they play the scene.
   Then the "B's" think of their favorite food, and eat it in front of their partners. But this time "A" is to imagine that he or she also loves this food and is sorry not to have some too.

Reflect and Evaluate: After they have played, discuss what they tasted, and whether or not their mouths watered. Was it difficult for the partners to react to the food being eaten, if they really like or dislike the food in reality? If so, they might try to imagine how they react to a different food which they either like or dislike, and transfer that reaction to the food their partner is eating.

Assessment: Ask them to write down at least six adjectives which help describe their favorite food. Adjectives can deal with taste, texture, temperature, smell or appearance. They should then write a paragraph about the food, incorporating those adjectives. Some may want to read their paragraphs aloud to see how others in the class respond.

SMOKE

Drama Objectives: Recall the smell of smoke; react to smoke in the house, playing different characters

Related Objectives:

Language Arts: Use nonverbal communication; use a variety of words to express feelings and ideas; participate on committees in group problem-solving activities; use a set of reasons to persuade a group

Physical Education: Develop and practice behavior reflective of safety

Science: Predict cause and effect relationship

Health: Practice general emergency procedures; recognize hazards in the environment and acquire skills necessary to avoid injury and to prevent accidents; recognize the health of the family is dependent upon the contributions of each of its members

Introduce:

Smells may mean different things at different times. For instance, if we were sitting around a beach fire, we would hardly notice the smell of smoke. But what if you were in bed at night and woke up smelling smoke?

Ask students to find a place on the floor and imagine they are sleeping in their own beds. Suddenly they become aware of smoke. What would they do? If there is a fire in the house, how would they escape? Maybe it is not a fire, how would they find out? Give the signal to begin the action.

Discuss their reactions to the smoke. People react in different ways— some become panicky, some are very calm and efficient about what to do.

Plan: Divide the class into groups of four. There are four characters: a young toddler, a parent, an aged grandparent, and the family dog. They are all sleeping when one of them smells smoke.

Allow a couple of minutes for them to plan their scenes, answering questions about who smells the smoke first, what that character does, how each will respond, and how, or if, they all escape.

Act: The groups can act out their scenes simultaneously. Afterward, one or two groups might like to repeat the scene for the rest of the class.

Evaluate: Discuss the reactions of the various characters. Did they make it seem as if there really was a smoke filled house? Could they make it clearer?

Assessment: Note those who were able to concentrate on the task and make it really seem as if there was smoke. You may want to discuss the difference between really using the senses to recall smoke and just pretending to go through the motions. The actions of those really using their senses are likely to be realistic and believable, whereas the reactions of others are likely to be exaggerated and unbelievable.

Concept: Develop body awareness and spatial perception through *pantomime*

COOPERATIVE PANTOMIME

Drama Objectives: Cooperate to pantomime an activity in pairs and small groups; use details to describe action observed

Related Objectives:

Language Arts: Employ active listening in a variety of situations; use nonverbal communication; use a variety of words to express ideas; participate in group problem-solving activities

Science: Use skills in acquiring data through the senses

Introduce: Ask them to think of something they do during the day that requires only one person to do it. Examples might include brushing teeth, combing hair, playing a video game. Each one should find his or her own space and go through the pantomime. You can sidecoach them about using their senses—feeling how heavy or light an object is, how it feels in the hand, and so on.

They pair up and each pantomimes the activity for the partner. While the partner is watching, he or she is to describe exactly what is going on in the activity, using as many details as possible.

> For example: *"I see you taking the cap off the toothpaste and putting it down. You are squeezing a lot of toothpaste on the brush. You are turning on the faucet and wetting the toothbrush. You are brushing your teeth and it is very foamy . . . ."*

You may want to model such a description for them while someone is doing a pantomime. The reason for giving such feedback is two-fold: one, it helps the observer focus on the pantomime and, two, the person doing the pantomime can adjust and clarify what is being done if the observer is not describing it correctly.

155

Plan and Act: Each pair then decides on an activity that might take two people. For example, making the bed, washing and drying dishes, one taking a picture of the other. They practice it and, at a signal from you, join up with another pair. Each pair pantomimes their activity, while the observing pair gives them continual feedback.

Next, the groups of four are to decide on an activity that might take four people. If you want to make the activity more challenging, tell them they may not choose to pantomime a game. The groups present their pantomime for the entire class. This time the observers are silent until after the pantomime is completed.

Reflect and Evaluate: After each pantomime, ask the observers to write down what the activity was and three details they noticed about it. When all are completed, discuss cooperation, asking them to think of as many things as they can that require cooperation in life.

Assessment: How well did the groups work together? Rate them on their pantomimes. Collect their papers and rate them on how closely they observed.

PASS THE SPACE SUBSTANCE, PLEASE

Drama Objective: Pantomime using an object so all know what
it is

Related Objectives:
Language Arts: Use nonverbal communication
Science: Use skills in acquiring data through the senses

Introduce: "Space substance" is an imaginary substance. For instance, if you hold your hands as if you were holding something the size of a basketball, you could say you were holding "space substance." Obviously the size can change at any time.

Plan and Act: You can use this activity with the whole class in a circle, or you may want to divide into two or three small circles. Tell them that you are going to give one person in each group a space substance which can become anything they want it to be. They can make it grow bigger or smaller, blow it up like a balloon, squash it down, cut it or shape it in any way they want to. The point is to make an object out of the substance and to handle it so that everyone in the group knows what it is.

You might demonstrate by shaping a flower, for example, with a stem, leaves, and petals, and then smelling it, or picking petals off it. When the group has correctly identified the object, it is passed to the next person, who reshapes it into another object.

Reflect: Ask them what makes a pantomime easy to guess. Not only are details important when pantomiming, but the activity has to be something the observers know about either through their own experience or by someone else's, on television, for example.

Assessment: Rate them on the achievement of the objective.

ADVERB GAME

Drama Objective: Communicate different meanings by changing the way a movement is executed

Related Objectives:
Language Arts: Use nonverbal communication; use modifiers correctly

Materials: Index cards

Introduce: The game they are going to play today has to do with adverbs. Ask them how an adverb works in a sentence. Then ask for examples of adverbs and write a few on the chalkboard. Ask them to perform a simple action in a number of different ways. For example, the action might be "Write a letter." They do the same action 1) frantically, 2) sneakily, 3) thoughtfully. Ask them what effect the adverb had on the way they performed the action.

Plan: Divide the class into two teams, A and B. Each team takes a minute to write down three different adverbs, making sure the opposing team doesn't hear them discussing the words. (If you prefer, you can work with four teams.)

Act: One person on Team A picks a card from Team B and looks at it. The rest of Team A, one at a time, calls out actions for their teammate to do in the manner of the adverb. For example, "Tie your shoe." Team A continues to instruct the person to do actions until they determine the correct adverb.

If a team is having a lot of trouble finding the right adverb, ask the team that wrote the adverb to give the player an action that fits the adverb well. (Obviously not all adverbs fit well with all verbs.)

Reflect and Evaluate: When were the adverbs easiest to guess? What were some examples of clear pantomime? How would a good vocabulary of adverbs (adjectives, too) help an actor bring a character to life in a play?

Assessment: Note the level of concentration in the game by the performers and the observers.

Concept: Develop body awareness and spatial perception through *emotional recall in character*

THE MOOD CHANGES

Drama Objective: Establish contrasting moods

Related Objectives:
  Language Arts: Use nonverbal communication; use a variety of words to express feelings and ideas

---

Introduce: With the class, choose a situation in which the characters are obviously in a happy mood. Examples:

  Astronauts who have made a successful landing on Mars;
  Explorers who have just found buried treasure;
  Hikers who have successfully climbed a mountain.

They act out the scene, establishing the mood clearly.

Plan: Then ask what could happen to change the mood so they would always shudder to remember that day. Select one of their ideas.

Act: They act it out, beginning with the previous happy mood and going through what happens to change the mood.

Reflect and Evaluate: Discuss what various characters did that showed their feelings had changed. Ask what kinds of things cause their own moods to change, either for better or for worse.

Assessment: How effectively were they able to create the mood change?

EXPRESSING FEELINGS

Drama Objective: Express a character's feelings in a given situation

Related Objectives:

Language Arts: Use nonverbal communication; follow logical organization of an oral presentation; use a variety of words to express feelings and ideas; adapt content and form of oral language to fit the purpose and audience; recall specific facts and details that support the main idea and/or conclusion; draw logical conclusions; experience and relate to the feelings and emotions of characters

Materials: Prepare two sets of index cards: one set lists actions, the other lists feelings. Examples:

ACTIONS:	FEELINGS:
bury a pet	sadness
read a letter	happiness
enter an empty cabin at night	fear
clean the house or yard	anger

Introduce: Talk about situations in which they have experienced strong feelings of sadness, happiness, fear, anger. Actors often recall those feelings when they are playing a character who is supposed to feel a certain way. They may never have been in the specific situation the character in the play is in, but they have experienced the feelings. For example, in the lesson on mood changes, the students have obviously never been in the situation of landing on Mars, but they have experienced happiness from having accomplished something.

In this lesson, they may be given an unfamiliar situation, but they will know about the feeling the characters are to portray.

Plan: Students work in groups of three. Each group selects an Action card and a Feeling card at random. It is possible that the two don't seem to go together. For example, the action card may say "Bury a pet," and the feeling card may say "Happiness." The group will have to figure out reasons why they might honestly be happy in such a situation, unlikely though it seems. They decide *who* they are and what their relationship is (family, friends, workers, and so on), and *where* the action takes place. They are working for truthful and honest expression of feelings.

Act: After they all try out their scenes simultaneously, several groups might like to share their scenes with the class.

Reflect and Evaluate: After each scene is presented, the audience identifies the characters, the action, the setting, and the feeling. Ask about any difficulties they may have had trying to act out the characters' feelings.

Assessment: Were the feelings shown by the characters believable?

Concept: *Voice*

"COME HERE"

Drama Objective: Communicate different meanings by
changing the intensity, pitch and rhythm of the voice

Related Objectives:
    Language Arts: Adapt content and form of oral language
to fit the purpose and audience

Introduce: Discuss how the voice can be used to communicate different ideas, even when the words are the same. How many ways can the students think of to say the words, "Come here"? Those two words could be said with a variety of intentions, such as disgust, urgency, pleading, enticement, patience, anger, joy, questioning. Experiment with different ways.

Act: Then ask the students to do the same thing with other words. While they walk around, for instance, they say "Hello" to other students, each time in a different way. Other words or phrases can also be used, such as "Yes," "No," "Goodbye," even "Please pass the gravy."

Reflect: Talk about how they used their voices for different intentions. That is, if they were pleading, were their voices high or low, loud or soft? Were their words fast or slow?

Assessment: Note if they were really trying to experiment with different ways to use their voices.

WHISPER

Drama Objectives: Move the mouth and lips to form words clearly; stress beginning and ending consonants

Related Objectives:

Language Arts: Employ active listening in a variety of situations; adapt content and form of oral language to fit the purpose and audience; participate in group problem-solving activities

Introduce: The point of this lesson is to provide practice in articulation. Clear articulation is necessary in speaking aloud, as well as in whispering.

Whisper a simple direction to the class, such as, "Look out the window at the bird." Do *not* emphasize articulation or speak slowly. Some of the class may understand you, but most will not. Ask why they didn't understand you. Don't they understand whispering? Repeat the direction, this time whispering clearly and slowly, stressing beginning and ending consonants. Ask them why they understood you better that time.

In pairs, each one whispers one or two things they did after school yesterday. They whisper clearly enough so that the partner can understand every word without asking to have it repeated.

Ask a student to stand up and whisper something to the class. If they do not all understand, the student should repeat. Two or three others may also want to try.

Ask what they found themselves doing differently when they were trying to whisper clearly. Tell them to think of the way they used their mouths and lips and to repeat what they said earlier to their partner. They do it the same way, only they say it out loud instead of whispering.

Plan: Divide the class into groups of four or five. Each group is to develop a scene in which it would be natural to whisper rather than talk aloud. Examples:

163

someone is sick;
robbers are entering a house;
police are laying a trap;
children are getting a midnight snack;
people are trying not to set off an avalanche.
The students will be able to think of their own ideas.

Act: Each group acts their scene for the class.

Evaluate: The class talks about whether they could understand what the characters said and the situation they were in.

Assessment: Rate them on how well you could understand them.

VOICES AND FEELINGS

Drama Objective: Express different feelings through variation of pitch, volume, and rate of speed

Related Objectives:

Language Arts: Employ active listening in a variety of situations; adapt content and form of oral language to fit the purpose and audience

Introduce: Discuss how one can tell what mood another person is in by listening to his or her voice. What do adults in their family sound like when they are in a very good mood? A bad mood?

Act: Describe the following situations. They all act simultaneously, right after you describe the situation. There is no need for planning time.

1. *You just received your report card. You made all A's. You are overjoyed, and run to tell your best friend about it. Imagine you are talking to your best friend.*
2. *Your friend is not so happy. Your friend's report card was not good. You try to cheer your friend up.*
3. *It is dark and your pet hasn't come home. You are afraid something has happened to him. You go out to call for him.*
4. *Your bike has been stolen. Talk to your friend about it.*

Reflect: Ask them to think about how they used their voices in each situation. Describe in terms of pitch, volume and rate of speed.

Assessment: Ask them to describe, in writing, how the voice would sound in these situations:

1. *A mother or father is trying to comfort a crying baby and get it to go to sleep.*
2. *A mother or father is cheering for a child's soccer team.*

Grade their papers.

PLAYMAKING/PLAYWRITING:
COLLABORATIVE IMPROVISATIONS

Concept: Dramatize original stories using *pantomime*

THE STOOGES

Drama Objectives: Use exaggerated pantomime and movement
to communicate a story; develop cooperation skills in group
problem-solving

Related Objectives:
Language Arts: Arrange events in sequential order when
sequence is not stated; understand cause and effect
relationships; predict probable future outcomes or actions;
participate in group problem-solving activities

Materials: Old ragtime or honky tonk piano music, such as
"Chinatown, My Chinatown," would provide an appropriate
background for the action

Introduce: Ask the class if they have ever seen the Three Stooges cartoon
on television. They are three characters who can never do anything right,
and are constantly getting into trouble. They might be described as corny,
zany, idiotic, stupid. Are there any other characters on television that are
like that?

Plan: Describe the situation: *The Stooges have decided there is no reason
why people can't fly like birds. They are in the process of completing a kite-
like apparatus which they are sure will fly.*

> *What kinds of things do you think might occur as they put the
> finishing touches on the kite?*
> *Where will they choose to fly from?*

Think of what might happen and what they might do as a result.
Other situations could be used instead of, or along with, the above:

The Stooges decide to go into the plumbing business.
They decide to join a circus—wild animal acts, aerial acts, and so on.
They need to leave town in a hurry in their old jalopy.
They go on a safari.

Divide the class into groups of three. They are to plan the scene, which is to be acted in pantomime, no dialogue.

Talk about group problem-solving responsibilities and skills. Write criteria on the board, such as the following:

1. *Each person contributes ideas.*
2. *Each person listens carefully to ideas of others without putting them down.*
3. *They evaluate the ideas according to the problem they are working on.*
4. *They reach consensus in selecting the ideas they want to use and putting them in a logical order.*
5. *Consensus may mean making compromises.*

While they are planning, put the music on. Remind the class that they are cartoon characters, which means that their actions are exaggerated. Allow them several minutes to plan.

Act: All groups can play simultaneously. Have them start by getting into a beginning pose, as if a camera had snapped a picture of them. When they are all posed, start the music as a signal to begin. After they have played about 30 seconds, tell them to continue in *slow motion*. Then tell them to continue in *double time*. You can alter the speed several times. After they have all played, some of the groups may want to share their scene with the rest of the class.

Evaluate:

How did the characters seem cartoon-like?
What were some examples of clear pantomime?
Could the ending of some of the scenes be improved?

Assessment: Using the group problem-solving responsibilities and skills you listed on the board, ask each student to evaluate, in writing, how well their group worked together to solve the problem. You will be able to compare the product (scene) they created with their self-evaluations. For example, if the scene was not well done, but each group member gave high marks for their problem-solving skills, there is a discrepancy you will want to discuss with them.

Concept: Dramatize original stories using *improvisation* which reveals an understanding of *conflict in a plot*

CONFLICT CAUSED BY PEOPLE

Drama Objectives: To improvise a scene in which the major conflict stems from people having different objectives; develop cooperation skills in group problem-solving

Related Objectives:
Language Arts: Arrange events in sequential order; understand cause and effect relationships; predict probable future outcomes or actions; draw logical conclusions; experience and relate to the feelings and emotions of characters; participate on committees in group problem-solving activities; use a variety of words to express feelings and ideas

---

Introduce: Tell the students to close their eyes and listen. Then open and close the door quietly, but with some sound, as a person might who is sneaking in. Then tiptoe across the floor. Ask the class what they heard.

Next, tell them they will hear the same sounds, but as they listen they are to picture the following:

> *who might be coming in,*
> *what room or building the door is opening to, and*
> *why the person is entering in such a manner.*

Repeat the sounds and discuss their ideas.

No doubt many of their ideas would make a very interesting beginning of a play. And several might indicate a conflict. Ask them how they would define conflict. A conflict is a problem which needs solving, or an obstacle that keeps someone from doing what he or she wants to. Often a conflict arises when two people have different objectives. For example, if two friends decide to go to a movie, but each one wants to see a different movie, they have a conflict.

Plan: Divide the class into groups of three. They are to develop a scene with conflict, based on the beginning discussed before—the door opening and closing and footsteps crossing the room. They need to decide

> who the characters are,
> what the conflict is,
> what happens, and
> how they will end the scene.

Act: After a few minutes of planning, each group plays simultaneously. Then, if there are groups who would like to share their scenes with the rest of the class, they may do so.

Evaluate: Ask the students to point out who the characters were, what the conflict was, and how the scene ended. Did the conflict happen because the characters had different objectives? (For example, did one want to rob a bank and the other want to guard the money?) Tell them to try to figure out the conflict in the next television program they watch.

Assessment: Instead of discussing each of the scenes, ask the students to respond in writing to two of the scenes:

1. *Who were the characters?*
2. *What were the objectives of each of the characters?*
3. *What was the conflict?*
4. *How was the conflict resolved?*

Ask them to evaluate their group's problem-solving skills, as in the preceding lesson. In addition, ask them to evaluate how well they personally worked with the group to accomplish the assigned task.

CONFLICT CAUSED BY THE ENVIRONMENT

Drama Objectives: Improvise a scene in which the environment causes the conflict, or problem; develop cooperation skills in group problem-solving

Related Objectives:
    Language Arts: Arrange events in sequential order; understand cause and effect relationships; predict probable future outcomes or actions; draw logical conclusions; experience and relate to the feelings and emotions of characters; participate on committees in group problem-solving activities; make organized oral presentations
    Science: Describe changes in objects and events; predict cause and effect relationships

Materials: Cards with beginning ideas on them. (Described below.)

Introduce: Tell the class that they have learned that one of the causes of conflict is people—when people want to do different things, often a conflict arises. They may have examples to share from television.

There are other causes for conflict too. Sometimes the environment causes a problem. Do they know anyone who has allergies? Allergies are caused by the environment—foods, pollen, dust, etc. Talk about why allergies are a problem, or a conflict. What other things in the environment could cause a conflict? (Fire, floods, storms, drought, tidal waves, air pollution.) The lesson today will focus on conflict that is caused by the environment.

Plan: Divide the class into groups of three or four. Each group is given a card indicating what they are doing before the conflict arises. They are to determine what the environmental conflict will be, what they will do and how they will end the scene. Examples of cards follow. It is all right if more than one group has the same card. Comparing their scenes will be interesting.

1. You are way out in the ocean in a boat, enjoying the day and fishing.
2. You are exploring a deep cave in the rocks by the beach.
3. You have been camping and you are enjoying a hike in the woods, a long way from your campsite.
4. You are enjoying a day at the beach.
5. You are shopping in a crowded mall.

Act: After they have planned their scenes, let each group act out their scene for the rest of the class. They should start by clearly establishing where they are and what they are enjoying doing before the conflict arises.

Evaluate: Following each scene, ask the class to tell what they were doing first, what the conflict was, and how the conflict changed their plans.

Assessment: Rate the groups according to the following:
Did the conflict stem from the environment?
Was it made clear both by actions and words of the characters?
Did they resolve the conflict in a logical way?

Again, ask them to evaluate their group's problem-solving skills and how well they personally worked with the group to accomplish the assigned task.

CONFLICT CAUSED BY ONESELF

Drama Objective: Improvise a scene in which the conflict comes from within the character

Related Objectives:
Language Arts: Arrange events in sequential order; understand cause and effect relationships; predict probable future outcomes or actions; experience and relate to the feelings and emotions of characters; use a variety of words to express feelings and ideas; participate on committees in group problem-solving activities; make organized oral presentation
Social Studies: Follow standards of ethical and moral conduct

This lesson has two distinct parts to it. You may choose to do the second part on a different day from the first part.

Part One:

Introduce: Tell the students to close their eyes and imagine they are in their own bed at home. Sidecoach the following:

> *Remember the way your room looks — try to recreate it in your imagination. Remember where the closet is, where various pieces of furniture are, where the door to the room is.*
>
> *Imagine that it is late at night. You and your mother are alone in the house. Other members of the family are away for a few days. The house is completely dark.*
>
> *You have wakened from a deep sleep for some reason. All of a sudden you feel very much alone. You hear the creaks in the house, but somehow they seem louder and different tonight. All sorts of ideas go through your mind. You begin to get a little scared, but you stay in your room.*
>
> *Finally you can't stand it any longer. You call out to your mother. No one answers.*
>
> *Call again. No answer.*
>
> *You are frightened. You run into your mother's bedroom. She isn't there. Now you really are frightened.*
>
> *You hear footsteps at a distance. What will you do? The steps are coming closer.*
>
> *The lights turn on. And there is your mother.*

Fear is a feeling that comes from within and it can cause a big problem or conflict if we let it. Briefly talk about times when they may have been frightened for what turns out to be no good reason, for example, going off a diving board for the first time, playing in a recital, or nightmares.

Fear is just one conflict that comes from within us. We create conflicts for ourselves in other ways as well. Have you ever wanted to do something, but you know you shouldn't? One part of you says "Do it!" The other parts says, "You know you shouldn't."

Act: While they are at their desks, ask them to act out this situation.

Each of you is a boy or girl of your same age, taking a test.
The test is important because if you do well, your parents have promised to get you something you've wanted for a long time.
You are stuck on one part of the test.
You are quite sure that the person sitting next to you has the right answer, but it has always been against your principles to cheat.
Go through the process you think this boy or girl would go through.

After about 15 seconds, tell the class that when you count to five, the test papers will be collected. This is their last chance. What will they do?

Evaluate: Be open and receptive to students' individual opinions. Talk about how cheating on a test is not acceptable behavior and will hurt the student in the long run.

Part Two:

Introduce: Sometimes our mouths get us into trouble or conflict.

Have you ever said something and then immediately were sorry you said it?

Sometimes we become so angry that we say or do things we are sorry for. Or sometimes we just don't think of the other person's feelings when we say or do something. Often we can do something to make up for our actions. But other times, nothing we say or do seems to help and only time will heal wounded feelings.

Plan: Divide the class into groups of two or three. They are to create a scene in which one or all in the group feel inner conflict of some sort. List some titles on the board that may help them think of an idea. Examples:

1. "I dare you!"
2. "Do you still have to do everything your parents say?"
3. "There's no such word as 'can't'."
4. "How was I to know?"
5. "It's too dark."
6. "You're just too dumb."
7. "Mama's little helper."
8. "Why did you tell?"

Allow a few minutes for them to plan their scenes. They need to figure out a good beginning and ending for the scene.

Act: Groups may volunteer to show their scenes to the rest of the class.

Evaluate: If you find that it is hard for them to act out the scenes seriously, or with good concentration, it is probably due to embarrassment at expressing deep rooted feelings. Focus discussion on the content of the idea, rather than how they acted it out. Recognize that this sort of thing is difficult to do, but encourage them to do their best, just as the actors on television do.

Assessment: Ask them to write a sentence describing the inner conflict after they see each scene, and before they discuss it. You will be able to determine their understanding of the concept.

Introduce: A scenario is an outline of a play. It provides all the character and plot information necessary for actors to improvise upon. Playwrights often write a scenario first, and then they fill it in with the dialogue of the characters.

The following is an example of a scenario based on a familiar story. Instead of presenting the scenario to them you may want to develop it with them, using their words, and write it on the chalkboard. Any familiar story may be used. You may want to use one they have read recently in their literature books. This one is based on *The Three Billy Goats Gruff*, which they should remember from when they where small.

Setting: There are two hillsides. One hill has almost no grass. The other hill is full of tall, green grass. In between the two hills is a bridge.

Time: The story takes place on a morning in Spring.

Characters:

> **Little Billy Goat Gruff,** light and a bit wobbly on the feet. It has a tiny voice.
>
> **Middle Billy Goat Gruff,** sure on the feet, but not very confident. It has a medium voice.
>
> **Big Billy Goat Gruff,** powerful and strong, with ram's horns. It has a deep, gruff voice.
>
> **Troll,** greedy, mean and ugly, with "eyes as big as saucers" and "nose as long as a poker." It has a loud, raspy voice.

Sequence of Events:

1. The goats wake up hungry. There is no grass left on their hill. Their **objective** is to eat food on the other hill. They know they must cross the bridge to get to the other hill. **Conflict:** they also know there is a mean Troll under the bridge who is hungry, as well. They make a plan.
2. Little Billy Goat Gruff crosses the bridge and is confronted by the Troll. Troll lets Little Goat cross when it hears about bigger goat to come.
3. Middle Billy Goat Gruff crosses the bridge and is confronted by the Troll. Troll lets Middle Goat cross when it hears about huge goat to come.
4. Big Billy Goat Gruff crosses the bridge and is confronted by the Troll. The Big Goat challenges the Troll to a fight. The Troll accepts. **Climax:** they fight. **Conflict resolved:** Big Goat knocks Troll over the side of the bridge.
5. **Objective achieved:** Goats feast on the grass.

Plan and Write: Divide into groups of three. Their assignment is to write a scenario for a television play. Give each group a couple of pages from a newspaper. They are to read the headlines and select one that seems to have interesting dramatic possibilities. They may read the accompanying story, but they do not have to stick to all the facts in the newspaper if they don't want to. In other words, they may add or delete characters and events.

  After they agree on a headline to use, they should brainstorm possibilities regarding the characters to be included, the conflict, the events. Together they write the scenario, according to the outline above.

Evaluate: Ask them to exchange scenarios with another group. They imagine they are a team of television producers reading a scenario submitted for possible script development. They evaluate it according to the following:

1. *Can you visualize the setting from the description?*
2. *Is the time stated?*
3. *Are the characters clearly described?*
4. *What is the conflict? Is it clear?*
5. *Is the sequence of events logical?*
6. *How is the conflict resolved?*
7. *What audience might be interested in seeing a show based on this scenario? (For example, children, teenagers, families)*
8. *What suggestions do you have to improve the scenario?*

Assessment: Grade each scenario and its evaluation.

Concept: Dramatize literary selections in which *attitudes* are revealed in *characterization*

THE FROG WHO WANTED TO BE A SINGER

Drama Objective: Show how the attitude of characters affects the way they act

Related Objectives:
Language Arts: Use a variety of words to express feelings and ideas; present stories for entertainment; recall specific details that support the main idea; become acquainted with a variety of selections, characters, and themes of our literary heritage; explain and relate to the feelings and emotions of characters

Materials: A piece of boogie-woogie music, with or without words, that the frog can sing and play along with during the last scene

---

Introduce: Discuss what it means to be frustrated. The story they are about to hear starts right out asking whether they have ever been frustrated. It is a story in a wonderful collection of African American tales told by storytellers, called *Talk That Talk*. This particular story is called "The Frog Who Wanted to Be a Singer."

Present: *THE FROG WHO WANTED TO BE SINGER*

Linda Goss

Well, friends, I got a question for you. Have you ever been frustrated? That's right, I said *frustrated*. Tell the truth now. Everybody in this room should be screaming. "Yeah, I've been frustrated," because you know you have, at least once in your lives. And some of us here are frustrated every single day.

How do you tell when you are frustrated? Do you feel angry? Do you feel depressed? Are you full of anxiety? Are you tense? Are you nervous? Confused? Sometimes you can't stop eating. Sometimes you don't want to eat at all. Sometimes you can't sleep. And sometimes you don't want to wake up. *You are frustrated!*

Well, friends, let's go back. Back to the forest. Back to the motherland. Back to the days when the animals talked and walked upon the earth as folks do now.

Let's examine a little creature who is feeling mighty bad, mighty sad, mighty mad, and mighty frustrated. We call him the frog. There's nothing wrong in being a frog. But this particular frog feels that he has talent. You see, he wants to be a singer. And there's nothing wrong in wanting to be a singer except that in this particular forest where this particular frog lives, frogs don't sing. Only the birds are allowed to sing. The birds are considered the most beautiful singers in the forest.

So, for a while, the frog is cool. He's quiet. He stays to himself and practices on his lily pad, jumping up and down, singing to himself. But one day all of his frustration begins to swell inside him. He becomes so swollen that frustration bubbles start popping from his mouth, his ears, his nose, even from his eyes, and he says to himself (in a froglike voice): "You know, I'm tired of feeling this way. I'm tired of holding all this inside me. I've got talent. I want to be a singer."

The little frog decides to share his ambitions with his parents. His parents are somewhat worried about his desires, but since he is their son, they encourage him and say: "Son, we're behind you one hundred percent. If that's what you want to be, then go right ahead. You'll make us very proud."

This makes the frog feel better. It gives him some confidence, so much so that he decides to share the good news with his friends. He jumps over to the other side of the pond and says, "Fellows, I want to share something with you."

"Good!" they reply. "You got some flies we can eat."

"No, not flies. I got talent. I want to be a singer."

"Fool, are your crazy?" says one friend. "Frogs don't sing in this place. You'd better keep your big mouth shut."

They laugh at the frog, so he jumps back over to his lily pad.

He rocks back and forth, meditating and contemplating his situation, and begins to realize that perhaps he should go and talk with the birds. They seem reasonable enough; maybe they will allow him to join their singing group.

He gathers up his confidence, jumps over to their tree house, and knocks on their trunk. The head bird flies to the window, looks down on the frog's head, and says: "Oh, it's the frog. How may we help you?"

"Can I come up? I got something to ask you," says the frog.

"Very well, Frog. Do jump up."

Frog enters the tree house, and hundreds of birds begin fluttering around him.

"Come on in, Frog. Why don't you sit over there in the corner," says the head bird. Frog sits down but he feels a little shy. He begins to chew on his tongue.

"Frog, how may we help you?"

"Uh, well, uh, you see," says Frog, "I would like to become a part of your group."

"That's wonderful," says the head bird.

"Yes, wonderful," echo the other birds.

"Frog, you may help us carry our worms," said the head bird.

"That's not what I had in mind," says Frog.

"Well, what do you have in mind?"

Frog begins to stutter; "I-I-I-I-I want to-to-to sing wi-wi-with your group."

"What! You must be joking, of course. An ugly green frog who is full of warts sing with us delicate creatures. You would cause us great embarrassment."

"B-b-but . . ." Frog tries to plead his case, but the head bird becomes angry.

"Out! Out! Out of our house you go." He kicks the frog from the house. Frog rolls like a ball down the jungle path.

When he returns home, he feels very sad. The frog wants to cry but doesn't, even though he aches deep inside his gut. He wants to give up, but he doesn't. Instead he practices and practices and practices and practices.

Then he begins to think again and realizes that even though the birds sing every Friday night at the Big Time Weekly Concert, they don't control it. The fox is in charge. The frog jumps over to the fox's place and knocks on his cave.

"Brother Fox, Brother Fox, it's me, Frog, I want to talk to you."

The fox is a fast talker and a busy worker, and really doesn't want to be bothered with the frog.

"Quick, quick, quick, what do you want?" says the fox.

"I want to be in the concert this Friday night."

"Quick, quick, what do you want to do?"

"I want to sing," says the frog.

"Sing? Get out of here, quick, quick, quick!"

"Please Brother Fox. Please give me chance."

"Hmmm," says the fox, shifting his eyes. "Uh, you know something, Froggie? Maybe I could use you. Why don't you show up Friday, at eight o'clock sharp, okay?"

"You mean I can do it?"

"That's what I said. Now, get out of here. Quick, quick, quick!"

Oh, the frog is happy. He is going to "do his thing." He is going to present himself to the world.

Meanwhile, the fox goes around to the animals in the forest and tells them about the frog's plans. Each animal promises to be there and give the frog a "little present" for his singing debut.

And so Monday rolls around, Tuesday rolls around, Wednesday rolls around, Thursday rolls around, and it is Friday. The frog is so excited, he bathes all day. He combs his little green hair, parts it in the middle, and slicks down the sides. He scrubs his little green fingers and his little green toes. He looks at his little reflection in the pond, smiles, and says, "Um, um, um, I am *beauuuutiful!* And I am going to 'do my thing' tonight." And soon it is seven o'clock, and then it is seven-thirty, and then it is seven forty-five, and there is the frog trembling, holding on to the edge of the curtain.

He looks out at the audience and sees all the animals gathering in their seats. The frog is scared, so scared that his legs won't stop trembling and his eyes won't stop twitching. Brother Fox strolls out on stage and the show begins.

"Thank you, thank you, thank you, ladies and gentlemen, we have a wonderful show for you tonight. Presenting, for your entertainment, the frog who thinks he's a singer. Come on, let's clap. Come on out here, Frog, come on, come on. Let's give him a big hand." The animals clap and roar with laughter. The frog jumps out and slowly goes up to the microphone.

"For-for-for-for my first number, I-I-I-I—"

Now, before that frog can put the period at the end of that sentence, the elephant stands up, pulls down a pineapple, and throws it right at the frog's head.

"Ow!" cries the frog. And the lion pulls down a banana, throws it, and hits that frog right in the mouth. "Oh," gulps the frog. Other animals join in the act of throwing things at the frog. Some of them shout and yell at him, "Boo! Boo! Get off the stage. You stink! You're ugly. We don't want to hear a frog sing. Boo, you jive turkey!"

The poor little frog has to leap off the stage and run for his life. He hides underneath the stage. Brother Fox rushes back on the stage.

"Okay, okay, okay, calm down—just trying out our comic routine. We have some real talent for your enjoyment. Presenting the birds, who really can sing. Let's hear it for the birds." The audience claps loudly. The birds fly onto the stage, their heads held up high. Their wings slowly strike a stiff, hypnotic pose as if they are statues. They chirp, tweet, and whistle, causing the audience to fall into a soft, peaceful nod.

Everyone is resting quietly except the frog, who is tired of being pushed around. The frog is tired of feeling frustrated. He leaps over the fox. He grabs him, shakes him, puts his hands around the fox's throat, and says, "You tricked me. You tried to make a fool out of me."

"Leave me alone," says the fox. "If you want to go back out there and make a fool of yourself, go right ahead."

"Hmph," says the frog. "That's just what I'm going to do."

Now that little green frog hippity-hops back onto the stage. He is shaking but determined to sing his song.

"I don't care if you are asleep. I'm gonna wake you up. I came here to sing a song tonight, and that's what I'm going to do."

In the style of what we call boogie-woogie, the frog begins to "do his thing":

DOOBA DOOBA DOOBA DOOBA DOOBA DOOBA DOOBA DOOBA
DOOBA DOOBA DOOBA DOOBA DOOBA DOOBA DOOBA DOOBA

The frog bops his head about as though it were a jazzy saxophone. His fingers move as though they were playing a funky bass fiddle.

DOOBA DOOBA DOOBA DOOBA DOOBADEE DOOBADEE DOOBADEE DOOBADEE
DOOBA DOOBA DOOBA DOOBA DOOBADEE DOOBADEE DOOBADEE DOOBADEE
DOOBA DOOBA DOOBA DOOBA DOOBA DOOBA DOOBA DOOBA DOOBA! DOOB! DOOP-DEE-DOOP! . . . BLURRRRRRP!

The elephant opens one eye. He roars "Uuumphf!" He jumps from his seat. He flings his hips from side to side, doing a dance we now call the "bump." The lion is the next animal to jump up from his seat. He shouts: "I love it! I love it!" He shakes his body thisaway and thataway and every whichaway, doing a dance we now call the "twist." Soon the snakes are boogalooing and the giraffes are doing the jerk. The hyenas do the "slop" and the fox does the "mashed potato." The birds also want to join in: "We want to do Dooba Dooba, too." They chirp and sway through the trees.

Tweet Tweet Tweet Dooba
Tweet Tweet Tweet Dooba

The whole forest is rocking. The joint is jumping. The animals are snapping their fingers. They are *dancing,* doing something that they have never done before.

The fox runs back on the stage, grabs the mike, and shouts: "Wow, Frog, you are a genius. You have given us something new."

From then on, the frog is allowed to sing every Friday night at the Big Time Weekly Concert.

And, as my granddaddy used to say, that is how Rhythm and Blues was born.

DOOBA DOOBA DOOBA DOOBA DOOBA DOOBA DOOBA DOOBA! DOOBA! DOOP-DEE DOOP! . . . BLURRRRRP!

Plan: Trace the frog's frustration levels from the first scene when he is practicing on his lily pad through to the crisis scene when the animals throw things at him. *As his frustration increases, what happens to the way he acts?*

Plan the crisis scene, discussing the feelings of the frog and then the other animals.

> *How was the frog feeling when he first went out on stage? What do you suppose was going through his mind when the elephant threw the pineapple at him? What about when the other animals joined in throwing things and yelling? How would you feel if you were in the frog's shoes? What does "humiliated" mean? After he runs off and hides under the stage, he hears Brother Fox introducing the birds and hears them perform. What is he thinking while that is going on? What finally drives him to confront the Fox and take matters into his own hands?*
>
> *What about the other animals—why did they start throwing things at the frog? How did they feel about him? What did the actions of the Fox have to do with their attitudes?*

Divide the class in half. Half will act the part of the frog, half will be various animals in the audience. Each should become a specific animal and decide how that animal would behave, what it will throw and what it will say to the frog. If there is some question about why there are so many frogs, explain that they are simply trying on the characters now, in order to experience the feelings of the particular characters. Each person who is being a frog will be reacting as he or she thinks the frog would.

186

Act: It would be helpful if you would take the part of the sly fox, introducing the frog in an exaggerated fashion, winking at the audience and so on. After the frog runs off the stage, say a few words to calm the audience down and end the scene by introducing the birds.

Reflect and Evaluate: Ask the frogs how they felt during the scene. What are some specific things they saw the animals do that made them feel humiliated, afraid or angry?

Ask the other animals how they felt. What people do often reveals how they feel or what their attitudes are. What are some other things the characters could do to show how they feel?

Reverse the roles and replay.

Plan: Discuss the climax of the story, from the time the frog hippity-hops back onto the stage to when the fox says his last lines.

> *What does the frog say to the audience?*
> *How does he feel?*
> *How would he say the lines?*

Have several people demonstrate.

> *How does the frog feel when he begins to "do his thing"?*

At this point, ask them each to try on the role of the frog, while you put on music for them. They can use their voices and pantomime playing various instruments.

The story says that at the beginning of this scene the other animals have been lulled almost to sleep by the singing of the birds. They are definitely mellow.

> *What do you think goes through the animals' minds when the frog*
> *   comes back on stage?*
> *What happens when he begins to perform?*
> *What do they do?*

You might want to reread that part of the story to refresh their memories. As before, they should think of specific animals to be and decide how that animal would move. Let them experiment with their animal dances.

Act: *If you were going to choose one word to describe the mood of this scene, what might it be?* Possibilities might include triumphant, celebratory, joyful, happy. This time, choose one volunteer to be the frog, while the rest are animals in the audience. You can continue to be the fox, participating in the celebration and ending the scene on a triumphant note.

Reflect and Evaluate:

How successful were you at creating the mood of the scene?
What were some particularly effective actions?
What would you change to make it better?
What do you think the author of the story was trying to communicate?

Assessment: Note how well they communicated the attitudes of the various characters in action, and how accurately they verbalized the attitudes during the discussions.

Concept: Dramatize original stories in which *attitudes* are revealed in *characterization*

GETTING UP IN THE MORNING

Drama Objective: Show how the attitude of a character affects the way he or she acts

Related Objectives:
Language Arts: Employ active listening in a variety of situations; use nonverbal communication; understand cause and effect relationships; experience and relate to the feelings and emotions of characters; draw logical conclusions

---

Introduce: Ask the students to imagine a very simple action. Sidecoach:

> *You are in bed sleeping. Your mother tells you it is time to get up. You get out of bed and go in the bathroom to brush your teeth. Close your eyes a movement and think through all the little actions you take in order to do this. Do you stretch first? Check the weather out the window? How do you remove the covers?*
> *Do you put your slippers and robe on or do you just walk barefoot? How does the floor feel on your feet? Is there a light that needs turning on? Is there a cap on the toothpaste?*

Plan: Tell them that the basic action of getting up in the morning is what they will be working with, but the way they do it will change according to the situation you will describe. They will all act simultaneously.

Act:

THE FIRST SITUATION:

Imagine that it is a bright sunshiny day. You have had enough sleep and feel good. You are looking forward to going to school because your class is going to have a party today. The way you get up and brush your teeth should tell us you feel great.

Begin the action by calling them to get up like the mother might.

THE SECOND SITUATION:

It is February and you are sick of going to school. The day is gloomy and rainy. Get up and brush your teeth like you would on such a day.

As mother, you may have to prod them a little to get going.

Repeat the exercise with other attitudes and situations. Examples:

You haven't had enough sleep and have a hard time waking up.
This is the day for a big test. You know you must go to school but you are very worried.
Your little brother hides the toothpaste and you are in no mood for games.
You are angry for some specific reason.

The class may be able to think of other circumstances that would alter the way they proceed.

Evaluate: In each playing, the action was the same. Ask the students what made each one different. Circumstances and the resulting attitude affect the way the character does the action. Point out that when thinking about developing characters in drama it is important to understand the characters' attitudes. Suggest that at supper they see if they can notice different attitudes of the people at the dinner table.

Assessment: How appropriately do they adjust their actions to each situation?

ATTACHMENT

Drama Objective: Reveal the attitude of a character through action and dialogue

Related Objectives:
Language Arts: Employ active listening in a variety of situations; use nonverbal communication; understand cause and effect relationships; experience and relate to the feelings and emotions of characters; use a set of reasons to persuade; adapt content and form or oral language to fit the purpose and audience
Social Studies: Respect the rights of others to behave in ways consistent with personal value system

Materials: A "costume box," with various miscellaneous items of wearing apparel, including hats, jewelry, and accessories. The students may want to contribute to the box, or you may find many items at garage sales for very low cost. The costume box can be used for many lessons.

Introduce: Each student is to choose one item to wear. After they have put it on, they find a place to stand or sit and listen while you guide their thinking. Each person answers the questions silently.

> *Think of a character who might be wearing what you have on.*
> *Are you old or young?*
> *What do you do—do you work?*
> *Do you have a family?*
> *What kind of house do you live in?*
> *How do you feel—are you grumpy, cheerful, kind, mean, sad?*
> *For some reason, you are very attached to the article of apparel you put on. You are so attached to it that you never want to take it off. You are always making excuses for leaving it on. Think of why you are so attached to it.*

Plan: Ask then to find a partner, and then describe this situation for them:

> *The two of you have just met. You are at a party talking to each other. As you talk, each of you notices the piece of costume that the other has on and you become fascinated with it. You try very hard to get the person to take it off. You may use any method you like to get the person to take off the article in question, except physically forcing it off. What will the reaction be?*
>
> *What will your reaction be when your partner wants you to remove the article you are so attached to?*
>
> *What excuses will you invent?*
>
> *Keep in mind who you are and your attitude toward the costume piece, as well as your attitude toward the other person.*

Act: There is no need for the partners to plan ahead. Everyone acts simultaneously when you give the signal to begin. After they have played awhile, tell them they have one minute to end the scene in some way.

Evaluate: Discuss what they did.

> *What was your partner's attitude toward the piece of clothing?*
> *How could you tell?*
> *What were some of the excuses your partner invented?*
> *How did you end the scene?*

Assessment: Give them this situation about the characters they have just developed:

> *You notice that a lot of people think you are very strange because you insist on always keeping your costume piece on. Write a letter, to be kept in your safe deposit box, explaining your attachment to the object, just in case something bad happens to you.*

They are to write in the first person, as the character.

Concept: Dramatize original stories using *puppetry*

THE ADVENTURES OF . . .

Drama Objectives: Construct sock puppets, invent a plot; act out a play

Related Objectives:

Language Arts: Use a variety of words to express feelings and ideas; participate in group problem-solving activities; adapt content and form of oral language to fit a purpose and/or audience; understand cause and effect relationships; draw logical conclusions; follow a set of directions; select and narrow a topic for a specific purpose; experience and relate to the feelings and emotions of characters; present a story

Art: Discover, explore, examine, and apply art elements including line, color, shape, texture, value, form and space; express individual ideas, thoughts, and feelings in simple media including construction and modeling three dimensional forms

Materials:
Socks;
Lightweight cardboard, or 3″ x 5″ index cards;
Material for stuffing the head—cotton, old stockings, etc.;
Fabric remnants, handkerchiefs, bandanas;
Yarn, buttons, felt scraps, various kinds of trim;
Scissors, needle and thread, glue, rubberbands, masking tape

193

Introduce: Ask the class what an adventure is. Solicit ideas for what they think would be good adventures. Then tell them that they may be able to go on some of those adventures—except it won't happen to them, it will happen to the puppets they create.

They are each to think of a character they would like to create. Maybe it is Detective Dog, or Cranky Crocodile, or Grim Granny, or Fabulous Felicia. The character can be an animal or a person. They can be thinking of the character they want to make while they construct the basic puppet figure. After that, they will add the features and costumes which will give the puppet its own unique personality.

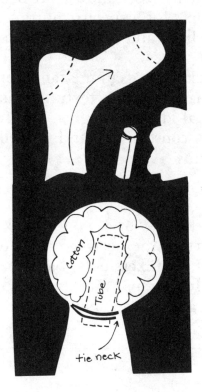

CONSTRUCT:
1. Make a tube of cardboard, about 5 inches long and wide enough to fit the index finger. Put the tube into the toe of the sock.
2. Stuff the toe of the sock with cotton or old stockings. This will become the head of the puppet.

3. Tie a string around the base of the head, around the tube to create the neck.

4. Cut slits in the side of the sock for the thumb and third finger.

5. Make a simple basic costume:

Cut a hole in the center of a bandana size piece of material.

Pull the bottom of the sock through the hole and tie it with thread or a rubberband around the neck.

Put the puppet on and gather the material around the thumb and middle finger (the puppet's arms) and secure with a rubberband. The puppet is now basically ready to perform — it just needs a personality!

6. Sew or glue features on. Add yarn or other material for hair. Add anything else to the basic costume that will help it come "alive."

Plan: Divide the class into groups of three or four. They should discuss their puppets and devise an adventure for the characters, writing it down in scenario form (See pp. 177–179).

If there are any props needed for their puppets, they should gather them together or construct them. Do they want sound effects? Those can be tape-recorded.

The stage can be as simple as a table top which they kneel behind. The front should be draped with material or paper to conceal the puppeteers in back.

Act: Each group should rehearse several times before presenting their puppet adventure for the class. Even these simple puppets are capable of a variety of movements. It is important that there is movement on stage — the puppets don't just appear and "talk," without using appropriate head and arm gestures. Ask them to think about puppets they have seen on television and how they move.

Evaluate: Afterward, talk about their adventures, and especially the plot structure.

> *Was the action of the story clear?*
> *What was the conflict?*
> *What was the climax?*
> *Could the play have been improved?*

These puppets can be used in a variety of ways and in many combinations for future puppet plays.

Assessment: Grade them both on the written scenario and the acting of the puppet adventure.

RESPONDING AND CONSTRUCTING MEANING: DEVELOPMENT OF AESTHETIC SENSIBILITIES

Concept: View theatrical events emphasizing
analysis of character attitude revealed in behavior;
recognition of kind of conflict;
prediction of plot resolution;
evaluation and aesthetic judgments

NOTE: Viewing theatrical events means going to a theatre, or seeing a performance by a touring group who comes to the school. Most theatre companies will provide study guides to help prepare the children for a performance, and to further their understanding through follow-up activities.

The following lesson is based on a play, *The Squire's Bride*, included here. The lesson serves as a model of how to analyze certain aspects of a play. The play can either be performed by the children, or simply read out loud.

THE SQUIRE'S BRIDE

Drama Objectives: Analyze the characters' attitudes as they are revealed in behavior; recognize the source of conflict in the play; predict the resolution of the plot; evaluate and make aesthetic judgments

Related Objectives:
Language Arts: Recall facts and details that support the main idea; understand cause and effect relationships; draw logical conclusions; evaluate and relate to feelings and emotions of characters; predict probable future outcomes; participate in group problem-solving activities; evaluate and make judgments; respond to various forms of literature; become acquainted with a variety of selections, characters, and themes of our literary heritage

---

Introduce: Ask the class to give examples of times when someone has insisted they do something they really didn't want to do. How does that make them feel?

The play they are about to read deals with that kind of situation and the clever solution that was found. Tell the children to picture the characters, as they read, and how they look when they respond to what happens.

Present: *THE SQUIRE'S BRIDE*

Characters

Squire	Jim
Mary Jones	Ned
Farmer Jones	Wedding guests
Mary's father	(8 to 10)
Horse	Narrator

A play in four scenes.
Scene 1   The farm
Scene 2   Later, on the farm
Scene 3   The Squire's house
Scene 4   Living room of the Squire's house

SCENE 1

NARRATOR:

There was once a very rich Squire, who had everything he could buy with money, but he was not happy because he was lonely. He had a wife at one time but she died, so the Squire decided to look for another bride. One day when he was out in his yard, he saw Mary Jones, the daughter of the farmer who lived next door, working in the field. She was pretty and very strong and the Squire thought she would make a good wife. He knew her family was poor, and so he was sure that Mary would want to marry a rich man like himself! The fact that the Squire was fat, bald, and much older than Mary didn't seem to bother him at all. He was sure that his money would be all any girl could want. So the Squire crossed the field to where Mary was working and began to talk to her.

SQUIRE:
Hello, Mary. Fine day, isn't it?

198

MARY: (Keeps on hoeing the field)
Hello, Squire. Yes, it is.

SQUIRE: (Sighing)
It's hard to feel sad on such a beautiful day, but I do.

MARY: (Keeps working and doesn't look up)
Oh really?

SQUIRE:
Yes, I've been lonely since my wife died last year. In fact, I think it's time that I married again.

MARY:
Maybe some nice, older lady will want to marry you.

SQUIRE:
Oh, I wasn't thinking of an *older* lady. In fact, I was thinking of you!

MARY:
Me? Oh, no thank you. I don't want to marry you.

SQUIRE:
Mary, don't be silly. I have so much money you would never have to do hard work again as you are doing now. Of course you want to marry me!

MARY:
But I like to work outdoors. And even if I didn't, I would not marry you!

SQUIRE:
You know, Mary, you are being foolish. Very few girls have the chance to marry a man as important and rich as I am.

MARY:
Well, I'm sure you'll find someone who cares for your money as much as you do, but it's not me! Goodbye! (Leaves the stage)

SQUIRE:
Mary! Mary! Come back!

FARMER JONES: (Enters)
Hello, Squire. Is something wrong?

SQUIRE:
Yes, there is, to be sure. I have done your daughter the great honor of asking her to be my bride and she refused!

FARMER JONES:
Refused? So fine a gentleman as you? I don't understand.

SQUIRE:
Neither do I, Farmer Jones. I think maybe she is just too young to know what is good for her. As her father, maybe you should make the decisions for her. In fact, I will make a bargain with you. When you convince her to marry me, I will cancel the debt of money that you owe me, and I will give you that piece of land you wanted, down in the meadow.

FARMER JONES:
Well, that's mighty generous of you. You just leave things to me. I'll bring Mary to her senses. She doesn't know what's good for her.

SQUIRE:
It's nice to deal with a reasonable man. I'll be going home now. I think you should talk to her right away.

FARMER JONES: (While Squire exits)
Oh yes, I certainly will. Just leave everything to me. I'll convince Mary! Mary! Mary! Come here, please.

MARY: (Enters)
Did you want me, Father?

FARMER JONES:
Yes, I did, child. What's this I hear about you not wanting to marry the Squire?

MARY:
I don't want to marry that old goat. I not only don't want to marry him, I'm not going to marry him!

FARMER JONES:
Now, daughter, he is a rich man and if you marry him, we'd never have to worry about money again.

MARY:
I don't care how rich he is. I wouldn't have him if he sat buried up to his neck in gold!

FARMER JONES: (Sternly)
Mary, as your father, I order you to marry the Squire!

MARY:
And as your daughter, I refuse! (Leaves stage)

FARMER JONES:
Come back here, Mary! Mary! Oh my, that girl has a mind of her own, just like her mother. What shall I do now? The Squire wants an answer right away and I can't tell him she said no! Oh my.

SCENE 2

NARRATOR:
The farmer stayed away from the Squire for several days, but finally the Squire insisted on knowing what Mary would do. The only plan the farmer could think of was this: First, the Squire was to get everything ready for the wedding, and then the Squire was to send for Mary as if he wanted her to do some work for him. When she arrived, they would be married so quickly, she would not have time to think about it. The Squire agreed to the plan and went home to prepare for the wedding. He invited his guests, and when everyone had arrived he sent two of his servants to the farmer's house. They were to say to the farmer, "We have come for what you promised the Squire."

JIM:
Well, Ned, here's the farm. Where's the farmer?

NED:
I don't know. Farmer Jones! Farmer Jones!

MARY: (Enters)
Hello, did you want something? I'm Mary Jones. My father's not here.

JIM:
Oh. Well, the Squire is in a big hurry to have your father send him what he promised him.

MARY:
A hurry? Why?

NED:
Oh, he's having a big party! And those were his instructions.

MARY:
Oh, I see! (To herself) I've been wondering what father and the Squire were up to! I think I'm beginning to understand. (To Ned and Jim) Oh yes, now I remember. What you want is that little horse of ours, over in the field. Better go and get her. It isn't right to keep the Squire waiting.

JIM:
All right. Thank you. Come on, Ned.
(Both go up to the horse and lead her back to the Squire's house while the Narrator speaks.)

SCENE 3

NARRATOR:
Now, audience, we ask you to imagine that this is a real horse. She doesn't speak but, as you may know, she is very important to our play. The boys took the horse back to the Squire's house. They left the horse in front of the house and went in to report to the Squire.

SQUIRE:
Well, did you get her?

NED
Oh yes, sir. She's outside.

202

SQUIRE
Well, while I take care of my guests, you take her to the room my mother had.

JIM: (Bewildered)
But how can we do that, Master?

SQUIRE:
You'll have to figure that out. Get some more people to help, if you can't manage her alone. (Leaves the room)

JIM: (Jim and Ned go off stage and return pulling and shoving the horse.)
Come on, Ned. Push harder!

NED:
Are you sure Squire wants this horse in the bedroom? Seems crazy to me!

JIM:
Me too, But that's what he said.
(Both struggle with the horse, who does not want to go with them. Finally, they get her in the bedroom.)

(Squire and Jim both go into the living room from different directions at about the same time.)

JIM: (Hot and panting)
Well, Squire, we did it! I was the hardest job we've ever had to do around here.

SQUIRE:
Never mind. There was a good reason for it. Now send a maid to help her dress in the wedding clothes on the bed.

JIM:
Dress? But Master . . .

SQUIRE:
No back talk! Tell the maid not to forget the veil and wreath.

JIM:
Yes sir.

(Squire exits.)

SCENE 4

NARRATOR:
Jim told a maid in the kitchen to go upstairs and dress the horse in the wedding clothes, so she would look like a bride. Jim and the others thought the Squire was playing a joke on his friends. So the woman laughed and did as she was told. In the meantime, the Squire brought his guests into the living room.

SQUIRE: (Entering with guests)
Good friends, as you no doubt have guessed, we are about to have a wedding in this house. The bride has been feeling a little shy about being a part of all this splendor, but I told her you were all good friends of mine and she was not to worry.

JIM: (Enters and interrupts the Squire, whispering to him.)
She's ready.
(He goes out, giggling. The guests whisper excitedly among themselves, wondering who the bride is.)

SQUIRE: (Proudly)
Quiet, everyone! Here comes my bride!
(He majestically turns away toward the audience, so that he doesn't see the horse enter. The guests do see the horse and they begin to giggle. Jim and Ned are pushing the horse, who clatters into the living room.)

SQUIRE: (Still facing away, but putting his arm out to the side.)
Mary, my beautiful bride, come here by me.
(He is smiling and turns to greet his bride. His smile freezes on his face as his eyes grow wide with astonishment. He laughs feebly and falls over in a faint.)

NARRATOR:
The guests laughed about that wedding for months, and as for the Squire, he never went looking for a bride again!

Discuss the characters: The following questions can be used to help the class plan how they will perform the play, or just to discuss after they have read the play. Some of the answers are found directly in the script. Others rely on the students' imaginations, as they picture what a particular character might be like.

Mary Jones:

In the opening of the play, how does Mary behave that lets you know how she feels about the Squire?
Why doesn't she want to marry him?
What does she think about her father?
How do you know she has a sense of humor?

Squire:

What does he look like?

Based on what he does and says, what kind of person is he?

Why does he keep insisting that Mary marry him?

What is his attitude toward Mary?

How does he behave when he is with her?

What is his attitude toward Jim and Ned?

How does it happen that he doesn't find out that the bride is a horse until the very end?

Farmer Jones:

Why is he so anxious to have his daughter marry the Squire?

How does this show when he talks with Mary?

Do you think Mary often does what he tells her to?

How does he feel when she refuses to marry the Squire?

Jim and Ned:

What is their attitude toward the Squire?

What do they think when the Squire tells them to take the horse to the bedroom?

What does Jim think when the Squire tells him the horse is to be dressed like a bride?

Wedding Guests:

How do they feel about the Squire?

Why did they want to attend the wedding?

What do they think when the "bride" comes in?

How do you think they reacted?

The "Bride":

Assuming two people are playing the horse, what do you think the attitude of the horse is to all that is happening?

How might the horse move that would show how she felt?

Discuss the conflict and plot resolution:

Based on knowledge of the three kinds of conflict, what kind of conflict does this play represent—person against person, person against environment, or person against him or herself?

What is the Squire's objective? How does that put him in conflict with Mary? How does Farmer Jones contribute to the conflict?

What is the high point, or climax, of the play?

At what point in the play did you get the first clue about what might happen? (When she sends the horse.)

What was the second clue? (When the horse is to be dressed as a bride.)

What makes it funny? (Our sympathies are with Mary—no one likes to be forced into doing something, especially something so important as marriage. The play is funny because the audience is aware of what is happening, but the Squire is totally unaware until the very end. The audience enjoys the trick played on him.)

Stage Considerations: Even if the students are not performing the play, they can discuss the staging. They should keep the audience in mind when solving the following problems:

How will you "create" the horse? What can be used to costume the horse?

The bedroom, where the horse is dressed, can be off stage. But the horse should be pushed and pulled into the living room, on stage, and then out through the door into the bedroom. Decide where the doors should be.

Be sure that the Squire is never in a place where he would be able to see the horse, until the very end. Plan out exactly where everyone will stand, or sit.

Evaluating and making aesthetic judgments: Since a theatrical event is a thing witnessed, not just read, one must see a performance in order to judge it. If the class has actually performed *The Squire's Bride*, you can evaluate it. If not, talk about a television show or movie most of them have seen. Questions such as the following can be tailored to most shows:

1. *What did you like about it?*
2. *Were the characters believable within the context of the plot? Were their objectives clear? Did you know how they felt about what was happening at any given time?*
3. *Did the conflict and tension build through the play until the climax was reached?*
4. *How did the costumes help you know what the characters were like?*
5. *How did the scenery help you know where the action was taking place?*
6. *What might be done differently to improve the play?*

Assessment: There are a number of assessment possibilities, depending on whether you use this lesson just for analysis or for acting. You might want students to respond to the questions about conflict and plot resolution in writing, since plot development has been emphasized in this year's work.

SEEING A PLAY

Drama Objectives: Use appropriate audience behavior; respond to the play by drawing, dramatizing and discussing

Related Objectives:
Language Arts: Communicate verbally and nonverbally; use a variety of words to express feelings and ideas; identify the main idea; recall important facts and details that support the main idea; respond to various forms of literature
Art: Express individual ideas, thoughts and feelings in simple media

Before the play: Most theatre companies provide a study guide for teachers to use with students both before and after the play. Such a guide can help prepare the students for seeing the play. The better prepared they are, the more they are likely to enjoy the performance. They will anticipate what is about to happen, and know something about the plot and characters.

If the play is based on a story or book, you may want to read the story, or excerpts from the story, to the class. They will understand the play better if they know the basic plot beforehand.

You might want the students to act out a few of the more exciting scenes before they see the play. You could also ask them to recall and enact times when they were afraid, or sad, or joyous, just like the characters in the story. They will find it interesting to compare what they did with what the actors do in the play.

If there are any concepts or words you think they might not understand, these should be reviewed beforehand.

If the play is set during a particular historical period, you might want to bring in some pictures of the period. Discuss the types of clothes people wore, what kind of transportation they used, what kind of homes they lived in.

After the play: Providing a variety of ways for students to respond to seeing the play is important to reinforce their learning. If you were given a study guide, you may find follow-up suggestions that will appeal to your class. The following is a list of activities which many teachers have found useful. Obviously these are "generic" suggestions, and you would want to tailor them to fit the particular play the class saw.

1. **Draw**
   a. *Draw your favorite character, or the most exciting scene.*
   b. *Draw the set.*

2. **Dramatize**
   a. *Show how each of the characters walked.*
   b. *Choose one scene from the play to act out. Why was that scene selected?*
   c. *Act out a different ending for the play.*
   d. *Act out a scene from another story which shows courage, feeling afraid, reaching a goal—whatever is appropriate to the play that was seen.*

3. **Discuss:**
   a. *What was the most exciting part of the play? How did you feel during that part?*
   b. *Who was your favorite character? What did you like about him or her?*
   c. *What was the objective of each character?*
   d. *Select three words to describe each of the characters in the play.*
   e. *How was the play the same, or different, from the story or book it was based on? (If appropriate.)*
   f. *What was the main conflict? How was the conflict resolved?*
   g. *What could have happened to change the ending?*
   h. *How did the designers of the scenery, costumes, props and lights use their imaginations?*
   i. *When you think about the production you saw, which colors come to mind?*

Assessment: Give them opportunities to respond to at least one part in each of the sections—draw, dramatize, discuss (in writing). Their responses will illustrate their understanding.

Concept: Recognize similarities and differences among television, film and live theatre, emphasizing the *time* of action and *special effects*

THE SAME, BUT DIFFERENT

Drama Objectives: Describe how the time of action can be indicated in a play and in a film; describe special effects used in the theatre and in film or television

Related Objectives:
   Language Arts: Describe the time and setting of a story; use a variety of words to express feelings and ideas; explain processes; evaluate and make judgments

---

Introduce: Ask the class to imagine they had seen *The Squire's Bride* on television. How might it be the same? How might it be different? Discuss their answers.

Plan:

1) **Time of Action**

There are four scenes in the play.

When does each scene take place? How do you know in the play version that Scene 2 takes place several days after Scene 1? The Narrator says so. If you saw it on television, there would probably not be a narrator. (Not all plays have Narrators, but this one did.)

On television, how might you know that the time of the action was different, without a narrator? In television, a play is not filmed as one continuous play, going from the beginning to the end.

Many different scenes can be filmed and then edited to give a sense of the passage of time. For example, we might see the conversation between the Squire and Farmer Jones making their plan. Then we might see the Squire and others making preparations for the wedding and the final wedding day results.

211

There would also be time for costume changes, which would indicate passage of time.

Apply: Assign students to watch a 30 minute television show and write down all the ways that passage of time is indicated.

2) Special Effects

There are few special effects necessary for *The Squire's Bride,* although on television one would probably see a real horse being dressed in wedding finery, instead of people pretending to be a horse. But television and film can use a much wider variety of special effects than can be used on a stage. For example, if the script calls for someone to catch on fire, that can be done on television, but would be difficult, if not impossible to do on stage. For one thing, the actor puts on a special costume. The camera shoots the burning for only a few seconds and there is a whole team of people on the set with fire extinguishing equipment.

Apply: Ask the class to think of other special effects on television or in the movies. Science fiction films provide good examples.

If possible, show the class a film, such as *The Making of E.T.* or *Making of Star Wars.*

Reflect: Although the plots may be the same on film as they are on the stage, going to the theatre requires more from the audience. The audience members need to use their imaginations more when seeing a play in a theatre. Ask the class why this is so.

Assessment: Use their assignment about the passage of time as a basis for grading.

Concept: Recognize that *playwrights, critics* and *actors* all have different responsibilities as they work on a play.

SWAPPING SCENARIOS

The following unit may be used as a culminating project for the drama class. Students will be involved in group problem-solving as playwrights, critics and actors. The unit is divided into separate, but sequential, parts. You may choose to do one or more parts per day over several days. The unit presupposes that the students have participated in the earlier lesson "Writing Scenarios," on pages 177–179.

Drama Objectives: Use cooperative skills to
1) develop and write a scenario;
2) critique a scenario;
3) improvise from a scenario

Related Objectives:

Language Arts: Select and narrow a topic for a specific purpose; use chronological order; describe the time and setting of story; use a variety of words to express feelings and ideas; use fundamentals of grammar, punctuation, and spelling; present plays for entertainment

Materials: A collection of photographs or drawings in which there is inherent tension. An excellent book for this is *The Mysteries of Harris Burdick,* by Chris Van Allsburg. An opaque projector would be helpful to show the pictures to the class for discussion purposes

---

Part One: *THE SCENARIO*

Introduce: Tell the students what the drama objectives of the unit are. One of the differences between the final improvisation in this unit and other lessons they have had is that they will be acting out a scenario written by another group, rather than their own group. The scenarios, therefore, need to be very clear since the improvisation will reflect back on the playwrights' work.

Good plays usually contain dramatic tension of one sort or another. Dramatic tension occurs when you are not sure just what is going to happen next. A car hanging part way over a high cliff is one example of dramatic tension, a cat stalking a mouse is another. Ask the class for other examples.

Show them selected pictures or photos, using the opaque projector, if possible. If the Van Allsburg book is used, tell them the title of each picture. Ask where the dramatic tension is in the picture.

Plan: Divide the class into groups of three or four. If possible, each group should have the same number in it. If that doesn't work out, try to make sure each group has a corresponding group that matches it in number. The reason for this is that they will be developing the same number of characters as they have people in their group, and in Part Four they will be swapping scenarios for improvisation purposes, so the number in the group should be the same.

Give each group a picture or photo. They are to develop a scenario based on the picture. One constraint is that they must create the same number of characters as they have in their group.

Ask them to discuss the following questions in their groups:

1. *What is happening in the picture? Describe the dramatic tension.*
2. *What are the conflict possibilities?*
3. *What scenes might have preceded this picture? That is, what happened earlier?*
4. *What might happen next?*
5. *Who is in the picture?*
6. *What other characters might be involved? Are they human? (You don't need to include all the characters in all the scenes.)*

Write: After they have discussed character and plot possibilities, they are ready to make some choices and write a scenario. The scenario needs to be detailed enough that someone else reading it would know what the characters are like, what the conflict is, what the major events are, how the conflict is resolved.

The scenario form is found on pages 177–178.

Reflect and Evaluate: After they have written their scenarios, talk about the process. What seemed easy to do and what seemed difficult? Ask each one to evaluate how well he or she worked with the group to solve the problem of writing a scenario. To do that they are to answer, in writing, the following questions:

1. *I (did or did not) contribute several ideas to the discussion and planning.*
2. *I (did or did not) listen respectfully to the ideas of others in my group.*
3. *I felt others (did or did not) listen respectfully to my ideas.*
4. *I concentrated on our task (all the time, sometimes, very little).*
5. *When there was an argument about what might happen next, I (helped or did not help) the group work out a solution.*
6. *I (was or was not) satisfied with our product (in this case, the scenario).*
7. *Our group (needs or does not need) to learn how to work together better.*
8. *These are ways I could be more helpful to our group:*

Each student should exchange evaluations with one other member of his or her group to find out whether that person agrees with the evaluation. If not, which points does the person question? If the writer agrees, the answer can be changed.

Assessment: Collect the evaluations. You may find some of the groups need help working together. The same forms will be used in other parts of the lesson, so progress can be noted.

Part Two: THE CRITIQUE

Introduce: *School is not the only place where work is evaluated. It is difficult to think of a profession in which the work of an individual is not evaluated in some way. It may not receive a letter grade, like school work, but it is evaluated nonetheless. How, for example, is a physician's work evaluated? A car mechanic's work?*

When a play or movie opens, reviewers write about it in the newspaper, either encouraging or discouraging people from attending. Long before the opening, the script is submitted to producers to see whether they might be interested in funding it. Sometimes they are interested in the idea but they think some changes should be made before the play is cast and rehearsals are scheduled. The playwright can either agree to the changes, or refuse to make them, or negotiate a compromise.

Students have had one experience looking at someone else's scenario and critiquing it. (See Writing Scenarios, pp. 177–179.) This will give them another opportunity.

Those who are evaluating the creative work of others have a great responsibility. They must learn how to make comments that are helpful, not hurtful.

Compare these two comments: "That scene stinks—get rid of it." And, "I'm not sure how this scene fits in with the rest of the plot. Maybe the point of the scene needs to be clarified, or maybe the scene belongs somewhere else."

Plan: Have groups swap scenarios. (For this exchange, it doesn't matter if the size of the groups are the same.) If possible, copies of the scenarios should be made so each person has one to look at. They are to imagine they are a team of producers reading a scenario submitted for possible script development. They are eager to find good scripts, so they will be making constructive remarks about what they like and what needs additional work.

They should read the scenario through once, either silently or orally. Each part of the scenario should be discussed and evaluated. The questions on page 179 may be helpful. They might also ask themselves: *"If we were given this scenario to act out, could we do it? What additional information would we need?"* It is important that the group work together and that they agree on the evaluation and the way the remarks are made.

Write: They are to write their comments on a separate piece of paper, rather than on the scenario. The purpose for writing is to be as clear and helpful as possible to the playwriting group. If there is something in the scenario they don't understand, they should write a question about it.

Reflect and Evaluate: Use the same process as for Part One.

Assessment: Read their critiques for how thoroughly they seemed to consider the scenario and how clear and helpful their remarks are. Since there is one product, each member of the group receives the same grade. If there seems to be an imbalance in effort, you will no doubt be able to catch that from their self-evaluations.

Part Three: *THE REWRITE*

Introduce: Ask students what they think might go on in a playwright's mind once the scenario is sent off and he or she is waiting for a response in the mail. Have they ever waited for something special to come in the mail? What is it like to wait?

Today the "mail" has arrived. Each playwriting group will receive the critique from the producers. If this were happening in real life, the producers' response could either make the playwrights very depressed or ecstatically happy. Even if they have more work to do on the scenario, that will mean the producers think it is promising.

Plan and Rewrite: Distribute the critiques. The members of the groups should read the remarks aloud and discuss each one. If they don't understand a particular remark, they can ask the "producers" to clarify.

Then, they rewrite the scenario. If they have thought of improvements themselves since it was first written, those should be included as well. They should keep in mind that the next group to see the scenario will be the "actors."

Reflect and Evaluate: Use the same process as before.

Assessment: Compare the original with the rewrite to see how changes were incorporated.

Part Four: *THE PERFORMANCE*

Introduce: The producers have said they want to see the scenario performed. They want to try it out to see how the play might work. The actors have been cast. They are a troupe of improvisational actors, who make up their own dialogue to fit the characters and action of the plot. How do you think they feel while they wait to have a first look at the scenario?

Plan: Distribute each scenario to a different group from the "producers" who critiqued it in the last lesson. This is the exchange where it is important to have the same number in the action group as there are characters in the scenario. If the gender make-up of the acting group is different from that of the characters, they can deal with that either by having the actor pretend to be a different sex, or by changing the name and other gender-specific references to the character.

They read the scenario through and decide who will play the various roles. They plan and rehearse each scene, adding any details they need to make the action clear. If there are several distinct scenes, marked by passage of time, or change in locale, they can use a narrator to inform the audience, or make signs to hold up between scenes.

Each actor needs to make certain decisions about the character: what he, or she, or it, looks like; how the character moves; how it talks and what it says; what the objective of the character is; how it feels about the situation and other characters in the play.

If they think costumes or props would help, they can find or make their own.

If, as they rehearse, they think of something they would like to add that is quite different from what is in the scenario, they should first check with the playwrights.

Act: After they have had ample time to rehearse, each acting group performs for the rest of the class.

Evaluate: Ask for responses from the playwrights and the producers of each scenario.

219

What did they like?
Were there any surprises?
What still needs to be more clear?

Ask those who were not familiar with the scenario beforehand to respond:

What was the conflict?
Where was the dramatic tension?
Who were the characters?
Was the ending clear?
What suggestions do you have?

Ask each acting group to do a self-evaluation like the ones they have done before.

The point should be made that when they see a play or watch television or a movie, the responsibility for the success, or failure, of the product rests on a whole lot of people—not just the actors. There are the playwrights and the producers. Who else is involved? Ask them to notice the credits listed before or after the next movie they see. The can count the kind of jobs included—sometimes there are 50 or more!

Assessment: How much detail were the performers able to add? Were the characters they created believable? Did they stay in character the whole time?

This unit created a number of products to assess: the scenario, the critique, the performance, and the self-evaluations are four. To those can be added the discussions and the group cooperation skills observed each day.

Chapter IV:

Grade Six

Sixth graders, who have been participating in the theatre arts curriculum, have had experiences in *movement, sensory awareness, emotional recall, pantomime,* and *original dialogue.* Those expressive skills are applied and reinforced in the sixth grade.

Students will continue to develop their original stories for dramatization. Up to this point they have learned about plot structure and the nature of conflict. This year, they will learn how the *setting* and the *time of action* affect the plot. They will also learn to recognize *themes.* With regard to characterization, they have learned about physical attributes, objectives, and attitudes. This year their work will focus on how *speech* reveals a character. They will also participate in activities which stress *role playing in situations* which are of current interest and concern to the students. They will have the opportunity to understand their own and *others' points of view* by playing out scenes from several vantage points. And they will learn how to develop and write a *scenario* and *dialogue* for characters.

When they *view theatrical events,* the students will have the chance to see how the play and the acting reflect the concepts they have been learning in their other theatre arts lessons. They will learn how to *evaluate* and make *informed aesthetic judgments.* A play script is included as a *model for analysis.*

If the students have not attended a live theatre performance before, they may benefit from the lessons on audience etiquette and the player-audience relationship in Chapter Two. In fact, a review of those points would be helpful for all students.

In the sixth grade, the students continue to explore the *similarities and differences among television, film, and live theatre.* This year the emphasis is on *camera angles* and the *position of the audience.*

A multi-faceted unit, called "Making Decisions," culminates the year's work, providing opportunities for students to enter into the roles of *playwright, designer* and *actor.*

Critical thinking skills and *self-assessment* are important features of the sixth grade work in drama. To that end, it is suggested that students keep a journal, which the teacher will read periodically. Specific journal assignments are recommended in many of the lessons. Others may be added by the teacher or students.

In the event that a class has not had prior experience in classroom drama, the Cross Reference Guide included here provides a ready access to concepts and page numbers. Classes may benefit from activities described in the fifth grade before they work on the activities for the sixth grade. In any case, the teacher may wish to review some of the earlier lessons. Refer to the Scope and Sequence, pages 28–29, to see when concepts are introduced.

The following on-going personal and interpersonal behaviors may be set up in a chart form in the student's journal. They should evaluate themselves periodically on how well they are doing. The student's self-assessment can be compared with the teacher's assessment of the student's behaviors.

1. *I follow class directions and rules.*
2. *I cooperate with others.*
3. *I show respect for others by listening to and watching their presentations.*
4. *I listen and respond to the ideas of others.*
5. *I contribute ideas.*
6. *I respect the space of others.*
7. *I volunteer and participate appropriately in drama activities and scenes.*
8. *I concentrate on assigned tasks.*
9. *I demonstrate appropriate audience etiquette.*
10. *I show respect for others' feelings by carefully phrasing evaluative comments.*
11. *I respond appropriately to constructive criticism.*

THEATRE ARTS
Cross Reference Guide

Essential Elements	Grade Five	Page No.	Grade Six	Page No.
Acting: Expressive use of the body and voice	Develop body awareness and spatial perception using			
	· *movement*	140–148	· *movement*	228–236
	· *pantomime*	155–158	· *pantomime*	243–244
	· *voice*	162–165	· *voice*	249–258
	· *sensory recall*	149–154	· *sensory recall*	237–242
	· *emotional recall in character*	159–161	· *emotional recall in character*	245–248
Playmaking/ Playwriting: Collaborative improvisations	Dramatize original stories using		Dramatize original stories using	
	· *pantomime and dialogue*	166–168	· *pantomime and dialogue*	259–262
	· *puppetry*	193–196		
	· *conflict*	169–177	· *setting* · *time*	263–270
	· *characterization* emphasizing · *attitude revealed in behavior*	180–192	· *speech revealing character*	271–283
Responding and Constructing Meaning: Development of aesthetic sensibilities	View theatrical events emphasizing · *player-audience relationship* · *audience etiquette*	197–210 197–210		
	· *analysis of character's attitude revealed in behavior*	197–210	· *analysis of how speech reveals character*	284–298
	· *recognition of kind of conflict*	197–210	· *recognition of kind of conflict*	284–298
	· *prediction of plot resolution*	197–210	· *prediction of plot resolution*	284–298
	· *evaluation and aesthetic judgments*	197–210	· *evaluation and aesthetic judgments*	284–298
	Compare television, film and live theatre emphasizing · *time of action* · *special effects*	211–212 211–212	· *camera angles* · *position of audience*	299–301 299–301

A NOTE BEFORE BEGINNING: The sentences which are in italic are stated as if the teacher is talking directly to the children. They are either directions, questions, or sidecoaching comments. Sidecoaching means that you are observing the children and making comments while they are acting, in order to spark their imaginations, suggest new ideas, or encourage their good work.

The italicized sentences are intended only as suggestions. Each teacher has an individual style, and should tailor remarks and questions to that style, as well as to the needs of the particular class.

GETTING STARTED

Drama Objectives: Develop an initial understanding of drama, through discussion and action; demonstrate understanding of action and reaction

Related Objectives:
    Language Arts: Use nonverbal communication
    Physical Education: Develop coordination, reaction, and balance

Materials: A control device, such as a drum, or tambourine

Introduce: Structure the discussion around a television show the students are all likely to be familiar with and like. Ask why they like the show.

> *One reason we like certain shows is that we believe for the moment that what is going on is actually happening, even though we know the people are really actors, who go home from work just like everyone else.*
>
> *For example, when you see a fight on television, what makes it seem so believable? It isn't just that they have a little capsule of fake blood that releases on impact. It is all based on action and reaction, and, of course, very careful planning of each move (called choreography). If (name student in class) went over to (another student) and pretended to hit him in the stomach and (2nd student) just stood there, we wouldn't believe he had been hit at all.*

226

What would (2nd student) have to do to make it believable? He would have to double up in some way, reacting to the action of the imagined punch.

As soon as I give you the signal, imagine you have been punched in the stomach. (All students play simultaneously.)

Plan: This would be an appropriate time to establish the use of the drum or tambourine as a start and stop signal, as well as a signal for them to freeze their positions.

Try it again. Remember if you are really hit, your face reacts as well as your body. Imagine you are really being hit, when I give you the signal.

Drama is just like life, in that it is a constant series of actions and reactions.

Imagine you have come home from school and you smell your favorite cookies. How would you react?

Act: Give them a series of suggestions to react to, using the start and stop signal each time. All the students can play simultaneously. They are to physically react, not just talk about what they would do. You may use the following ideas or some of your own:

You are walking down the street, and you sense that a stranger is following you.

You are walking down the street when you see a hundred dollar bill.

You are walking in the rain and you see a bedraggled little kitten who seems to be lost.

You are walking down the street when a huge thunderstorm starts.

Relfect: Ask them which situations seemed most real to them and why. Stress the use of imagination and concentration on what is happening.

Assessment: Make particular note of those students who may have had difficulty participating. If no progress is apparent after three lessons, hold individual conferences with them.

ACTING:
EXPRESSIVE USE OF BODY AND VOICE

Concept: Develop body awareness and spatial perception through *movement*

DIAMONDS

Drama Objective: Synchronize movement

Related Objective:
    Physical Education: Develop flexibility, coordination and reaction

Materials: A piece of slow, flowing music

Introduce and Plan: This is a variation of a mirror activity. If the students haven't done mirroring before, you may want to begin with the activities on pp. 139–140 and save this activity until they have done those.

Tell students that in this lesson they are going to see how "together" they are. Divide them into groups of four. Each group should stand up and form a diamond shape. The points of the diamond should be far enough apart so they have ample room to move. Everyone is to face the front of the room. (See drawing.)

That means that in each diamond group, B, C and D can see the back of A. Person A is the leader and begins making slow, flowing movements to the music; persons B, C, D follow as exactly as they can. At some point Person A will turn and face another direction, which means they will be looking at someone else's back in their group. That person them becomes the leader.

Act: All groups move to the music, as described above. If necessary, you might sidecoach them about using different levels of space for their movements.

Reflect: Ask for their reactions to the activity. How well were they able to synchronize their movements? What do they like about the activity?

Assessment: Rate them on how well they accomplished the objective. This activity can be repeated on different days. They ought to improve each time.

BACK AND FORTH

Drama Objective: Focus concentration on controlled movement
Related Objective:
    Physical Education: Develop flexibility, coordination and reaction

Introduce: Tell students this lesson will test their concentration skills. It starts off very easily, but "Beware"!

Act: Sidecoach:

Move your arms in a gentle, swaying, swinging rhythm. Add the rest of your body, using large, swinging movements. Think of a word that might fit your rhythm. Whisper the word and fit it to the rhythm. Keep whispering it. Now say it out loud—louder, and louder.

Now move in a jerky rhythm. Start with your arms and then add the rest of your body.

Think of a word that fits that rhythm. Whisper it. Now say it out loud—louder, and louder.

Now switch back and forth. Start with the gentle swaying rhythm. When the signal is given, switch to the jerky rhythm. Back and forth.

To create some tension, allow less and less time between the switches.

Reflect: *At what point did you begin to have trouble concentrating? Why does that happen?* Share experiences of having so many different things to do that concentration becomes difficult. Talk about possible ways to handle that problem.

Assessment: Note how quickly they were able to make the changes. Concentration should increase with practice.

OPEN AND CLOSE

Drama Objective: Use the quality of movement to reveal a
character

Related Objectives:
Language Arts: Employ active listening; follow the logical
organization of an oral presentation; use a variety of words
to express feelings and ideas; explain and relate to the
feelings and emotions of characters
Physical Education: Develop flexibility, coordination and
reaction

Introduce: Ask students to open and close their hands rhythmically.
Explore other parts of the body that can open and close. Work up to the
point where the entire body is closed, including the face, and then the
entire body is open. Inhale when open, exhale when closed. End with the
entire body closed, but in a standing position.

Act: Ask them to move around, maintaining the closed position. While
they are moving, sidecoach:

Think about what kind of person might be closed like that.
What might he or she be doing?
What kind of mood is the person in? Why is he or she in that mood?
As you move around, say "Hello" to other people you pass as you
think this person would.

Reflect: Afterward, ask them to tell something about the characters they
were.

Act: Repeat the last part of the open and closed movements again. This time end with a very open position and ask them to move around in that position. Do the same sidecoaching as before.

Reflect: Afterward:

> *How were the characters in the open posture different from those with the closed posture?*
> *How did they feel toward the world and other people?*
> *Have you ever felt particularly closed or open before?*
> *How does posture reflect a person's mood or attitude?*

Assessment: Set a scene in which they are to portray one of the two characters they developed. For example, they have been invited to a party. They decide to go even though they don't know anyone else. How do their characters handle the situation? You might want to play music to help the party mood. Only half the class acts at one time. The other half is to jot down open and closed characteristics they see.

Assess both what they did and the notes they hand in.

COLOR

Drama Objective: Interpret color through movement

Related Objectives:

    Language Arts: Follow the logical organization of an oral presentation; use a variety of words to express feelings and ideas; respond to thoughts expressed by others through clarifying, qualifying and extending ideas; generate material for writing

    Physical Education: Develop flexibility, coordination and reaction

    Art: Discover, explore, examine, and apply art elements including line, color, shape, texture, value, form, and space

    Music: Move to express mood and movement of music

    Science: Observe phenomena and apply knowledge of facts theories, laws, structure, and concepts

Materials: Colored paper or fabric; Spotlights or slide projector; Colored gelatins for lights

    Music: For the warm-up use one piece of smooth, swinging music; another of fast, percussive music

There are two parts to this lesson. You might want to do the first part on one day, and the second on another day.

Part One:

Warm-up: Ask them to stand where they have plenty of space.
Sidecoach:

> *You have all this space around you. In a way, this space is like a blank piece of paper. On a piece of paper you could make patterns by using paints or crayons.*
>
> *You can also make patterns in space by moving your bodies in various ways. See if you can move your body so it makes a curved pattern in your space. It is almost like using your whole self to fingerpaint.*

Make the curved pattern move. (You can use a smooth but swinging piece of music here, if you wish.)
Now use your bodies to make a pattern that is full of moving angles—all corners and sharp edges. (Fast, percussive music could be used here.) *Now try a twisted pattern. Remember there are different levels in space: very low, very high, and in-between. Fill all the levels with the moving, twisting patterns. And relax.*

Introduce: Show students a piece of bright red paper or fabric.

The reason we see colors is because of light. Light is not stationary; it moves very fast. Some colors seem to move and vibrate. If the red you are looking at now could show us how it is moving, how might it move? What kind of pattern in space would it like to make to express its "redness"?

Act:

Find your own place in space—a place where you have enough room to work without touching anyone else. Close your eyes, and at the signal begin to move in the pattern you think red would made. The reason for closing your eyes is that right now you each have your own idea, which may be very different from somebody else's idea. Each idea is right because it is the way you think about this particular color. If your eyes are closed, you will be able to create the color movement you are thinking about, without being influenced by someone else.
While you move in your own space, say the word "red" in a way that fits your pattern—it could be long and drawn out, or it could be repeated fast and loud. It could be one note or many notes.

Reflect: Discuss their interpretations. If they wish, half could do the red movement again, while the other half watches to see what different aspects of the color seem to come across in the movement. Then reverse players and audience.

Repeat the process with at least one other color, such as green or blue.

234

Part Two: This part of the lesson holds high appeal for students. The experience of being *in* a color is quite different from observing the color on paper or fabric. If at all possible, try to get the equipment necessary. The point is to bathe the playing area in intense color.

You can paint blank slides very intense colors—one color per slide—and use one or two slide-projectors. Or you can use two spotlights with high intensity colored gels in them. If your school does not have lighting equipment, the spotlights can be made by inserting a strong light into a two-pound coffee can. Colored gelatins—a cellophane type of material—are placed over the opening. You may have some students who would be interested in making them for class use. For this activity, each light should have the same color gel on it. The lights should be placed in front of the playing area.

Introduce: Turn out all lights except the red spotlights. Ask the students to sit quietly, observing the space around them and feeling the color. Suggest that as they feel the color, it will cause them to want to move in some way or to do some activity. Give them a few moments to think, then give the signal to begin. If some students have trouble coming up with an idea, either realistic or abstract, suggest that they just begin moving and an idea is likely to occur to them.

After they play for a while, turn the regular lights on and discuss how the color makes them feel. Repeat with a different color.

Plan: Divide the class into groups of four or five. Assign a color to each group, or allow them to choose their own color. It won't matter if more than one group has a certain color, since interpretations are bound to vary. Each group interprets their color in any way they wish. For example, they could choose one aspect of the color, such as fire for red, and work out a scene around fire. Or each person in the group could do something different that might be illustrative of the color.

Act: Each group shares their interpretation.

Reflect and Evaluate: After the groups play, discuss what they did that communicated the color.

Assessment: This would be a good time to introduce the idea of keeping a journal, if you haven't already done so. Time can be allotted in class for writing, or journal homework can be assigned. Periodic checks on the journal will be of great assistance in determining the progress students are making in their understanding of various aspects of drama. For this lesson they could address questions such as the following:

How well do you think your group accomplished the objective for the day?

What improvements could have been made?

What is your favorite color and why?

How do colors affect your moods?

If you could redecorate your room, what colors would you include?

Write a poem about color. (See Hailstones and Halibut Bones, by Mary O'Neill, for ideas.)

What colors would you expect a set designer to use for a mystery play? For a comedy?

Concept: Develop body awareness and spatial perception through *sensory awareness and sensory recall in character*

HOW AWARE ARE WE?

Drama Objective: Observe closely

Related Objective:
    Science: Organize data

Introduce: Tell students the game they are about to play will test how much they really see.

Plan: Divide the class into two groups, A and B. Each group chooses a person in their group and writes a series of twenty questions that can be answered "Yes" or "No" about the person's appearance and habits. For example:

> Are John's eyes blue?
> Does he wear glasses?
> Does he part his hair?
> If so, is it on the left side?
> Does he write left-handed?

Act: The person Chosen by Group A leaves the room, or goes somewhere where he or she can't be seen. Group A asks Group B their set of questions. Then the person chosen by Groups B leaves, and Group B asks Group A their set of questions. The team with the most correct answers is the winner.

Reflect: Ask them to rate themselves privately on how closely they observed, using a scale of one (low) to ten (high). Discuss occupations in which close observation is necessary. They may discover that almost every occupation requires close observation of some kind.

Assessment: Journal assignment:

Find five things in the room you sleep in at home that you weren't aware of before.

Watch one of your favorite television programs and carefully observe what the main characters are wearing. What do their costumes reveal about them? (Note that even what may seem to be everyday clothing is a carefully chosen costume for the character.)

SHAPE UP!

Drama Objective: Replicate the shapes observed
Related Objectives:
    Language Arts: Use nonverbal communication
    Physical Education: Develop flexibility, coordination,
    reaction and balance

Introduce: This is another observation activity. Watch for details.

Act: Divide the class into groups of four. One person is to make a shape with his or her body. The second person adds to the shape in some way so that together they look like a single sculpture. The other two members have their backs turned until the sculpture is ready. Then they look at it very closely for about fifteen seconds. The first two return to normal positions, while the second pair make themselves into the same shape as the first pair. The first pair check to see if everything is correct. Then reverse roles.

    Do the same with groups of six. Three make the statue, three duplicate it. The only rule is that no one is to climb on another person's back. Then use groups of eight, and ten, if they can handle it.

Reflect: Afterward, discuss how trying to duplicate the shapes of five people is different from duplicating two people. In the larger group it is necessary for each person to be responsible for the shape created by one person, rather than knowing how everything goes together exactly.

Assessment: Note any students who aren't able to accomplish the objective. Try to determine whether it is a concentration problem or a commitment problem and discuss it with the student. You may want them to write about it in their journals.

THE CAVE

Drama Objective: Use the senses to establish the reality of being in a cave

Related Objectives:
Language Arts: Follow the logical organization of an oral presentation; relate to the feelings and emotions of characters
Physical Education: Develop flexibility, coordination and reaction

Materials: A record of electronic music, or some kind of dissonant music. "Poem Electronique" or "Integrales" by Edgar Varese would be appropriate.

Introduce: The students each find their own place on the floor and imagine what they would do if suddenly they woke up in a cold, dark cave. Ask them to close their eyes as if they were asleep. Play music to set the "eerie" mood.

Act: While they play, sidecoach:

> *Even before you open your eyes, you begin to feel that you are in a strange place. Feel the dampness. Maybe you can hear a dripping sound. Smell the dampness. Feel the cold, hard ground under you. Open your eyes. It is very dark. Sit up and try to see through the darkness. Smell the mildew and the mold. Feel the walls. They are rough and uneven. Try to get a feeling of the shape and size of the cave. You run into a spider web. Everything about this place is frightening. You must find a way out of here. You must escape. Try to find a way, even though you can see no light at all.*

Let them work to the music for awhile. Some will escape, some will still be working on it when you give the signal to stop.

240

Reflect: Discuss what they saw, and felt, and heard.

Act: Play the same thing, but this time they are to imagine they are someone different from themselves. How might a four-year-old react? How might an old, feeble person react? Remind them that in interesting stories, the person always encounters severe difficulties which need to be overcome.

Reflect: Discuss the responses of the different characters.

Assessment: Journal assignment:

Write about ways people you know react to disappointment, such as losing a game or not being allowed to do something they want to do, or receiving a poor grade at school. Use fictitious names when writing.

REACTING TO A SOUND

Drama Objective: React to a recalled sound

Related Objectives:
    Language Arts: Use nonverbal communication; use a variety of words to express feelings and ideas; explain and relate to the feelings and emotions of characters; respond to thoughts expressed by others through clarifying, qualifying, and extending ideas
    Physical Education: Develop flexibility, coordination and reaction
    Social Studies: Compare and contrast opposing viewpoints

Materials: A recording of the sound of waves would add to the mood

---

Introduce:

Imagine you are on a beach, sleeping in the sun.
You are wakened by the sound of waves.
How would you react?
What if you were a parent who fell asleep in the sun, while your two-year-old was playing in the waves? How would you react when you woke up?
What other characters might react to the sound of the waves in still other ways? For example, how might a non-swimmer, who was floating on a raft, respond to the waves if he or she woke up and found the raft had drifted a long way from the shore?

Discuss several possibilities for characters and what they might do.

Act: Each person decides on a character and plays the scene according to the way he or she thinks the character would react. They all play, simultaneously.

Reflect: Discuss the various reactions. The point to make is that people react differently to the same stimulus, in this case the sound of waves, depending upon who they are, their past experiences, and the situation they are in.

Assessment: Journal assignment:

Using a different sound stimulus, such as a siren, write three different ways people might react.

Concept: Develop body awareness and spatial perception through *pantomime*

WHERE?

Drama Objective: Pantomime being in a specific place
Related Objective:
    Language Arts: Use nonverbal communication

Introduce:

> *Events in a play always occur in a certain place, whether it is an ordinary living room or outer space. It is up to the actors to let the audience know through their actions just where they are.*

Plan: Direct the students to sit down in one large circle. The center of the circle can be any kind of place they want it to be—a jungle, a snowbank, a dungeon, any place. Each one should think of an idea for a place, but not say it aloud.

Act: One person is to enter the center of the circle as if it were the particular place imagined, and do something that helps communicate where that place is, without telling. As soon as others in the circle think they know what the place is, they join the first person, doing *something else* that would be appropriate for that space. For example, if the first person establishes that he or she is snow skiing, others could enter and either ski in a different way, or build a snow man, or have a snowball fight—whatever would be appropriate to do in the snow. Before too long, almost all the students will be pantomiming in the place set by the first person.

Reflect:

> *What was your first clue as to the location? Were all of you imagining the same place?*

If not, what happened?
Since the goal was for everyone to see and be in the same place, what could have been done, without talking, of course?

Discuss the need for close observation of details on the part of those watching, and clear, specific pantomime choices on the part of those initiating the acting.

Assessment: Note how detailed their pantomime is and how well they are concentrating on the goal.

CHARADE PANTOMIME

Drama Objective: To pantomime activities determined by
 selecting cards at random
Materials: Index cards

Introduce: Divide the class into four teams. Each team has four cards on which they write activities, such as building a fire, buying groceries, and so on. The cards are collected and shuffled.

Act: Each team, in turn, picks a card and quickly pantomimes the activity. The other teams try to determine what the activity is in as little time as possible. Use a stop watch to see how may seconds it takes to guess correctly.

 The emphasis is on clear pantomime, so the team guessing correctly *and* the team doing the pantomime both get the number of seconds as their score. The team with the fewest number of seconds at the end, wins.

Reflect and Evaluate: Discuss what people did to make their pantomimes clear.

Assessment: Note any progress of individuals on using details in pantomime.

Concept: Develop body awareness and spatial perception through *emotional recall in character*

WAITING

Drama Objective: Realistically express a character's feelings

Related Objectives:
   Language Arts: Follow the logical organization of an oral presentation; use a variety of words to express feelings and ideas; explain and relate to the feelings and emotions of characters; respond to thoughts expressed by others through clarifying, qualifying, and extending ideas
   Social Studies: Compare and contrast opposing viewpoints

Introduce: The students are to think of an adult character they find interesting—either a real person, or a type of person. The person is about to enter a bus station to catch a bus to another city for a very important reason. The students must decide on such things about the character as

   the age,
   occupation,
   important reason for going on the bus,
   personality type.

Act: The characters walk in and take a seat to wait for the bus. They can talk to one another in character, if they wish. Tell them you will play the part of the station attendant.

   After a minute or so, announce that the bus will be delayed half an hour. After a little while longer, announce that the bus has room for only five passengers. Since they all have tickets, how will they decide which five will go?

   Then, later still, announce that the bus has broken down and will not be leaving at all.

Reflect: Discuss how their characters felt and why.

How did different characters show their emotions?
Do people always show their emotions in real life?
If not, what do they do?
What are the advantages and disadvantages of showing emotions?

Assessment: Journal assignment:

Recall and write about a situation in which you felt very happy.
How did you react?
What did you do and say?
Do the same for a situation which made you feel angry.
What are some healthy ways to deal with angry feelings?

SOMETHING HAPPENS

Drama Objective: Develop an improvisation based on two different emotions

Related Objectives:

Language Arts: Use a variety of words to express feelings and ideas; explain and relate to the feelings and emotions of characters; respond to thoughts expressed by others through clarifying, qualifying, and extending ideas; describe the time and setting of story

Materials: Make two sets of cards, or ask the class to compose a list of words which will go on the cards.

Each card in Set 1 has a word on it that expresses a happy mood, such as

joyous, delighted, gay,
cheerful, glad, lucky,
jolly, exhilarated, or playful.

Words for Set 2 expressing an uphappy mood might include

sad, angry, anxious
quarrelsome, frustrated,
disappointed, grouchy, or glum.

Introduce: Talk about moods. Share experiences where a person is in a good mood and then something happens to change that mood.

Plan: Divide the class into groups of three or four. Each group picks a card from each set. They are to develop a scene in which the mood changes from either the happy mood to the unhappy, or the reverse. The change of mood can come from an *outside* force, such as

a phone call, a letter,
an item in the newspaper, a person coming in,

or from one or more of the people *within* the group, such as
    an announcement being made,
    a quarrel, an accident.
They must decide
    who they are,
    where they are, and
    what they are doing, as well as
    what happens to change the mood.

Act: Groups can volunteer to share their scenes.

Reflect and Evaluate: After they have played their scenes, discuss them:

    How was the change of mood made apparent?
    Were the changes believable?
    How could they be even more believable?

Assessment: Rate them on their achievement of the objective.

Concept: *Voice*

GIBBERISH

Drama Objectives: Communicate feelings through vocal tone, pitch, volume and rate of speed; listen for clues about how a person is feeling

Related Objectives:
   Language Arts: Follow the logical organization of an oral presentation; manipulate rate, volume in oral presentation; explain and relate to the feelings and emotions of characters
   Music: Develop the voice for clear diction; perform contrasts including high/low, up/down, fast/slow, loud/soft, long/short

---

Introduce:

   If you were in a foreign country where you did not know the language, how might just the sound of a person's voice tell you that the person was sad?

Tell them that they are to describe something sad, maybe a pet dying, only they are to do it in a made-up language, called gibberish. They all speak at once.

Then ask them to tell someone who sits near them to come quickly. There is an emergency and help is needed. Again, they use gibberish.

Discuss the differences in the sound of their voices in the two situations.

Act: In groups of six or seven, have them tell a very spooky story, using gibberish. One person starts the story, then after a couple of "sentences," the next person picks it up. The story gets more and more exciting. Finally the last person in the group ends it.

Reflect: Afterward, ask them how they knew when there was an exciting part of the story being told, and how they knew what the ending was like.

Act: In the same groups, one person at a time answers the phone. They are to let their voice, actions and words convey how they feel about the person on the other end of the line. The can use English this time. Remind them to give the other (imaginary) person time to speak and really imagine what he or she is saying before responding.

The rest of the group listens, with eyes closed, to determine if they can tell how the person answering the phone seems to feel about the caller. The idea is to think of different attitudes and notice how they are reflected in speech.

Reflect and Evaluate: Discuss vocal clues they picked up while they listened to the person speaking.

Assessment: Journal assignment:

> *Pay particular attention to members of your family. How do their voices let you know how they feel in specific situations?*

TIMING

Drama Objective: Vary the rate of speed according to the circumstances

Related Objectives:
  Language Arts: Manipulate articulation, rate, volume, and physical movement in oral presentations; vary word choice to accommodate the purpose and audience
  Music: Develop the voice for clear diction; perform contrasts including high/low, up/down, fast/slow, loud/soft, long/short

---

250

Introduce: Actors need to know how the rate of speed affects the meaning of what they are saying. Have the class try out the following ideas, all together.

> *Imagine you are a mother or father explaining carefully to your three-year-old that he is not to cross the street alone. Use gibberish to talk to him.*
> *Now imagine that you have left him playing in the yard. You look out the window and see him step into the street. A car is coming. React in gibberish.*
> *What did you notice about your voice in those two situations?*
> *How did the rate of speed change?*
> *Often a person's objectives determine the rate of speed. How did the objectives of the parent differ in those two instances?*

Repeat the situations. This time they respond in English.

Plan: In pairs, let them try out this situation:

> *One person has been kidnapped and is being held for ransom. The scene begins with the kidnapper bringing the bound and gagged person in the door. The kidnapper has to go downstairs for something. The victim tries to get to the telephone to tell the operator to get the police at once.*

Give the pairs a few minutes to plan the setting—where the doors are, where the telephone is. Tell them not to plan an ending to the scene, but to let the ending occur spontaneously. They may use English or gibberish.

Act: All play simultaneously. One or two pairs may like to show their scene to the rest of the class.

Evaluate: Discuss the speech, with particular emphasis on rate of speed.

Assessment: How effectively were they able to vary their rate of speed?

SWITCHING STATIONS

Drama Objective: Speak clearly and with variety in vocal inflection

Related Objectives:
> **Language Arts:** Manipulate articulation, rate, volume, and physical movement in oral presentations; vary word choice to accommodate the purpose and audience
> **Music:** Develop the voice for clear diction; perform contrasts including high/low, up/down, fast/slow, loud/soft, long/short

Materials: Tape recorder and blank tape

Introduce: Discuss commercials they have heard on the radio. In their view, what makes a good commercial?

Plan: Divide the class into groups of three or four. Each group is to plan a radio commercial which uses sound effects, as well as voices. They should practice it several times.

Act: Then record their commercials, but interrupt them frequently, by pretending to switch stations. When you return to their "station," they should pick up right where they left off before.

Evaluate: Listen to the tape and discuss the use of sound and voice.

Assessment: Journal assignment:

> *Why is it important for an actor to know how to use his or her voice in a variety of ways?*

STORYTELLER'S RAP

Drama Objectives: Speak clearly, with variety in vocal inflection; cooperate in a group to accomplish goal

Related Objectives:

Language Arts: Listen to appreciate sound devices; manipulate articulation, rate, volume and physical movement in oral presentation; adapt content and formality of oral language to fit purpose

Music: Create new words to songs; perform contrasts including high/low, up/down, fast/slow, loud/soft, same/different, long/short

Introduce: Ask how many students listen to rap music. What is it that is fascinating about rap? One thing is the rhythm and the beat. Ask them to describe the rhythm and beat of rap. Most people can't help but move in some way when they listen to rap. The rapper has to speak very distinctly in order to be understood, because the words come very fast and the rap usually has a story to tell.

Tell students that today they will be working on a rap. It is a rap of a storyteller talking to popular rap groups.

Warm-up: First, however, they need to limber up their lips and voices. Practice these tongue twisters for accuracy and speed first. Then practice them using a wide range of pitches—traveling up and down the scale, for example.

1. *BUDDA GUDDA BUDDA GUDDA* (repeat over and over)
2. *RED LEATHER, YELLOW LEATHER, RED LEATHER, YELLOW LEATHER* (repeat)
3. *What a ta do to die today at a minute or two to two, a thing distinctly hard to say, but harder still to do. For they'll beat a tatoo at twenty to two, a ratata, tatata, tatata to, and the dragon will*

come when he hears the drum at a minute or two to two today, at
a minute or two to two.

Present: Give them a couple of minutes to read through the rap. The numbers in the left margin have been added for easy referral in the lesson.

SPREAD THE WORD: A STORYTELLER'S RAP

Linda Goss

1. *I'm a story teller*
   With a story to tell
   I can tell'em loud
   I can tell'em well
   I don't need a microphone
   When I talk
   I don't need a chair
   'Cause I'm going to walk
   I can strut and stroll
   'Cause I'm bad
   And I'm bold
   Gonna tell it "like it is"
   This aint' no show biz
   Gonna tell my own story
   Tell it to the world
   For all the boys
   For all the girls
   From the mountain top
   To the valley low
   Gonna "talk dat talk"
   Gonna go-go-go
   CALL: *Have you heard?*
   RESPONSE: *SPREAD THE WORD*
   CALL: *Have you heard?*
   RESONSE: *SPREAD THE WORD*
2. *Yeah, storytelling is the thing to do*
   It's also brand new
   Medicine for the spirit
   Healing for the soul

254

It's for the young
And it's for the old
It's for the rich
And it's for the poor
For the sick at heart
And what's more
It's for Black people
White people, Brown people too
Red, Yellow, Orange
Green, Purple, and Blue
From the break of day
Till the cool midnight
I can weave a tale
That's outta sight
Yeah, storytelling is what I'm about
I can run my mouth
Till my eyes pop out
CALL:　　　*Have you heard?*
RESPONSE:　*Have you heard?*
CALL:　　　*SPREAD THE WORD!*
RESPONSE:　*SPREAD THE WORD!*

3. *Listen good people*
  All over the world
  Start telling stories
  Start Spreading the Word
  In the tradition
  Is a natural condition
  You just pass it on down
  Hand it on around
  It's mythical, it's history
  It's magical, it's mystery
  Use your imagination
  Talk about your dreams
  Talk about your heroes
  Plans and schemes
  Talk about your family
  Life or love
  Talk about the Master
  up above
  Talk about the birds

Talk about the bees
Talk about zebras
Talk about trees
A little common sense
A little sense of humor
Let it all hang out
But don't drop your bloomers
CALL: *Have you heard?*
RESPONSE: *Have you heard?*
CALL: *SPREAD THE WORD!*
RESPONSE: *SPREAD THE WORD!*

4. (Improvise)
Tell the truth, snaggle tooth
What's your story, morning glory?
You don't miss your water
Till your well runs dry
Anansi is a trickster
Brother Rabbit is sly
Bocka booka bocka booka bocka bam bam bam
Bocka booka bocka booka bocka bam bam bam
Bocka booka bocka booka bocka bam bam bam
Bocka booka bocka booka bocka bam bam bam
Bocka booka bocka booka bocka bam bam bam

5. *I know I might look crazy*
I might sound strange
I'm a story teller
I ain't ashamed
You can steal my style
You can steal my rhyme
But I'll be back
Just give me time
You've heard my tales
You've heard my rap
And if you don't like it
You can bust on dat!
CALL: *Have you heard?*
RESPONSE: *Have you heard?*
CALL: *SPREAD THE WORD*
RESPONSE: *SPREAD THE WORD*

Plan:

1. Students stand up and read the first section, through the first Call and Response a couple of times. Work for clarity and speed, which will increase as they become familiar with the words and establish the rhythm and beat. You may find it helpful to be a "cheerleader" for them at first, until they lose their self-consciousness about doing something unfamiliar.

Rappers seldom stand still. How might the rapper move during this rap? Have them add movement to the rap.

2. Divide the class into four groups. Tell them that each group will be assigned a section of the rap. The goal is to use clear diction and movement to perform the rap together. Ask them what they will need to do in order to accomplish the goal. List their ideas on the board and ask for consensus (commitment) for each idea. The list might include ideas such as "Contribute ideas to the group," "Listen carefully to each idea," "Be willing to compromise," "Cooperate," "Speak clearly," and so on. Tell them you will be looking at their group cooperation skills today, as well as their vocal and movement skills.

Assign a section (1, 2, 3, 5) of the rap to each group. (Do not assign section 4 yet; they will all work on that later.) When it comes to the Call and Response, the whole class gives the Response. They are to work out the vocalization and the movement for their section of the rap.

Act: After they have had sufficient practice time, each group gets into position, ready to perform so that the rhythm isn't broken between sections. You may want to "conduct" them, at least on their entrances.

Plan: Section 4 allows opportunity for improvisation. Note that the rhythm is set in lines of two, before the "bocka bookas." Each group should make up one or two couplets. The whole class can do the "bocka bookas"—adding movement, of course.

Practice Section 4 until the rhythm and beat are well established.

Act: Perform the rap! Preferably more than once!

Reflect and Evaluate: Ask for reactions to what they did. What parts worked especially well? If they were professional rappers, what would they want to perfect? How clear were the words?

There are a number of musical groups about the same size as the groups they worked in. What are some of the fun parts about working with a group that size? What are some of the difficulties?

On a piece of paper to be handed in, ask them:

1. *How well do you feel your group accomplished its goal on a scale of one (low) to ten (high)? Why did you choose that rating?* (This questions could be answered individually or you could ask them to meet in their groups and reach consensus about a rating and a rationale.)
2. *How would you rate your own contribution to the group goal on a scale of one to ten? Why did you choose that rating?*

Assessment: Grade groups on accomplishment of the objective and how well they were able to work as a group and handle problems. Give each student a rating on cooperation skills and see how it compares with the student's self-assessment. If there is a wide disparity, discuss it with the student.

If you have had students rate the group goals individually, you might want to meet with the group and tell them the ratings they came up with, not giving the names of the raters. Discuss the rationales they gave. Such a discussion could help them gain some insights into the group process.

PLAYMAKING/PLAYWRITING: COLLABORATIVE IMPROVISATION

Concept: Dramatize original stories using *pantomime*

MUSIC SETS THE MOOD

Drama Objectives: Write two scenarios based on contrasting moods; pantomime the scenes

Related Objectives:
Language Arts: Select and narrow a topic for a specific purpose
Music: Move to express the mood of the music

Materials: 1. A record which has a happy, carefree mood to it. There are many possibilities. Records by Chuck Mangione or Hap Palmer provide several options. 2. A contrasting piece of music which might suggest a mood of mystery, or struggle. Examples: *Music for Strings, Percussion and Celesta,* by Bartok; "Hall of the Mountain King," from *Peer Gynt Suite,* by Grieg; *Pictures at an Exhibition,* by Mussorgsky; *The Planets Suite,* by Holst.

Introduce: Play the first piece of music. Ask the students to close their eyes and imagine they are listening to the sound track for a movie. They are to think of what might be happening with that music as a background. Afterward, ask them to describe the mood of the music and some of the pictures they saw as they listened.

Plan: Divide the class into groups of four or five. Each group is to pantomime a scene to the music. The scenes should have a clear beginning, middle, and end. They can be very simple. For example, the recess bell rings; the students rush out on the playfield and begin to play; recess is over.

Act: All groups can play their scenes simultaneously, or they can share them, one at a time. Ask the audience to see how they capture the mood of the music.

Evaluate: Ask what the group did that fit the happy, carefree mood of the music. Did they seem to be enjoying themselves? What could be done to establish the mood more clearly?

Plan, Act, Evaluate: Proceed in a similar way, using a contrasting piece of music, such as those suggested above. Due to the more dramatic nature of the music, it will probably suggest a more definite plot line to the students.

Assessment: Grade them on the second pantomime.
   1. To what extent did they establish a mood which matched the music?
   2. Did they have a clear beginning, middle and end?
   3. How well did they maintain their concentration?

HALLOWEEN

Drama Objective: Pantomime the characteristic movements of each character

Related Objectives:
   Language Arts: Use nonverbal communication; use a variety of words to express feelings and ideas; experience and relate to the feelings and emotions of characters; manipulate articulation, rate and volume in oral presentations; relate stories for entertainment; generate material for writing
   Music: Move to express the mood of the music

Materials Music: *Danse Macabre, Opus 40,* by Camille Saint-Saens

Introduce: Ask the students to close their eyes while they listen to the music, and decide what they think is happening at the very beginning. Play the opening portion of *Danse Macabre,* from the clock striking and into a bit of the dance.

Accept all their ideas, but the one pertinent to the music is the clock striking twelve. Play that part again. Then ask them what is special about twelve o'clock midnight on Halloween. According to legend, that is the one night of the year that ghosts, skeletons, witches, zombies, vampires and other such characters come alive and celebrate.

Tell the name of the music and explain the word "macabre." The man who composed the music was inspired by a poem called the "Dance of Death," by Henri Cazalis. (The poem is excellent for choral reading, incidently.)

Present:

> Click, click, click . . .
> Death is prancing;
> Death, at midnight, goes a-dancing
> Tapping on a tomb with talon thin,
> Click, click, click
> Goes the grisly violin.

Plan: Listen to the music.

What kind of beings do you see and what is the setting like?
How would a skeleton move differently from a ghost?

Try the movement just using the hands. Each student decides on what kind of creature to be and where the creature appears from, such as a tombstone, or a tree. While playing the music, sidecoach:

Maybe you are a bit stiff at first from being still so long.
How does it feel to be free for these few hours? Make your creatures show how they feel.
Suddenly the cock crows indicating it is dawn. Show what happens.

Act:

It is hard to create a skeleton or ghost with just the hands. This time use your whole body to rise from the tomb or wherever you are. Find a place and a good starting position.

Some of the students could be playing the "grisly violins," sitting on tombstones, and watching the revelry. You may want to darken the room somewhat.

Evalute:

What difference did you see between the way the skeletons danced and the way the ghosts danced?
What signs did you see that they were glad to be free?

You can add to the activity by planning what the creatures might do if a couple of young children happened to come and spy on them. Use the ideas as the basis for a play.

Assessment: Rate them on how totally they are able to use their bodies to move in appropriate ways for each character.

Concept: Dramatize original stories using *improvisation* which focuses on the *setting* and *time of plot*

PLOT: SETTING

Drama Objective: Develop a scene based in a specific place

Related Objectives

Language Arts: Relate stories for entertainment; generate material for writing; vary word choice to accommodate purpose and audience; respond to thoughts expressed by others through clarifying, qualifying, and extending ideas; describe the setting of the story

Materials: Cards with places, or settings, written on them, such as a dark forest, a supermarket, an airplane in flight, a deserted house, a lake, a telephone booth

---

Warm-up: Use the **Where?** activity on page 243.

Introduce: It is important to establish where a scene or play takes place. In fact, the setting often affects what happens in the plot.

Divide the class into groups of three or four. Each group is to invent a plot with a problem, complications and solutions, around the sentence "Help me." Each group will be given a card with the name of a place written on it. The action of the scene will occur in that particular place.

Plan: They are to work out what happens in the scene and then plan the details of the place they are in. They can rearrange chairs, tables and other things in the room, if that will help show where they are. Sometimes a chair or table can be used in a way that shows it is something else. For example, some chairs put together could be a log crossing a ravine, or a sofa. After they have planned the action and the setting, they should rehearse the scene once or twice.

Act: One group shows its scene while the rest watch. The audience is to try to get a feeling for what the setting is and watch for as many specific details about the place as they can.

Evaluate: After each scene, instead of discussing what happened and what the setting was, given each person a piece of paper. Tell them to make a quick sketch of the place they envisioned because of what they saw the players do. Allow only two minutes for the sketch. Artistry is not important. They can use symbols and label them if they wish. The people who played the scene should make a sketch, too. If the ideas of students in the same group are quite different, they might discuss why it is necessary to work with the same basic plan.

Assessment: Ask students to write a description of their setting with enough detail that someone else could make a drawing based on the description.

PLOT: TIME

Drama Objective: Develop a scene in which the action occurs at a certain time.

Related Objectives:

Language Arts: Relate stories for entertainment; vary word choice to accommodate purpose and audience; respond to thoughts expressed by others through clarifying, qualifying, and extending ideas; describe the time of the story

Materials: Cards with a certain time written on them: 15,000 B.C.; 3000 A.D.; New Year's Eve; Halloween; 3:00 a.m.; 4:00 p.m.

Introduce: Briefly discuss things that are different today from when their grandparents were children. *When* something occurs can be very important to the plot of a play. Even the hour of the day can make a big difference. For example, if you hear a knock on the door at three o'clock in the afternoon, you would think nothing of it. If you hear a knock at three in the morning, that would be quite a different matter.

Plan: Divide the class into groups of three or four. Each group is to improvise a scene around the same object, such as a glistening stone. you may or may not have the object on hand. Each group is given a card with a certain time in which the action of the scene is to occur. Allow them time to work on the scene, deciding

who the characters are,
where they are,
what happens.

Act: Each group acts its scene before the rest of the class, without telling them what the time of their scene is. Ask the audience to watch for the ways the time of the scene affects the action.

Evaluate: Use the question directed to the audience before the scenes were played.

Assessment: Did they clearly reveal who the characters were, where they were, and what happened at the particular time assigned to their group?

WHO, WHERE, WHEN

Drama Objectives: Improvise scenes based on given characters, settings and times; write a scenario

Related Objectives:
Language Arts: Relate stories for entertainment; generate material for writing; vary word choice to accommodate purpose and audience; respond to thoughts expressed by others through clarifying, qualifying, and extending ideas; describe the time and setting of the story

Materials: Blank index cards—three for each student

Warm-up and Introduce: Tell the students to start walking briskly around the room, with no talking. While they walk, call out various characters. When a character is named, they are to do something immediately that they think that character would do. After they do the character action for a few seconds, they resume walking until the next character is called. A drum beat for the walking would be effective. Examples:

an old man,
a firefighter,
a doctor,
a teacher,
a dog,
a frog,
a sprinkler,
a surfboard.

There are so many interesting characters and places and situations to make plays about. Pass out three cards to each person. They should label each card first:

Who, on one card;
Where, on another;
When, on the last.

Then they are to think of an interesting character or group of characters and write the idea on the "who" card, for example, astronauts. Collect the "who" cards. Do the same with the "when" and "where" cards, keeping each of the three piles separate.

Plan: Divide the class into groups of four or five. Each group picks a card at random from each pile. Then the groups develop scenes, using the information from the cards. All they need to decide is what the characters are doing. Allow a brief planning period.

Act: Each group shows its scene for the class, without having played it through beforehand. Encourage them to stay in character during the scene even if something unexpected comes up. They need to react to each other as their characters would.

Evaluate: Ask the audience if they could identify who, where, when for each scene. Was the action of the scene (the "what") clear? How might the scene be improved?

The cards can be used many times, both for drama and for creative writing.

Assessment: Shuffle the cards in each pile. Distribute one card from each pile to every student. They are to write a scenario:

Setting: The setting is listed on the card. They should describe it in more detail.
Time: The time is listed on the card. They may want to add to it.
Characters: They should provide enough details to help the reader. For example, if the card reads "Police officers," the student might add "One rookie police officer and one who is close to retirement."
Action: Briefly describe the sequence of actions from beginning to end.

WHAT IT IS REALLY ABOUT

Drama Objectives: Recognize themes in stories and plays; choose a theme and write a scenario around it

Related Objectives:

Language Arts: Use a variety of words to express feelings and ideas; explain and relate to the feelings of characters; select and narrow a topic for a specific purpose; recognize themes; use the fundamentals of grammar, punctuation, and spelling

Introduce: Works of literature, whether in the form of plays, stories or poems, have an underlying theme or message in them. Some are obvious because they are directly stated, as in fables. Choose one or two examples of fables, such as "The Boy Who Cried Wolf" or "The Tortoise and the Hare," and talk about the themes.

Other themes are less obvious, but are still there. Usually the main characters learn something because of what has happened, and that learning relates to the theme. Discuss a current popular television series and discuss some of the themes. For example, in programs of The Cosby Show, themes might include "Rules are meant to be obeyed," or "Shared laughter can heal wounds," or "We learn from mistakes," or "Trust has to be earned." Ask students to think of other themes.

Refer to the story "The Frog Who Wanted to be a Singer," on p. 180. Even if some of the students are familiar with it, read it to the class, or ask one or two of the best readers in the class to read it aloud. (You might want to ask them a day or two ahead of time, so they can practice it.) Before it is read, tell the students to be thinking about what the theme might be. Afterward, discuss their ideas. There are several possibilities and, of course, there are many ways of stating themes. Examples might include "Persistence pays off," "Have faith in yourself," "Don't let the opinions of others rule your life," "Follow your dream," and so on.

Plan and Write: Writers want to tell a good story that entertains, but they also have something important they want to say through their characters. Some writers start off with a theme in mind, others find that the theme emerges while they form the story and the plot.

Students work in groups of three. Either assign a theme to each group or tell the groups to choose their own theme. Possibilities are endless, of course. You may want to brainstorm a list of themes with the class. Or, you may want to choose from one of those already mentioned or the following list:

> Honesty is the best policy.
> Caring for the environment is essential.
> Everyone has a contribution to make.
> Say "No" to drugs.
> Consider the consequences of your actions.
> Don't judge a book by its cover.

The groups are to write a scenario that deals with their theme. They need to decide the following:

1. *Who are the characters?*
2. *Where are they?*
3. *What happens? What is the conflict? How is the conflict solved?*

Evaluate: Each group briefly describes its scenario and the other groups huddle together and decide what they think the theme was. If you want to make a game of it, give one point to the group (or groups) that comes closest to stating the theme correctly, as well as one point to the "writers" of that scenario for communicating the theme so well. If no one comes up with the correct theme, no points are given. Talk about the scenario and how the theme could have come across more clearly.

Assessment: Collect the scenarios as one basis for assessment. Be sure they state their theme on paper. You may also want to test their ability to recognize themes by asking them to read a story from their literature books and stating one or more possible themes.

Concept: Dramatize original stories focusing on *characterization,* and especially *voice* and *dialogue* which reveal character

---

BEYOND WORDS

Drama Objectives: Communicate through vocal pitch, intensity, volume, and rate of speed, as well as words; write dialogue for one character

Related Objectives:
Language Arts: Manipulate articulation, rate, volume, and physical movement in oral presentations; vary word choice to accommodate the purpose and audience; generate material for writing
Music: Develop the voice for clear diction; perform contrasts including high/low, up/down, fast/slow, loud/soft, long/short

---

Introduce: Discuss how a person's voice lets one know what kind of mood he or she is in. Ask the students how they can tell what kind of mood someone in their family is in at certain times.

Tell the students to close their eyes and listen to some sounds you are going to make. They are to see whether they can tell what kind of mood you are trying to communicate. Use a series of repetitive syllables, such as bum-bum-bum, or use the letters of the alphabet. Say them in a lilting, joyful manner, as if you are very happy. Afterward, ask what it was about your voice that let them know what mood you were expressing. For example,

Was there variation in pitch?
Was it loud or soft?
Was it fast or slow?

Then have them try expressing happiness all together, using gibberish.
Next, ask them to remember a time when they were really scared. They are to use the same sounds, no words, but make it seem as if they are scared.

Do the same thing with anger. Then discuss the differences in the way the voice was used in the different situations.

Plan and Act: Tell them to imagine that it is their birthday. They are opening a present and it turns out to be something they wanted very much. When you give the signal, they open the present, and run to someone else to tell them about the gift. They can use words, but they are to use their voices to communicate how they feel about their present.

Evaluate: How did the voices show their excitement?

Plan and Act: Now, ask them to imagine it is their birthday once again. They are counting on getting one special item they asked for. They have the present; it is the right size and weight for what they expect. They open the package, but it is not what they wanted at all. They are to let their voices show how they would feel if no one were around to watch and hear them.

Evaluate: Discuss the quality of the sounds.

Plan and Write: Using the last situation, they are to imagine they are talking on the phone to their best friend. They write what they would say to describe what happened and how they felt about it.

Act: They should rehearse their dialogue aloud several times. Choose some to share their dialogue with the class. They should remember to use the sound of their voices, as well as the words, to communicate.

Evaluate: Ask the class to point out effective bits of dialogue, and places where the words and the way they were said were a perfect match.

Assessment: Grade their written dialogue.

DIFFERENT INTENTIONS

Drama Objective: Use vocal contrasts to communicate different feelings

Related Objectives:
Language Arts: Manipulate articulation, rate, volume, and physical movement in oral presentations
Music: Develop the voice for clear diction; perform contrasts including high/low, up/down, fast/slow, loud/soft, long/short

Introduce: Ask the students to name as many different feelings as they can. List them on the board. A beginning list might include

    excitement,
    anger,
    anxiety,
    boredom,
    sadness.

Then write a simple sentence on the board, such as "I want that pen," or "Go home."

Act: The students are to say the sentence in a variety of ways to show various feelings. They should choose a feeling from the list, but not tell the class what it is.

Evaluate: What feeling did the person convery?

Assessment: How well did they accomplish the objective?

CHARACTERS AND VOICES

Drama Objectives: Use dialogue and vocal contrasts to reveal characters; write dialogue for three characters in script form

Related Objectives:
   Language Arts: Manipulate articulation, rate, volume, and physical movement in oral presentations; vary word choice to accommodate the purpose and audience; generate material for writing
   Music: Develop the voice for clear diction; perform contrasts including high/low, up/down, fast/slow, loud/soft, long/short
   Social Studies: Compare and contrast opposing viewpoints

Warm-up and Introduce: Tell the students to use movement and gesture, *not* voice, to say "Come here." Then have them do it like a witch might. Have them add a witch's voice to the movement. Repeat, doing it witchier. Repeat, with different characters:

   a giant,
   a demanding mother,
   a whining child,
   a pleading father,
   a frightened person.

Certain personalities seem to have voices that go with their personalities. Discuss examples. You may wish to illustrate by saying something like "I'm really a shy person," in a great booming voice. Ask if the words and the voice seem to fit together. Obviously they don't.

The problem for this lesson is two-fold:

One, to create characters in which the way they use their voices will tell what kind of characters they are; and

Two, to create those characters so that the kind of dialogue used also reveals what they are like.

If they don't know the word "dialogue," explain that it is the term people in the theatre use to mean what the characters say.

Plan: Describe the following situation:

> *Someone is throwing rocks at a post, not knowing that small children are near. One of the children gets hit with a rock. Although the child is not badly hurt, she tells her mother or father, who comes out furious that someone has been throwing rocks where children are playing.*

The main part of the scene is between the parent and the rock thrower. The way the rock thrower acts and talks depends upon his or her personality. Divide the class into groups of three, one being the child, one the parent, one the rock thrower. Each group is to play the scene three times:

> *One time the rock thrower is a basically shy, timid person;*
> *the second time, he or she is a belligerent bully;*
> *the third time, he or she is a confident, respectful teenager.*

Even the way the rocks are being thrown might differ, according to the personality of the rock thrower.

Act: All the groups can play at once. Tell them when to begin each scene. When they have finished the scene, they should sit down quietly until each group is finished. Then give the signal for the second playing. There is no need to show the scenes to an audience.

Evaluate: Discuss the differences they noted in dialogue and voice among the three various rock throwers, and the way the parent reacted to the different personalities.

Plan and Write: Each group chooses one of the scenes they just played and writes dialogue for the three characters. Some of the dialogue may be the same as they used when playing the scene, or they may choose to make some changes. They should use the format for writing a play, with the name of the character on the left, followed by a colon, then the words of the character.

Evaluate: Each group pairs up with another group and exchanges scripts. After they read each other's script, they discuss what parts of the dialogue they think work well and what parts could be improved.

Rewrite: The groups rewrite their scenes and hand them in.

Assessment: Grade them on the appropriateness of the dialogue written.

MOVE ONE CHAIR

Drama Objective: Enact situations from various viewpoints in order to better understand other people's view and feelings

Related Objectives:
Language Arts: Vary word choice to accommodate the pupose and audience; generate material for writing; respond to thoughts expressed by others through clarifying, qualifying, extending ideas; explain and relate to the feelings and emotions of characters
Social Studies: Compare and contrast opposing viewpoints; explain the role of compomise as a method of resolving conflicts; recognize that decisions made in one's self interest may benefit others

Introduce: This is a game in which students have the opportunity to play several different characters. Set up as many chairs as there are characters in a given scene. Each student sits in a chair and begins playing a certain role. When you say "Change," the students move to the chair on their left, and begin playing the role that was played by the person sitting in that particular chair before. They should pick up where the other person was, even if it was in mid-sentence. You can say "change" any number of times, giving more than one chance to play a given role in a scene. After they have played for awhile, tell them to find a way to end the scene.

Act: The following is a beginning list of situations which may be meaningful to your class. You and the class may come up with other situations which are relevant to them. They must be acted with sincerity and concentration, if the objective is to be accomplished.

1. A new student enters school in the middle of the year. He or she is shy and other students don't include the new student in their activities.

2. A student who was well liked at school suddenly seems to have a change of personality and makes hurtful remarks to his or her friends, and

doesn't do homework assignments. After some time, it is discovered that there are problems at home.

3. A student has asked for a certain present from the family. It is something the student has counted on for a long time. It is quite expensive. The family has come into financial difficulties and can't buy the present. They call their child in to talk about it.

4. A child finds 10 dollars on the counter at home. It is with a grocery list. The child is seen by a brother as she or he takes the money. The brother threatens to tell the parents if the money is not returned.

5. A student is caught cheating on a test. The principal has called a meeting of the student, the student's parent, and the teacher. The parent thinks the student can do no wrong.

6. There are three children and one parent. The oldest child stayed out too late. The parent decides to punish the child. One of the children is on the side of the parent; the other is on the side of the oldest child.

7. A mother is talking to her three children. She wants to go away on vacation, leaving the children alone.

Reflect: Discuss how they felt when they took various roles. Discuss other directions the conversations might have taken. What are potential solutions to the problems? Which solution would you think the most fair?

Assessment: Journal assignment:

> *Discuss the meaning of the Native American proverb: To know a person you must walk a mile in his or her moccasins.*

WALKING WITH THE CHARACTERS

Drama Objective: Write believable dialogue for two characters
in a scene

Related Objectives:
Language Arts: Explain and relate to the feelings of
characters; vary word choice to accommodate purpose; use
the fundamentals of grammar, punctuation, and spelling

Introduce: The Native American proverb discussed in the previous lesson
(p. 278) is appropriate for playwrights, too. The playwright needs to understand exactly how each character feels and what that character would do and
say in a certain situation.

Describe this situation to the students:

> *Maria's father and mother recently got a divorce. Now Maria only sees
> her father two weekends a month.*
> *What feelings might Maria be having about seeing her father? What
> does she want to happen most of all?*

Ask them to write as fast as they can for five minutes. They are to write in
the first person, as if they are the character, Maria, writing in a journal or
diary. (The boys may want to use the name Mario.) Assure them that this is
one time when you won't be checking for neatness, you just want them to
get as many of their thoughts on paper as possible.

After five minutes, ask each one to read just one sentence from what they
wrote. No comments are necessary.

Then have them switch to the character of the father.

> *What feelings might the father be having?*
> *What does he want to happen most of all?*

They are to write for five minutes, as before, in the role of the father.
Share one sentence, as before.

Plan and Write: Each student is to write dialogue for this scene:

> *Father has come to pick Maria up for their first weekend together since the divorce. They are riding in the car. Who speaks first? What do they say? How do they feel? How can their dialogue reflect how they feel?*

Give them a certain amount of time to write, like ten minutes. Ask if they are encountering any problems. Classmates may have suggestions. If some are having difficulty figuring out what to say, they might want to act out the scene with a partner and then write the dialogue down together, The "magic if" can be very helpful: **If** I were really excited to be seeing my daughter, what would I say? **If** I were feeling awkward, what might I say? Some students may be going strong and want to continue writing. They should write until there is a logical shift in the scene — they arrive where they are going and get out of the car, for example — or until they are "stumped" and don't know how to continue — or, until a certain alloted time is up.

Act: In pairs, have them read their scripts, each taking one of the roles. Tell them not to be concerned about whether they are reading a male or female part. They are just trying out the dialogue to hear how it sounds.

Evaluate: The pairs should talk about the dialogue — what seems realistic, what doesn't and what might work better.

Rewrite: Each should make any changes they want, and write the scene to hand in. (Possible homework.)

Reflect: Ask them how they felt about switching back and forth with the characters. Was it difficult? What was easy or hard? How successful do they feel they were in walking in each character's moccasins? They were only dealing with two characters. Some plays have ten or more characters in them. How do they suppose a playwright manages all those characters?

Assessment: You may want to collect the first two "diary" writings they did, as well as the script—not to grade, but just to see how well they were able to get into the situation. There may be some correlation between those and how well they managed the script. The "diaries" may also give you information about the attitude of the characters. For example, if the dialogue in the script seems strained and awkward, it may be that it relates to the feelings shared in the diary.

CROWDS

Drama Objectives: Create dialogue in a crowd scene; describe
how people affect one another in a crowd

Related Objectives:
Language Arts: Manipulate articulation, rate, volume, and
physical movement in oral presentations; vary word choice to
accommodate the purpose and audience; respond to
thoughts expressed by others through clarifying, qualifying,
extending ideas
Social Studies: Compare and contrast opposing
viewpoints; explain the role of compromise as a method of
resolving conflicts; support the principle of majority rule and
minority rights; recognize that decisions made in one's self
interest may benefit others

Introduce: Choose a situation, or have the class choose a situation, which
the students are currently very much aware of and which they care about.
Or choose a situation which they could easily imagine and would react to
strongly. Examples:

A school rule which they feel is very unfair;
School continuing until 5 p.m., or year around attendance;
A ban on extracurricular activities;
The closing of all beaches;
Teachers going through student lockers each day.

Plan: One rule in the playing: *no physical contact.* Decide on the setting
for the situation—the school hallway, outside, or some other appropriate
place. Before they begin playing, remind them to stay in character at all
times. It is important for each one to make it seem as if he or she cares
deeply about the situation at all times.

Play: You tell them verbally when to take each of the following steps.

1. In pairs, they are to begin discussing the issue, grumbling about it. They can walk as they talk.
2. Then each pair joins another pair and they continue the discussion. You can use a cymbal or a drum to indicate when they should merge with other groups.
3. Then fours join other fours, eights join eights. The discussion becomes more heated. This continues until the entire class is together in one group and they decide they must take some action.

If they decide to go to the governor or principal, you can take the role of that person. You can help heighten their antagonism by sending word that you will not see them at first. When you do see them, keep a desk or table between you and the crowd. The resolution depends upon the circumstances being played out. There may be a stalemate.

Reflect: Discuss their feelings at the beginning of the scene as opposed to the end. There may be new awareness of crowd psychology which they will be eager to discuss, relating to current demonstrations they may have read about and seen on television.

Assessment: Journal assignment:

> *Describe at least one experience you have had being in a crowd, such as at a party, a concert, a street fair, a church, a sports event. Imagine that while you were a part of that crowd, someone shouted "Fire!" What would be likely to happen? Describe a variety of possible reactions.*

RESPONDING AND CONSTRUCTING MEANING: DEVELOPMENT OF AESTHETIC SENSIBILITIES

Concept: View theatrical events, emphasizing
analysis of how voice and speech reveal character;
recognition of the kind of conflict;
suggestions for alternative courses of action;
evaluation and aesthetic judgments

NOTE: Viewing theatrical events means going to a theatre, or seeing a performance by a touring group who comes to the school. Most theatre companies will provide study guides to help prepare the students for a performance, and to further their understanding through follow-up activities.

The following lesson is based on a play, *The Hammer of Thor,* included here. The lesson serves as a model of how to analyze certain aspects of a play. The play can be either performed by the students, or simply read out loud.

THE HAMMER OF THOR

Drama Objectives: Analyze how speech and voice can reveal character; identify the kind of conflict represented in the plot; suggest alternative courses of action; evaluate and make aesthetic judgments

Related Objectives:

Language Arts: Select from an oral presentation the information needed; use a variety of words to express feelings and ideas; manipulate articulation, rate, volume, and physical movement in oral presentations; respond to thoughts expressed by others through clarifying, qualifying, and extending ideas; adapt content and form of oral language to fit purpose and audience; relate stories for entertainment; identify implied main idea of a longer selection; understand cause and effect relationships; evaluate and make judgments; respond to various forms of literature; become acquainted with a variety of selections, characters, and themes of our literary heritage; describe time and setting of a story; experience and relate to the feelings and emotions of characters

Introduce: Ask the students to give examples of times when they may have lost something of great value to them, and to describe how they felt about it.

> *Suppose you discovered that someone you know took the item. What would you do?*

The play they are about to read deals with that situation. It is an old Norse myth. The gods in Norse mythology were very powerful, but they had many human characteristics as well. They also had enemies who wanted to conquer them and take away their power.

Tell the students to be aware of the physical characteristics of the characters as they read the play, particularly the way their voices might sound.

Present: *THE HAMMER OF THOR*

CHARACTERS

Thor, the strongest god, protector of Asgard where the gods live
Sif, Thor's wife
Freya, a beautiful goddess
Heimdall, guard of Asgard
Loki, a god who gets into mischief
Thrym, a wicked giant
Thrym's Servants (about ten)
Narrator

This play has two scenes.
Scene 1: Asgard, the home of the gods
Scene 2: Thrym's banquet hall

SCENE 1

NARRATOR:
One of the most colorful gods of Norse legends was Thor. Thor was a huge god with flashing red eyes and a long red beard. His most valued possession was a big mighty hammer, which was extremely powerful and so heavy that it took ten men to lift it. No matter whom Thor threw the hammer at, it never missed its mark. And after it hit, it returned to Thor's hand. Because of the hammer's accuracy and power, Thor was able to protect Asgard, where the gods lived, from all its terrible enemies. But, one morning, disaster hit Asgard as Thor awoke to find his hammer missing.

THOR: (Sound effect of things being crashed and thrown around)
My hammer! My hammer! Where is my hammer?

SIF:
Calm down, calm down. Now it must be somewhere. Where did you put it?

THOR:
If I knew where I put it, I wouldn't be looking for it now!

SIF:

I know, but where did you put it last?

THOR: (Disgusted)

Don't ask such foolish questions. Look for it! I must have dropped it some-where.

SIF:

All right, all right!

NARRATOR:

Because of the shouting and crashing around Thor was doing, the other gods and goddesses were worried and came running to find out what had happened.

FREYA:

What's wrong, Thor? What's happening? Are you all right?

THOR:

Of course I'm all right! But I've lost my hammer!

HEIMDALL:

How terrible! Without it, how shall we keep the giants away?

LOKI:

We can't. The giant Thrym, our enemy, already has it.

THOR:

Loki! How do you know this? Where have you been? Have you seen my ham-mer?

HEIMDALL:

Quiet, Thor! Let Loki talk.

LOKI:

If you will all be quiet, I'll tell you. I was flying over Giantland and I saw Thrym on a hill. He called to me as I flew over. "Good morning, Loki. How is everything in Asgard?" "Fine," I answered. "Then no one realizes that Thor's hammer is gone yet," Thrym said. "What do you mean?" I asked. And he told me that he had taken Thor's hammer and hidden it eight miles deep in the earth—and that's not all. He will never give it back unless Freya becomes his bride.

(Pause—everyone looks at Freya.)

THOR:

Don't just stand there, Freya, get into your wedding clothes and hurry up. I've got to get my hammer back at once!

FREYA: (Very angry)

Never! I will never become Thrym's bride. I don't care what the reason is. He is big and fat and stupid and ugly and I will not marry him!

THOR:

This is no time to be choosy. We must get the hammer or we may lose Asgard to the giants!

FREYA: (Crying)

I won't go. I just can't do it.

HEIMDALL:

I have an idea. If Freya will not go, why not dress Thor up as a bride and send him as Freya? After all, Thrym is so ugly himself, Thor would seem beautiful to him.

LOKI:

Marvellous, marvellous! We can put a veil over his beard and give him Freya's beautiful necklace to wear. Find a dress for him, too, Sif. (Sif goes to a closet and gets some clothes. As soon as she gets them she and Freya begin to dress Thor. Thor does not cooperate very well.)

THOR:

Stop it! I will not make such a fool out of myself. I refuse to do this.

FREYA: (Mocking Thor)

This is no time to be so choosy.

HEIMDALL:

Now, Thor, you must do it! And Loki can go as your maid and talk to Thrym so he can't hear your booming voice. You just be sure to keep your face covered with your veil as if you are very shy.

THOR:(Shouting)

No! I won't do it! Loki has caused us enough trouble in the past and I won't let him speak for me now! Besides, if I wear this dress, all of Asgard will laugh at me.

LOKI:

Thor, we have no choice. Freya won't go, and if you really want your hammer back you must go yourself and get it!

THOR:

Oh, all right. If I must, I must. But you stop laughing, Freya, if you know what's good for you.

FREYA: (Laughing)

But just wait until you see how funny you look! Don't breathe too hard or you'll pop the seams on your beautiful white dress! It's too bad brides don't wear red dresses. Then your dress would match your lovely red eyes.

(Everyone laughs except Thor who frowns and shakes his fist at the others.)

SCENE 2

NARRATOR:

So Loki and Thor set out for Thrym's home dressed as Freya and her maid. Thrym had made everything ready for his bride. The floors were swept clean, a wonderful feast had been prepared, and Thrym himself was dressed in his best robe. As Loki and Thor drove up in their carriage, Thrym rushed forward to meet them.

THRYM:

Welcome, lovely Freya! I've waited so long and impatiently for your arrival. Let me help you. (Thrym takes Thor's hand. Thor grabs his hand away as quickly as he can.)
My goodness, Freya, you have such large hands and you have such broad shoulders too. You are larger than I thought you would be.

LOKI:

That is a sign of true beauty, sir. Look how wide and handsome *you* are!

THRYM:

Oh, my, do you really think so? Say, why doesn't your mistress speak?

LOKI:

Oh, she is much too shy. I will speak for her.

THRYM:

Well, come into the feasting hall and sit right here next to me, lovely Freya. Now, eat whatever you like, fair one. If you are still too shy to speak, just point at the things you would like to eat. Here comes a platter of fish.
(Servants bring in great trays of food.)
Here is the roast beef. Here is a tray of strawberries as large as watermelons. Ah, here comes a mountain of mashed potatoes. And a pitcher of ale to quench your thirst.

NARRATOR: (Thrym, Loki, and Thor pantomime eating while Narrator speaks.)
Thor eats and eats and eats — eight salmon, one whole ox, ten bushels of mashed potatoes, and forty gallons of ale. Loki keeps nudging Thor to try to stop him from eating so much but nothing can stop Thor's appetite. The huge appetite startles Thrym.

LOKI: (Whispering to Thor)
Slow down! Don't eat so much. Remember, you are Freya!

THRYM:
Never in my life have I seen anyone eat so much!

LOKI:
Well, you would be starving too if you hadn't eaten for eight days. Freya has been so excited since she got your message that she hasn't been able to eat a thing!

THRYM:
She was really so excited? I must give her a kiss. Let me lift her veil and see her lovely face!
(Thor glares at Thrym. Thrym gasps.)
Oh, her eyes—I only saw her eyes but they are so *red* and piercing!

LOKI:
Well, she also hasn't slept for eight nights because she was thinking about you! No wonder her blue eyes have turned red.
(Thor continues to eat, paying no attention to Thrym and Loki. Loki continues to nudge Thor to try to make him stop eating.)

THRYM:
Are her eyes really blue?

LOKI:
Oh my, yes. As blue as the skies on a lovely summer day.

THRYM:
Then let us be married right now. You, servants, clear the table for the wedding ceremony.

LOKI:
Wait, Thrym. Freya will not go through with the ceremony until you bring Thor's hammer here and she can touch it with her own hand.

THRYM:
We can do that later. (Thor leans toward Loki and whispers in Loki's ear.)

LOKI:
No. Freya refuses to be married until after she sees the hammer. I think you'd better humor her, Thrym. She can be very stubborn.

THRYM:
All right, all right. You servants, go fetch the hammer for Freya.
(It takes all the servants to carry the hammer. When it is brought, Thor grabs it.)

THOR: (Standing up and tearing off the bridal veil.)
Now I have the hammer, Thrym. This is the end for you and your kind.

THRYM: (Shocked)
Thor! You are not Freya! You are Thor!

THOR:
Yes, I am Thor! And this is for you, Thrym!

NARRATOR (Action is pantomimed as Narrator speaks)
As he said those words, Thor hurled his hammer at the wall of the banquet room. The timbers of the banquet hall creaked and groaned as they toppled over on the giants. Thor and Loki walked out of the ruins, smiling while they listened to the yells and shrieks of the terrified giants.

Discuss the characters: These questions can help the students plan to perform the play, or they can be used to analyze the reading.

Thor:

> *What did the play say about what Thor looks like and sounds like?*
> *How would his voice help the audience know he was one of the most powerful of the gods?*
> *Why is the hammer so important to Thor?*
> *Why doesn't Thor want to dress up like a bride?*
> *Why doesn't he talk at the wedding feast?*
> *Why does he eat so much?*

Sif:

> *How does she feel toward Thor?*
> *How does she try to help him find the hammer?*

How could her voice reveal how she feels?
How do you think she feels when she helps Thor dress as a bride?

Freya:

Why does the thought of marrying Thrym make Freya so angry?
How would her voice reflect how she feels?
Why does she laugh when Thor gets dressed up?

Heimdall:

He is the guard of Asgard. What do you think he looks like?
How do you know he is as clever as he is strong?
What do you think his voice sounds like?

Loki:

When Loki tells about talking with Thrym, he imitates Thrym's voice. How might that sound?
Do you think Loki minds dressing like the bridesmaid?
How does he make his voice sound like a girl's when he talks to Thrym?
What does he do to try to be charming to Thrym? How would his voice sound?
How do you know he gets nervous when Thrym notices how much Thor has eaten and how red his eyes are?

Thrym:

What do you think Thrym looks like?
Why did he steal the hammer?
Why does he want to marry Freya? What does he do that shows how anxious he is to marry her?
What does his voice sound like when he thinks he is talking to his bride?
How does he react to Loki's flattery?
What does he think when he sees that the bride is Thor not Freya? How would his voice reveal his feelings?

Servants:

Why are the servants very important in this play?

How do they bring in the heaping platters of food?

How do they bring in the hammer, to show how heavy it is?

What sounds might they make when the walls fall in at the end?

Discuss the conflict and alternative courses of action:

What kind of conflict is represented in this play? Is it person versus person, person versus the environment, or person against him or herself?

What is Thor's objective—what does he want?

What is Thrym's objective? Why does this cause the conflict?

Do you think Thrym really planned to give the hammer back to Thor? (Remember that the giants were always trying to overtake the gods.)

What other courses of action might Thor have taken instead of dressing up like Freya? How would other courses of action change the play? Would it be as interesting, or more interesting? Would it have been as funny?

Staging considerations:
You can discuss these, whether or not the class performs the play. Tell them to keep the audience in mind as they think of the following problems:

Will you use off-stage sound effects for the beginning of the play, or do you want Thor to make all the noise himself?

What parts of the stage can Thor and Sif use when they are looking frantically for the hammer?

The hammer is so large that it is probably better to pantomime using it. How can the servants make it seem very heavy?

What could be used for Thor's dress, veil and Freya's necklace?

What can be used for the banquet table? Who brings it in?

Where will the servants stand after they serve the food?

Do you want to use sound effects for the end, when the banquet hall falls down? How can pantomime help communicate what happens when the walls fall down?

294

Evaluating and making aesthetic judgments: Since a theatrical event is a thing witnessed, not just read, one must see a performance in order to judge it. If the class has actually performed *The Hammer of Thor*, you can evaluate it. If not, talk about a television show or movie most of them have seen. Questions such as the following can be tailored to most shows:

1. *What did you like about it?*
2. *Were the characters believable within the context of the plot? Were their objectives clear? Did you know how they felt about what was happening at any given time? How did the sound of their voices help communicate what their characters were like?*
3. *Did the conflict and tension build through the play until the climax was reached?*
4. *How did the costumes help you know what the characters were like?*
5. *How did the scenery help you know where the action was taking place?*
6. *What might be done differently to improve the play?*

Assessment: If they perform the play, use that as one basis for grading. Another basis could be the analytical quality of their discussions. Another could be on assigned written work from some of the questions listed in the lesson.

SEEING A PLAY

Drama Objectives: Use appropriate audience behavior; respond to the play by drawing, dramatizing and discussing

Related Objectives:
Language Arts: Respond to different forms of literature; explain and relate to the feelings and emotions of characters; describe the time and setting of the story; generate material for writing
Art: Express individual ideas, thoughts and feelings in simple media

Before the play: Most theatre companies provide a study guide for teachers to use with students both before and after the play. Such a guide can help prepare the students for seeing the play. The better prepared they are, the more likely they are to enjoy the performance. They will anticipate what is about to happen, and know something about the plot and characters.

If the play is based on a story or book, you may want to read the story, or excerpts from the story, to the class. They will understand the play better if they know the basic plot beforehand.

You might want the students to act out a few of the more exciting scenes before they see the play. You could also ask them to recall and enact times when they were afraid, or sad, or joyous, just like the characters in the story. They will find it interesting to compare what they did with what the actors do in the play.

If there are any concepts or words you think they might not understand, these should be reviewed beforehand.

If the play is set during a particular historical period, you might want to bring in some pictures of the period. Discuss the types of clothes people wore, what kind of transportation they used, what kind of homes they lived in.

After the Play: Providing a variety of ways for students to respond to seeing the play is important to reinforce their learning. If you were given a study guide, you may find follow-up suggestions that will appeal to your class. The following is a list of activities which many teachers have found useful. Obviously these are "generic" suggestions, and you would want to tailor them to fit the particular play the class saw.

1. **Draw**
   a. *Draw your favorite character, or the most exciting scene.*
   b. *Draw the set.*
2. **Dramatize:**
   a. *Show how each of the characters walked.*
   b. *Choose one scene from the play to act out. Why was that scene selected?*
   c. *Act out a different ending for the play.*
   d. *Act out a scene from another story which shows courage, feeling afraid, reaching a goal—whatever is appropriate to the play that was seen.*
3. **Discuss:**
   a. *What was the most exciting part of the play? How did you feel during that part?*
   b. *Who was your favorite character? What did you like about him or her?*
   c. *What was the objective of each character?*
   d. *Did you know how they felt about what was happening at any given time?*
   e. *How did the sound of their voices help communicate what the characters were like?*
   f. *Select three words to describe each of the characters in the play.*
   g. *How was the play the same, or different, from the story or book it was based on? (If appropriate.)*
   h. *What was the main conflict? Did the conflict and tension build through the play until the climax was reached? How was the conflict resolved?*
   i. *What could have happened to change the ending?*

j. *How did the designers of the scenery, costumes, props and lights use their imaginations?*

k. *How did the costumes help you know what the characters were like?*

l. *How did the scenery help you know where the action was taking place?*

m. *If you were the director, what might you have done differently to improve the play?*

Assessment: By now, students should be able to talk in fairly sophisticated ways about the play and about the quality of the acting and set design. They should be able to give reasons for value judgments they make. Use some of the questions in the lesson to determine their level of understanding.

Concept: Compare television, film and theatre, emphasizing *camera angles* and *audience position*

LIGHTS, CAMERA, ACTION!

Drama Objective: Describe the differences between the eye of the camera and the eye of the audience

Related Objectives:
  Language Arts: Describe the time and setting of a story; respond to thoughts, expressed by others through clarifying, qualifying and extending ideas; explain processes; evaluate and make judgments

Materials: If at all possible, use a video tape recorder, or a movie camera. Also use viewfinders which can be made from stiff paper, with a half inch square cut in the middle.

Introduce: Use the *The Hammer of Thor* as the basis for discussion. Ask the children to imagine they were seeing *The Hammer of Thor* on television.

How might it be different from seeing the play in a theatre?
> *One difference is that the camera can focus on one person at a time to watch what the person is doing, or to see how he or she is reacting to something that happened. The camera can zoom in for a close up of just one part of a person, such as the person's face. The camera actually tells us what to watch—it becomes our eyes.*
> *In the theatre, we usually see several characters at once, and we have to choose what or whom we are going to watch at any given time. Usually we watch the person who is talking or moving on the stage.*

How does the position of the audience make a difference about what is done?

> *Think of sitting in a theatre. How close are the actors to you?*
>
> *There is usually quite a lot of distance between the actors and the audience.*
>
> *Now think of sitting in a movie house. The* **screen** *may be some distance away, but how close do the actors seem?*
>
> *In the theatre, actors often need to use bigger movements, gestures and voices so that the audience will see and hear what is going on.*
>
> *In the movies the actors can use very natural movements and the camera will see that for us. In fact, in the movies, the characters are really much bigger on screen than in real life. If the actors exaggerated their movements or spoke very loudly they would seem grotesque.*
>
> *Also, in the theatre, the audience is seated facing the stage. The actors need to make sure that the audience sees their faces most of the time. They rarely talk with their backs to the audience. In film, the camera can move around and the microphone can pick up voices no matter where the actors are.*

Plan and Act: Use Scene 2, from *The Hammer of Thor,* where Thor, Thrym and Loki are seated at the banquet table. Ask three students to act out the scene. As the class watches, ask them to think of camera angles and close-ups that would help the scene if it were to be on television. For example, how would they film the following?

> *Thor's eating*
> *Loki's nudging him*
> *Thor's flashing eyes when Thrym wants to kiss him*

Replay the scene, with several students using viewfinders, imagining they are using a camera to film the scene. They can position themselves far away, move in close or move around the actors while they are playing the scene.

If you have a video camera, give several children the opportunity to film the scene. They can stop the scene at any time, and shoot portions again from different angles. If there is an editing device, they can even do that later. But, if not, they will still see the effect of different camera angles.

Evaluate: Play the video tape and ask them what worked well and what changes they might suggest. If you are working without a camera, talk about the kind of camera shots they imagined. Then ask them to review the differences and similarities in a play that might be done on television, film and in the theatre.

Assessment: Use their work on the play and subsequent discussion to determine their understanding of the subject.

Concept: Recognize that *designers, playwrights* and *actors* all have different choices to make as they work on a play

MAKING DECISIONS

The following series of lessons may be used as a culminating project for the drama class. Students will be involved in making aesthetic decisions from the points of view of a set designer, a playwright and an actor. They will be asked to reflect on their decisions as the project progresses and to evaluate the results of their efforts.

The project is divided into separate, but sequential, parts. You may choose to do one or more parts per day over several days. The last activity in each part is called "Reflect and Evaluate." For that, the students should keep a journal that carries through the entire project.

Note the materials needed for some of the lessons. You may want to ask the students to collect some of the materials, especially for Part Three.

PART ONE: LINES

Drama Objectives: Show how lines communicate feelings or moods; reflect on "lines" in the environment

Related Objectives:
　　Language Arts: Use a variety of words to express feelings and ideas
　　Art: Discover, explore, examine and apply the element of line; express individual ideas, thoughts, and feelings in simple media; experiment with art materials to understand properties and develop manipulative skills

Materials: newsprint; charcoal

Introduce:

1. Instruct student to fold a piece of newsprint in half, and then in half again, so the paper is divided into quarters. Give the following directions, allowing a couple of minutes after each direction for them to draw. Do not embellish the directions; there is room for creativity as each one interprets the directions.

   a. *In the upper left quadrant, use a charcoal stick to draw a series of straight vertical lines.*

   b. *In the upper right quadrant, use charcoal to draw a series of straight horizontal lines.*

   c. *In the lower left quadrant, use charcoal to draw a series of straight diagonal lines*

   d. *In the lower right quadrant, use charcoal to draw a series of curved lines.*

2. Students hold their papers so that at least several others may see them. Focus attention on one quadrant at a time. Ask questions such as the following:

   a. *What do the vertical (horizontal, diagonal, curved) lines make you think of?*

   b. *Notice that the lines are different depending on how the charcoal was used. What differences do you see?* (Dark/light lines; sharp/fuzzy; thin/thick; long/short; connected/disconnected.) *How do these differences affect what the lines remind you of?*

   c. *What is there in nature that gives the impression of having vertical (horizontal, etc.) lines?* (Possibilities for vertical lines might include trees, rain, heat, lightning, mountains.)

   d. *What other aspects of the environment include vertical (horizontal, etc.) lines?* (Possibilities for vertical lines might include skyscrapers, telephone poles, church spires.) *If someone was described as a very "vertical person," what might that mean?*

   e. *What feeling qualities do these lines evoke?* (List their words on the chalk board. Possiblities for vertical lines might include awe, rigidity, commanding, insistent, majestic, aspiring, domineering.)

Apply: After they have talked about the lines in each quadrant, direct students to choose one word from the lists of feeling qualities on the chalk board. On another sheet of newsprint, they are to use their charcoal sticks to communicate the word by the way they draw lines. They can use lines abstractly, or they can spell the word they have chosen, arranging it on the paper so that the feeling quality is expressed. They need to make decisions about how to draw their lines. (See 2. b. above.)

Discuss: Students, in partners, exchange papers and describe what they see in the other person's lines and the impressions the lines create. You may also wish to choose two or three papers which have used the same word and compare how the lines were used.

Reflect and Evaluate:
1. On the same sheet of newsprint, or in their journals, the students write about why they made the choices in the line they did, how effective they think they were, and what, if anything, they might do differently to make it "perfect."
2. In their journals, they should discuss their impressions about lines under three categories: lines in nature; lines in the people-made environment; lines created in bodies, both individually and in groups.
3. Ask them to grade themselves on how well they accomplished the objectives for this lesson. Use whatever method of grading they are used to—letters, numbers, descriptive words.

PART TWO: COLOR REVISTED

Drama Objectives: Show how color can communicate feelings or moods; reflect on color in the environment

Related Objectives:

Language Arts: Use a variety of words to express feelings and ideas

Art: Discover, explore, examine and apply the element of color; express individual ideas, thoughts, and feelings in simple media

Materials: paper; glue

Introduce: If the class has not done the lesson on color, p. 233, they should do that lesson now.

Each hue has a myriad of variations. Choose one color, such as red, and ask students to point out all the shades, tints or tones of red they can see in the classroom and on clothing. Ask if there is one red that seems more vibrant than the others, one that seems more stately, one that seems more calm, and so on.

Apply: Homework: each student should select one color and collect or create as many variations of the color as possible. Sources can be in nature, magazines, paint chips from a paint store, mixed tempera colors, and so on.

They bring their materials to class and create a collage.

Working with a partner, they are to write a title which captures the essence of each collage. Titles may be expressed metaphorically or literally. Share with the class

Reflect and Evaluate:

1. Discuss how the pieces of their collage could be rearranged to create an entirely different effect.
2. In their journals, they are to color, paint, or paste several different

colors and write phrases which describe how the particular color makes them feel.

3. Have them describe what it might be like to live in a world that consisted of only black and white, or in a world that consisted of only grey.

4. Ask them to grade themselves on how well they accomplished the objectives for this lesson.

PART THREE: DESIGNERS

Drama Objective: Make design choices which convey a particular mood

Related Objectives:
    Language Arts: Use a variety of words to express feelings and ideas
    Art: Discover, explore, examine and apply the elements of line, color, texture, shape; express individual ideas, thoughts, and feelings in simple media

Materials: One packaging box, approximately 11″ x 18″ x 16 1/2″, for every two students. The following are basic art supplies, plus an assortment of things one can readily get at a thrift store. Student may be asked to contribute items from home.

scissors	colored markers
staplers	tempera
glue	construction paper, various colors
pins	tissue paper, various colors
masking tape	yarn, various colors
foil	fabric pieces
cotton balls	glitter

Introduce: Students work in pairs as design collaborators. Each pair is given one box and a card with a word on it. They should not tell anyone else in the class what word they have. Possible words: peaceful, joyful, melancholy, mysterious, majestic, panicky. It is all right if the same word is given to more than one pair—later comparisons of their products can prove interesting.

Plan and Apply: Collaborators should discuss their word, what it means, and what kinds of lines and colors the word suggests. They are to create an environment inside the box that expresses their word, using any of the materials provided. They should be able to relate a reason for each choice they make. Allow at least half an hour for this task.

Discuss: When they are finished, allow them to look at the work of others in the class. The words should still be kept secret, until after the discussion.

Discuss each box with the class:

> *Describe the direction of the lines. How do they make you feel? How are the colors used? What words would you use to describe this environment? If you were to give this environment a title, what might it be?*

Ask the designers of the environment to reveal their word, and to talk about some of the design choices they made.

Reflect and Evaluate:

1. In their journals, they should respond to questions such as the following:
   a. *Which decisions were easy to make? Why?*
   b. *Which decisions were hard to make? Why?*
   c. *What happened if you and your partner had different ideas? How did you work it out?*
   d. *What are the advantages and disadvantages of working with a partner?*

e. *How did you feel when the class was discussing the environment you created? How successful were you in communicating your word visually?*

f. *After hearing the discussion, would you make any changes? What would you do?*

g. *What additional thoughts do you have about line and color?*

2. Ask them to grade themselves on how well they accomplished the objectives for this lesson.

PART FOUR: PLAYWRIGHTS

Drama Objectives: Make playwriting choices about theme, characters and action; write a short scenario; write the dialogue for one scene.

Related Objectives:
Language Arts: Select and narrow a topic; vary word choice to accommodate the purpose; use conventional play format

---

Introduce: In the last lesson, students functioned as design collaborators. For this lesson they will function as playwright collaborators, working with the same partner they had earlier, unless there is some reason to change. The environment each pair created in the box will serve as the setting for their play.

Plan: Each pair should brainstorm several answers to the following questions before making their final decisions. The questions do not have to be discussed in any particular order. They will ultimately want to make thoughtful, interesting choices since they will be acting the scene in the next lesson.

Characters:

> *What two characters might find themselves in that setting? Did they choose to be there, or not?*
> *Why are they there?*
> *What is the relationship between them?*
> *How old are they?*
> *How would an outsider describe special qualities of the characters?*

Theme: You may want to refer to the lesson they did on Themes, p. 268, to refresh their memories on possible themes.

> *What are some potential themes for your play?*
> *What could the characters learn, or discover, about themselves, other people or the environment?*

Conflict:

> *Describe the tension or conflict. Is it between the two characters? Or between the characters and the environment or the situation they are in? Or between the two characters and another, unseen character or force or event?*

Apply:

1. In pairs they write a scenario for a short play. They know who the characters are, where they are, and what the main conflict is. Now they need to decide what happens. The following is an outline to follow:

   Setting: Describe where the scene takes place
   Time: Describe when the scene takes place
   Characters: Name each one and give a brief description
   Prior action: Describe what took place immediately before this scene
   Sequence of Action: How does the scene open? How does the audience find out about the tension or conflict?
   What happens? Briefly describe one or more incidents.

309

How does the scene end? The conflict can either be resolved as if this were the end of the play, or this scene could be only one of a series that leads to a climax and eventual resolution. In any case, this scene needs to have an ending of some kind.

2. After the scenario is written, the pairs should improvise the basic action, paying particular attention to what each character would say. When they come up with bits of dialogue they like, they should pause and write them down. The improvisation/writing process can go back and forth until they have either completed the scene or, if the scene is a long one, until they have written two or three pages of continuous dialogue.

Reflect and Evaluate:

1. In their journals, they should respond to questions such as the following:
   a. *What themes interest you?*
   b. *Which playwriting decisions were easy to make? Why?*
   c. *Which decisions were hard to make? Why?*
   d. *What happened if you and your partner had different ideas? How did you work it out?*
   e. *Which parts of your scenario are you especially pleased with?*
   f. *Which parts still need some work? List any ideas you may have for improving them.*
   g. *What is easy and hard about writing dialogue? What kinds of things do you have to keep in mind as you create it?*

2. Ask them to grade themselves on how well they accomplished the objectives for this lesson.

PART FIVE: ACTORS

Drama Objectives: Make choices about physical attributes, objectives, and attitudes of a character; act out the scene created in Part Four

Related Objectives:

Language Arts: Use a variety of words to express feelings and ideas; manipulate articulation, rate, volume, and physical movement in oral presentation; act out plays for entertainment

Introduce: When they wrote their scenarios and the dialogue for one scene, they provided certain bits of information about the characters. With their partners, ask them to spend five or ten minutes making a list of things they know about the characters from writing the scenario and dialogue.

Alternative: They exchange scenarios with another pair and do the activities according to the scenarios they read and the dialogue that was written. They decide who will play which character.

Plan: A play doesn't reveal all the details about a character that an actor needs to make that character come to life. The actor needs to invent a lot of those details. Ask the students to stand up. Each one is to concentrate on the character he or she is going to play in their scene. They should not make visual or verbal contact with other students during this activity. Side-coaching suggestions follow:

> *Walk around the room, concentrating on your character. When I ask questions or make suggestions, respond to them as your character would—only do it silently, not outloud, unless I tell you to do so. While you walk, get a picture of the character in your mind. How old are you? How tall are you? What color is your hair? What is your posture like? Take on that posture as you walk. What is your walk like—is there anything particularly distinctive about it? If so, what makes it that way? Walk the way your character would.*

Stay in character, but find a place to sit—on the floor is fine.
What does your voice sound like? Do you generally talk loud or soft, fast or slow, high or low? As you answer the next questions to yourself, try to hear how your character's voice sounds. Imagine you are talking about your family. Are you the first-born—what position do you hold in the family? If you have brothers and sisters, how do you relate to them? Do you care about them? Where do you live? Do you live with other people or by yourself? Describe where you live—your own room.
I am going to tap you on the shoulder and ask you a question. Respond to me as the character would, using your character's voice.

Use a variety of questions, such as the following:

What do you do during the week—do you go to school or to work? What do you do on a typical day? Do you enjoy what you do? What do you do on the weekends? What is your favorite thing to do? Tell me about your friends. What concerns or problems do you have? What do you want out of life? (Add other appropriate questions.)

Discuss: They join their partners and talk about some of the things they learned about their character, adding to the list they started earlier. Ask them to discuss how this knowledge will help them create the characters in their scene. They should each be clear about the character's objective in the scene, how they feel about being there and toward the other characters.

Plan: Allow time for them to improvise the scene a couple of times. They may use the dialogue written before, or they may decide to use that only as a base from which to improvise, since they may not have time to memorize the lines. If the scenario isn't clear enough, they should check with the playwrights.

Act: They act their scenes out for the rest of the class, after showing the environment they built before and briefly describing it. They can introduce the scene, giving any information the audience needs to know before seeing the scene.

Reflect and Evaluate:

1. After each scene ask the audience one or two questions. You may want them to write their responses on index cards to give to the actors of the particular scene in question. They should write their own names on the cards, taking responsibility for their remarks. If you use this method, collect the cards and read through them yourself first. Their responses can reveal a lot about understanding of what they are doing and seeing.

   The following is a sampling of the kind of questions you might ask:

   > *Describe the conflict.*
   > *What was the relationship between the characters?*
   > *What was the objective of each character?*
   > *Use three adjectives to describe each of the characters.*
   > *How did the environment affect what the characters did?*
   > *What did you like best about the scene?*
   > *What needed to be more clear?*
   > *What changes would you suggest?*

And so on.

2. In their journals, ask them to respond to **some** of the following questions:

   a. *What kinds of choices did you make as an actor? Why are the choices an actor makes important?*

   b. *You didn't have very long to create the character. What would you work on, if you had more time?*

   c. *How well were you able to stay in character? Did you maintain your concentration?*

   d. *How well did you work with your partner while you were*

313

acting? What are some things you have to keep in mind while you are acting?

e. *Talk about how listening is important in acting.*

f. *If another pair acted out the scene you wrote, how close did they come to what you had in mind? If they were not at all close, what additional information could you have included in the scenario or the dialogue? What conclusions about playwriting can you draw from that experience?*

3. Ask them to grade themselves on how well they accomplished the objectives for this lesson.

4. Ask them each to evaluate the final results of their work by completing the following statements as honestly as they can. They should circle the response of their choice. After they are finished, they can talk about their responses with their partners to see whether they agree with one another. After discussion, they may want to change their responses to some of the statements. They should turn their papers in to you.

1. *The environment we designed to create the mood we were assigned communicated (poorly satisfactorily very effectively)*

2. *I could tell someone (0 2 4 6 8) things I learned about line.*

3. *I could tell someone (0 2 4 6 8) things I learned about colors.*

4. *I contributed (very few several many) ideas to create the environment.*

5. *My partner contributed (very few several many) ideas to create the environment.*

6. *The scenario we created (didn't fit fit) the environment.*

7. *The dialogue we wrote (didn't fit fit) the characters and the action.*

8. *I could list (0 2 6 8 10) things a playwright needs to keep in mind when creating a play.*

9. *I contributed (very few several many) ideas to develop the scenario and dialogue.*

10. *My partner contributed (very few several many) ideas to develop the scenario and dialogue.*

11. *I portrayed the physical attributes of my character (poorly satisfactorily very effectively).*
12. *I used my voice to portray the character (poorly satisfactorily very effectively).*
13. *I was (not clear clear) about portraying my character's objective.*
14. *All in all, I thought I portrayed my character (poorly satisfactorily very effectively).*
15. *I would give myself an overall grade of (F D C B A) for this whole project.*

Assessment Suggestions: You will want to assess the students' performance, as well as their ability to verbalize what they have learned. Some students will reveal their knowledge more by what they do than by how well they write about it. The reverse is also true—some can verbalize ideas but cannot apply them very effectively. Both ways of revealing knowledge are valuable.

Projects: There are several products to assess in this project: 1) the box environment, 2) the written scenario, 3) the written dialogue, 4) the acting of the scene. The success of each can be rated or graded according to how effectively the objective was accomplished.

Journals: Read their journals after Part One and make general comments about them to the entire class, so they understand what you expect from them. Either react to their journals after each part or at the end of the project. Journals can be rated or graded according to how completely and thoughtfully they answered questions, and the progress they seem to be making in their reflections.

Interviews: You can either interview each student or interview them in their working pairs or in small groups. There are a number of potential follow-up questions from their final evaluation, such as "What are the four things you learned about lines?" or "What was your character's objective?" or "What reasons can you cite for giving yourself an 'A' for the overall project?" and so on. You will be able to tell how thoughtfully they completed their evaluations by asking just a few questions. Questions may arise from what they have written in their journals, as well.

Chapter V:

OTHER SUBJECTS OTHER POPULATIONS

This chapter is divided into two parts. Part One provides suggestions for using drama to teach essential elements in English language arts, mathematics, science, health, physical education, fine arts, social studies, and other languages. Part Two discusses drama with other populations, more specifically, students with special needs—the academically gifted, the mentally, physically and emotionally challenged, and the economically deprived.

Part One
CORRELATING DRAMA WITH OTHER SUBJECT AREAS

Drama can be used as an effective teaching tool for other subject areas, as well as being an important subject in its own right. However, it is important that the students have experiences in drama as a subject, first, before applying the tool to other curriculum areas. Just as a child must learn to recognize and use numbers before applying them to solve problems, so the child must learn some of the essential elements of theatre arts before applying them to other subjects.

Drama is an effective teaching tool because it causes the student to become physically, mentally, and emotionally involved in the subject being studied. Because of this involvement, students generally remember more about the subject. Some students, who have difficulty grasping a concept through traditional teaching methods, will understand the concept when it is taught through drama. An additional bonus is that students find learning through drama *fun!*

The lessons in the preceding chapters list Related Objectives for other subjects when they seem appropriate for a particular objective. It is up to the teacher to adjust the teaching of the lesson so that a particular subject matter objective receives the desired focus. The following pages offer more ideas for correlating drama lessons with other curricular areas.

ENGLISH LANGUAGE ARTS

Many of the essential elements of English language arts are already so closely allied with the theatre arts lessons included in this book that, by using the drama lessons, you will be teaching essential elements in both theatre arts and language arts. These will be noted under the appropriate essential elements for language arts.

The following suggestions can be used and modified according to the grade level being taught. You may also find that a particular activity can be adapted to teach a different essential element from the one stated here.

Essential Element: Listening

Concept: *Listen to appreciate sound for each letter of the alphabet and devices of rhythm, rhyme, alliteration, and onomatopoeia*

1. Each student, in turn, says "I'm going exploring today." Then the student says his or her name and pantomimes an object to take along which begins with the first sound of the name. For example, "My name is Carlos, and I'm taking a (pantomime a camera)." The rest of the class guesses what Carlos has pantomimed.

2. Each student says his or her name, and then does a series of movements which are the same in number as the syllables in the name. For example, Maria might (1) put her arms straight up, (2) clap, (3) stretch her left arm out. The class repeats her movement.

3. The name is said, followed by a rhyming word, or nonsense syllables. For example, Andre—hombre.

4. Divide the class into pairs or threes. Each group is to decide on an animal. After they have decided, tell them they are to write a sentence about that animal, using as many alliterations as possible. Then they act it out and the class tries to determine both the animal and the alliterations. For example, "The tired turtle trudged to town."

Concept: *Employ active listening in a variety of situations*

All the lessons in this book require active listening either to the teacher or to other students. In many instances the students are listening to know how and when their characters must respond during an improvisation.

Concept: *Select the information needed from an oral presentation*

Many of the lessons in this book require students to listen to literary presentations or improvised scenes, in order to answer specific questions afterward.

Concept: *Detect the use of propaganda and overgeneralization*

Ask the students to watch commercials to find examples of propaganda and overgeneralization. Then, in groups have them create a commercial, using propaganda and overgeneralization. After they show their commercials to the class, ask the class to state what was propaganda and overgeneralization.

If you have a video cassette camera, you may want to tape the commercials.

Concept: *Determine a speaker's motive, bias, and point of view*

The word "motive" is similar to the word "objective" used in this book. It refers to what a given character wants to do. Whenever students are creating a character, they must decide on the objective of the character. The concept of character objectives is introduced in Chapter Two in this book.

In Chapter Four, the section on "situation role playing" lends itself to analyzing bias and point of view.

Essential Element: Speaking

Concept: *Develop fluency in using oral language to communicate effectively*

You will find that the lessons in this book deal with two or more communication skills, in which children are provided opportunities to

engage in creative drama activities and nonverbal communication;

use a variety of words to express feelings and ideas;

make organized oral presentations;

participate in group problem-solving activities;

manipulate articulation, rate, volume, and physical movement in oral presentations; and

respond to thoughts expressed by others through clarifying, qualifying, and extending ideas.

Concept: *Speak to persuade, using a brief set of reasons*

The students work in pairs in situations such as the following:

One student wants to see a movie, the other wants to play softball.

They have found a $10 bill. One wants to turn it in; the other wants to keep it, giving $5 to the friend.

One is a student, the other a teacher. The student is trying to persuade the teacher that a grade should be higher than it is.

A child is trying to persuade a parent to let him or her give a party.

One student is trying to get another to share lunch.

Concept: *Speak to entertain*

The lessons in this book provide many opportunities to present stories and plays for entertainment.

Essential Element: Reading

Concept: *Use comprehension skills to gain meaning from what is read; arrange events in sequential order; understand cause and effect relationships; predict probable future outcomes or actions; evaluate and make judgments*

Duplicate part of a short story for the students. In groups, ask them to discuss what they think will happen next, and act it out for the rest of the class.

In the creative drama lessons for Grades Five and Six, students are continually planning scenes in which they are focusing on plot development and the logical progression of what happens. Although they are not always *reading* to do this, they are gaining experiences in prediction which can apply to their reading, with assistance from the teacher.

The plot development lessons also relate directly to the concept of understanding cause and effect relationships, as well as to arranging events in sequential order including time and degree of importance.

The section on "Evaluation and Aesthetic Judgments," in Grades Five and Six, is a corollary of the concept in which students are to evaluate and make judgments about their reading.

Concept: *Develop literary appreciation skills to provide personal enjoyment; recognize that simile and metaphor involve comparison*

Part 1. Ask the students to move like a stalking cat. Then ask them to recall fog, and describe how it moves. Ask them to try to move like fog. The music, "Neptune," from *The Planets Suite,* by Holst, provides an excellent background for fog movement. Ask them to compare the movements of a cat and the movement of fog. How are they alike?

323

Read the poem, "Fog," by Carl Sandburg.

> The fog comes
> on little cat feet.
>
> It sits looking
> over harbor and city
> on silent haunches
> and then moves on.

Ask them questions to prepare them for acting the poem:

> *What words did Sandburg use that compared fog to a cat?*
> *What do you suppose the fog is watching? Might it see anything*
> *unusual? Where would it like to go so that it might see better?*
> *How does it move?*
> *What happens to fog when the sun comes out?*

Play the music again. The students are to be fog with catlike movements, moving in on the city and watching what is happening. After they have played for a couple of minutes, tell them the sun is beginning to break through, and the fog gradually evaporates into the air.

Discuss the difference between metaphor and simile and ask them which one was used by Sandburg.

Part 2. Ask the students to name other weather conditions and list them on the board. Divide the class into groups of three. Each group is to choose one of the weather conditions and think of an appropriate animal metaphor for it. They list words that compare the two. In fact, they can even write a poem—either using the Sandburg poem as a model, or coming up with one of their own.

Each group acts out their metaphor for the rest of the class. If they have written a poem, ask them to say the poem first, and then act it out.

Ask the class what two things were being compared, and whether the poem used metaphor or simile. If the poem used metaphor, ask them how they could change it so it was a simile, and the reverse for those that used a simile.

Concept: *Develop literary appreciation skills, recognizing personification as a literary device*

Use animal cartoons as a basis for discussing personification. In small groups, ask them to plan and act out a short scene, using animals who behave as humans do, but still keeping their basic animal shapes and movements.

Concept: *Develop literary appreciation skills, recognizing differences in first and third person point of view*

In groups, ask the students to plan an interview situation involved around the "Scene of the Crime." One person plays the victim, one or two others play the witnesses and one is the interviewer.

When watching the scenes, direct the students to notice the way the event is described, and the pronouns used by each person.

Concept: *Develop literary appreciation skills, describing the time and setting of the story*

Time and setting are important to any story, scene, or improvisation. Many of the lessons in this book ask where and when the action takes place. In Chapter Four, there are specific lessons dealing with setting and time.

Concept: *Explain and relate the feelings and emotions of characters*

This concept is applied in most of the lessons.

Essential Element: Writing

Many of the drama lessons in this book include writing activities. Written expression often becomes more imaginative, vivid, and colorful, following dramatization. In fact, the students are sometimes able to describe the dramatization in much more detail than was actually observed in their acting. The biggest danger comes from over-using this technique. If the students begin to realize that every time they do drama, they are going to have to write, they will lose their enthusiasm for both drama and writing.

Essential Element: Language

Concept: *Develop skills in using modifiers correctly*

1. The students begin walking around the room. You call out certain adverbs and they modify the way they walk accordingly. After you have called out several, invite them to call out other adverbs. Examples:

slowly, quickly, sadly,
proudly, happily, cautiously

This activity is also good for vocabulary expansion.

A similar activity can be done with adjectives. For example, the shy boy, the proud lion, the ferocious tiger.

2. With the assistance of the class, ask them to make a set of action (verb) cards and a set of adverb cards. In pairs or threes, each group picks a verb card and an adverb card at random. They are to pantomime the appropriate action and the class tries to determine what the words were.

This activity can be adapted to using nouns and adjectives.

MATHEMATICS

Essential Element: The basic operations on numbers

The "Machine Game" can be used effectly as a skill drill for all basic operation. Basically, the students create a human "Math Machine," using their bodies for the parts. The machine can be very simple, or quite complicated. The essential parts include a place for input, where the problem is put in (usually verbally), and a place for output. Some students like to form a calculator, with students responsible for each number, each of the signs, and an answer display. Other students have created a machine in which the imagined internal workings are displayed through movement and sound, until the answer is arrived at. Once a workable machine has been created, it can be used over and over again. Students vary which parts of the machine they play.

Essential Element: The use of probability and statistics to collect and interpret data

Concept: *Collect data and use to construct graphs*

The "Sleuth Game" can be used to add interest to collecting data, and constructing graphs. Divide the class into "sleuth teams" of two or three students. Each team is given a problem, which is to be kept secret. Therefore, they need to do their investigating in a way that the other students don't know what it is they are looking for. After the investigations, they construct a graphs which they may explain to the class, or which the other members of the class may interpret.

The following are just a few examples. No doubt, you will be able to think of many more.

> *How many students are likely to wear white socks on any given day? Collect data over a period of several days.*
> *How many students are likely to ask the teacher for a pencil on any given day?*
> *How many students are likely to be absent (or late) on any given day?*
> *How many scraps of paper are likely to be on the floor or in the waste basket at the end of any given day?*

Concept: *Construct sample spaces*

Using the creative drama lesson titled **Plot: Setting** on page 263, as a basis, ask the students to construct the setting to the scale of the space.

SCIENCE

Essential Element: The use of skills in acquiring data through the senses

Each grade has drama lessons in this book which focus on sensory awareness and sensory recall, which relate to this essential element in science.

Concept: *Observe the effects of phenomena associated with light*

See the lesson titled **Color**, page 233, for a direct application of this concept.

Concept: *Observe the cellular composition of organisms*

After observation, the students use movement and pantomime to demonstrate how the cellular composition works.

Concept: *Observe that energy can be changed from one form to another*

Energy changes can be demonstrated through movement and pantomime, with several students working together.

Essential Element: Experience in oral and written communication of data

Concept: *Describe changes in objects and events*

See the lesson titled **Fire**, on page 146, for a direct application of this concept.

Concept: *Describe animal behaviors*
Describe how plants and animals protect themselves

Each student chooses one plant or animal to investigate. After the data have been collected, use an interview technique. The student becomes the plant or animal, and is interviewed by another student. The plant or animal reveals the appropriate behavior, while talking with the interviewer.

Essential Element: Experience in skills in relating objects and events to other objects and events

Concept: *Relate knowledge and skills of science to careers*

Each student chooses a particular career to find out about. The question is, "How has new technology changed that career?" Hold small panel discussions in which the students "become" the persons in that particular career, and discuss how their jobs have changed. Career possibilities are vast, of course. They may vary from musician to banker to doctor to pilot to homemaker. All are affected by the new technology.

HEALTH

The students can use a variety of dramatic methods to promote knowledge and understanding of good health practices: puppetry, masks, improvisations, mock interviews, preparing a videotape, writing and acting out a play. They may want to prepare a performance of some kind for a lower grade.

In each of the grades, the development of self-concept is noted as being very important. Studies have found that participating in drama does promote a positive self-concept. The students learn that their ideas are valued and that they have a unique contribution to make. They each have the opportunity to be "in the spotlight" in a positive way.

PHYSICAL EDUCATION

Essential Elements: Motor skills that develop positive body image and confidence; rhythmic activities that develop coordination, self-expression, creativity, and endurance

The rhythmic and interpretive movement lessons in this book relate very closely to the physical education elements. They will both extend and reinforce the physical education activities in which the children participate.

Essential Element: Skills related to games and sports

Concept: *Develop and practice behavior reflective of good sportsmanship and safety*

Guide the students to construct hand puppets and create scenes which deal with sportsmanship. The children will be able to "hide" behind their puppets, and show how a good sport or a bad sport reacts and feels. They can use their voices to express the characters in a way they might feel self-conscious about without the puppet. Remind them that sometimes a person who wins a game behaves like a bad sport, as well as a person who loses.

Titles such as the following may spark imaginations for creating a short puppet scene:

Rufus wins the race, but loses friends;
Chris loses the race, but is cheered by all;
Everybody loses sometimes;
"The umpire (judge, referee) isn't fair";
"I'm never going to play with you again!";
"You got a bigger piece than I did";
"You tripped me on purpose";
"Congratulations!"

FINE ARTS

Art

Many of the lessons in this book lend themselves to follow-up activities in art. Generally, after students have explored ideas through drama, they are much more aware of details than before. Drawings and paintings become more vivid and colorful. Students can also be guided to create an abstract design or painting which reflects the mood of what has been improvised in drama.

Essential Element: Inventive and imaginative expression through art materials and tools

Concept: *Express individual ideas, thoughts, and feelings in simple media*

1. Show the students pictures or, better yet, actual examples of sculpture. Discuss the feelings evoked by the sculpture, as expressed by line and form. Discuss where sculptors get their ideas.

Divide the class into pairs. One becomes the sculptor, the other the piece of clay. The sculptor gently forms the clay into a sculpture expressing an idea, which is either realistic or abstract. Older students may want to express themes such as war, greed, love, joy and hope.

When the sculptures are completed, the class looks at them and reacts to the forms. Reverse the roles.

This can also be done with several people being the clay.

Some students may want to photograph the sculptures.

2. Students can be helped to understand the dynamics of line and form when they play out a series of "freeze-frame" movements. For example, two or more students are enacting a baseball play. One is the pitcher, another is up to bat. (Others can be the catcher, etc.) While they play, you periodically call out "freeze-frame." The players freeze their pose. Those who are watching discuss the line and form which communicates action.

Essential Element: Understanding and appreciation of self and others through art, culture and heritage

Concept: *Look at and talk about contemporary and past artworks*

If at all possible, take the class to an art museum. If not, use slides or other art visuals.

1. Look at a painting, such as one of the Old West, and talk about the sensory elements communicated by the painting: the sights, the smells, the tastes, the various textures.

What sounds can be heard by viewing the painting? (For example, horses' hooves, guns, yelling, bodies falling.)

331

Divide the class into groups and orchestrate a "sound sculpture" to go with the painting. Each group is responsible for a certain sound effect. When you point to any given group, they make the sounds they have decided on. You can build this so that it starts out quietly, builds to a crescendo, and then recedes.

2. Look at a painting and discuss what is happening in the painting.

What do you think happened just before the action in the painting?
What might have happened afterward?

Divide them into groups. Some of the groups will create a tableau of the "before scene," some of the "after scene." Have two groups create their tableaus at once. If possible, the "before" group will position themselves on one side of the painting, the "after" group on the other side. The class responds by giving their perception of what they see happening in each tableau.

Music

Essential Element: Singing concepts and skills

Concept: *Create dramatizations, movements, new words to songs*

Songs can be used in much the same way stories are used as a basis for dramatization. The lessons on pantomime and improvisation can help prepare the students to dramatize songs. Consider not only dramatizing while the music is playing, but using the song as a basis for a more complete and extended dramatization. Some songs also lend themselves to playing one verse, acting that out, playing the second verse, acting, and so on.

Concept: *Perform contrasts including high/low, up/down, loud/soft, fast/slow, long/short, smooth/jerky*

These contrasts can be reinforced by using body movements. For example, when higher notes are heard, the students move in the high level of space, when lower notes are heard, they move in the low level of space. Loud sound is accompanied by strong movements, soft sound by gentle movements.

Concept: *Recognize aurally the difference between repeated sections, contrasting sections, and sections that return after a contrast*

This concept can be effectively reinforced through movement. In groups, ask the students to create appropriate and very specific movements for a given section. Whenever that section of music is repeated, they repeat the movements. They can do the same for a contrasting section, selecting movements which are contrasting, as well.

Essential Element: Responses to music through moving and playing

Concept: *Move to express mood and meaning of the music*

The lessons on rhythmic movement and interpretive movement for each grade level relate to the music concept.

Concept: *Recognize visually letter names of notes on treble staff*

Students can become the notes on a staff, or on a keyboard. Whenever the C is read, for example, the person acting that note responds by a hand, or whole body, movement. Have them change the notes they act out, so they eventually have the chance to be (and recognize) every note.

SOCIAL STUDIES

Creative drama is an effective tool to teach many aspects of social studies because it helps the students internalize and understand the human interactions which underlie situations and events. People and events come "alive" for the students when they are acted out. Because the social studies content is so vast, the teacher must decide which specific subject holds the most dramatic possibilities and interest for the children. The most important aspect to explore is the feelings of the various people involved, and link those feelings to those the children have experienced. The following suggestions are only the tip of the iceberg.

Essential Element: Personal, social, and civic responsibilities

Concepts: *Support individuals' rights to have differing opinions*

Respect individuals' rights to hold different political and religious beliefs

Friends sometimes disagree about things, yet each one can be right. Discuss the following examples:

If you like baseball best and your friend likes football, who is right?
If one loves okra and the other hates it, who is right?
How could the person who hates okra react in a kind way to the one who loves it?

Ask the students to come up with examples in which their opinion is different from someone else's. In pairs, ask them to talk about a given topic in which each holds a different opinion. Then ask them to switch roles, so they are discussing it from the opposite viewpoint. The topics should be discussed on a peer to peer level, rather than child to parent. They can discuss topics as if they are both adults, if they wish.

One of the most wonderful things about living in the United States, of course, is that everyone has the right to hold different political and religious beliefs. Even though one person has a different belief from another, each should respected.

How can you show respect for another person's convictions?
How can you discuss different beliefs, showing respect for one another?

Hold a panel discussion with students who have different views about a topic which interests them. After each member of the panel talks about his or her beliefs, the class can join in the discussion. The point is to state one's views and listen and comment, showing respect for others.

Concepts: *Explain the role of compromise as a method of resolving conflicts*

Ask the students to act out situations from their own lives in which the people eventually compromise in order to solve a problem. For example,

> *On a beautiful Saturday, one family member wants to go biking, another wants to go swimming, another wants to go to a movie.*
> *Or, each wants to watch a different program on television.*
> *Or, each wants to do something different over the winter holidays.*

Ask the students to look in the newspapers for examples of how the leaders of nations have to use the method of compromise, too. They can hold a mini-United Nations, discussing a current issue.

Discuss the value of compromise.

Essential Element: Historical data about the United States and the world

Concepts: *Identify causes of historical events or actions in United States history; identify contributions of various cultures, past and present, to world civilization; identify significant individuals and their contributions to history*

Individuals are generally recorded in history because of something important they did for the good of the people. They usually accomplished something after having overcome great obstacles and problems. The problems and the feelings of the people are the heart of the drama. Choose situations to enact which show

> how things were before a particular change,
> how the people felt,
> what happened to make the change,
> and then how they felt after the change.

One such situation, for example, is the escape of slaves using the underground railroad.

> *What was the life of the slaves like?*
> *What kinds of things did they do?*
> *What would a typical day be like?*

How did they feel about their lives?
Why did many of them want to escape?

Ask the class to imagine they are slaves. They wake up in the morning, knowing that this may be the day they are to make their escape, if they hear the signal to go.

How will they get their things together and keep their masters from suspecting what is going to happen?
How do they feel about leaving some of their family and friends?
How will they go about their work until they hear the signal?
How did the underground railroad work?
What dangers were involved?

They all play out the situation simultaneously. You can sidecoach them as they go through the escape, heightening the drama by introducing complications such as the following:

You hear footsteps behind you in the distance. Can you find a place to hide?
You smell smoke. What will you do?
At last you reach your destination. How do you feel?

History is filled with very powerful, dramatic events. For example, play out how the people felt just before and then during the siege of the Alamo. You do not have to have opposing sides. They can imagine the siege and act out what happened to the men involved. Some of the students could make sound effects of the battle. Again, it is important to discuss what might have been going through the minds of the people, and how they felt.

The Revolutionary War is also filled with dramatic possibilities, especially since George Washington's troops had such difficulties for a long period of time. What must that winter have been like at Valley Forge, when there was not enough food or clothing, when 3000 soldiers died? Yet by spring, those who were there had turned into a well trained army. How could that have happened?

Individuals from many different countries have made significant contributions to our culture. Games can be played in which important inventions are pantomimed, with the first team to name the inventor winning a point.

In a similar vein, various countries are noted for specific contributions. As a review, groups of children could be assigned a certain country. They are to act out the "gifts" or contributions made by that country. For example, contributions from ancient Greece include democracy, public discussion of ideas, jury trials, tragic and comic plays, sculpture, epic poetry, the Olympic games. Each of these contributions holds possibilities for pantomime.

Essential Element: Local, state, national and world geography

Concept: *Know how landforms and climate interact*

Students can be greatly assisted in understanding the formation of mountains, plateaus, and so on, if they act out what happened physically. What causes eruptions, for instance, and what happens to the earth?

Concept: *Understand how people have adapted to and modified the physical environment*

Divide the students into groups, to depict how people lived—what they wore, what kind of housing they had, what they did, what they ate—that was directly influenced by where they lived and the climate. They may even want to use simple costumes, to give an idea of the people. Each group can enact a different region, to show the contrasts.

Essential Element: Psychological, sociological, and cultural factors affecting human behavior

Concepts: *Describe how traditions, customs, folkways, and religious beliefs differ among individuals and groups*
Identify holidays and celebrations in the nation that are cultural-group related
Identify the contributions of various cultures to the American way of life (art, literature, music, etc.)

There may be no better way to understand other cultures than by dramatizing the culture, and especially their holidays which include music, art, dance, costume, and foods. It is especially effective if a child, parent or community member can come to the class and talk about the festivities, their origin, and why they are important today. If such a person is not available, there is a wealth of information in books.

OTHER LANGUAGES

When trying to communicate with someone who speaks a language we don't understand, pantomime is the time-honored method for "speaking." Pantomime is also an effective way to reinforce concepts and vocabulary when teaching another language. In fact, one of the concepts listed for learning other languages is that the students "recognize the role of nonlinguistic elements in communication." Just as body language is the base for learning English, it is also the base for learning other languages. Out of body language, pantomime, grows the need for speaking. There are many opportunities for using drama in teaching other languages. A few examples follow:

Essential Element: Speaking

Concepts: *Reproduce sounds and intonation patterns in meaningful contexts; use words, phrases, or sentences as appropriate; and use expressions needed for daily life situations*

1. In teams, one team pantomimes a word or phrase. The other team determines what it is and they repeat it in the language. The team which guesses correctly in the least amount of time wins.

2. One student plays a teacher, another plays a child. The teacher gives instructions to the child, in the language, and the child follows the instruction. For example, "Turn off the lights."

3. Each student is given a card with a word on it. There are duplicate cards for each word. A volunteer pantomimes his or her word—"table," for example. When the student who has the same word recognizes the panto-

mime, he or she stands up and says the word. The same can be done with phrases or sentences.

4. Pantomime the actions to songs and simple stories.

5. The students can make sound effects at the appropriate time when you tell a story in the language. For example, the wind was blowing hard one night. (The class makes the sound of wind.) A clap of thunder shook the house.

Continue with the story.

Essential Element: Reading

Concept: *Read familiar material with comprehension*

If the children can read a story and then act out parts of it, you will know whether they comprehended the story or not.

Essential Element: Culture

Concept: *Experience various aspects of another culture*

All cultures have special days of celebration. Planning and participating in a celebration is one of the most effective ways of learning about the culture. Food, costumes, music, dance, decorations—all lend themselves to understanding the culture, as well as learning vocabulary.

You will find a number of helpful books in the library which tell of the customs and culture of specific lands. Two such books, for example, include a lot of information about Mexico: *Mexico is People, Land of Three Cultures,* by Barabara Nolen, published by Charles Scribner's Sons, 1973; and *Mexico, Giant of the South,* by Eileen Latell Smith, published by Dillon Press, 1983.

You may also want to refer to the section on anthologies and collections, in Appendix B of this book. There are many stories from various cultures which give the flavor of the culture and are suitable for dramatization by the students.

Part Two
USING DRAMA WITH
SPECIAL POPULATIONS

In a very real sense, all children, indeed all adults, are special. However, some children are set apart from what is considered "the norm," perhaps because of giftedness, mental, physical or emotional challenges or cultural difference. All of these children perceive themselves as "different," because society has cast them in that role. In fact, being children they are more "like" other children than they are "different." They all share some common needs: the need for acceptance, the need to communicate and express themselves, and the need for a positive self-concept. Experiences in the theatre arts address themselves to each of those needs in ways that provide great satisfaction to the child.

Children Who are Academically Gifted

Courses designed for the academically gifted are often rigorous and demanding, especially in the sciences and mathematics. Unfortunately, the social and creative aspects of development are frequently overlooked.

Even in the early grades, superior performance by gifted students is noticed by classmates, and unless the gifted child is also a social leader, he or she may not feel accepted by the other children. Through theatre arts activities, children can learn to work together and to respect one another.

Academically gifted children may or may not appear to be creative at first. But once the imagination is sparked, ideas will tumble out in rapid succession and even the most inhibited will find release in expression. These children are able to think of many things at once, understand structure, and perceive themes. They need a challenge and will be able to delve quite deeply into the material presented.

Children with Learning Disabilities

Mental challenges range from fairly mild to profound. The following suggestions are for those with mild learning disabilities—those children who are mainstreamed except for certain portions of the day—and those who are considered "educable mentally retarded."

1. Use coordination exercises, such as the rhythmic and creative movement activities in this book. Coordination exercises are often prescribed for children with learning disabilities.

2. Help them learn through their kinesthetic or muscle sense. Activities in which they physically use their bodies to represent a concept can be effective for retention of the concept:

    a. Draw large letters in the air.

    b. Walk the shape of a letter on the floor.

    c. Use the body to form the letter.

    d. Use the "Math Machine" activity on page 326.

    e. Act out words to reinforce their meaning and build vocabulary.

    f. Motivate the children to remember a story sequence by telling them they will be allowed to act it out after they read it.

3. Give directions which are "uncluttered," direct and clear.

4. Praise and encourage over and over again.

5. Repeat the same activities often.

6. Set up "pretend" environments for the educable mentally retarded. Often such children find it difficult to use their imaginations and relate to abstract ideas. Setting up a "restaurant" environment, for example, in one part of the room can be effective. Children show how one acts in a restaurant, looking at the menu, ordering, eating, and so on. They will enjoy pretending the food is really there—a leap in the imagination.

7. Key into the interests and needs of the children.

8. Provide a supportive and accepting environment. Helping the children develop self-confidence and a sense of self-worth is equally important as learning language and number concepts. They need experiences in which their contributions are valued and respected.

Children with Physical Disabilities

Theatre arts activities are readily adaptable to children facing various kinds of physical challenges. Furthermore, such activities bring great joy to the participants, and satisfaction to the teacher who guides them. Perhaps the most important thing to remember is to choose activities in which the child will feel successful, and proud of making a worthwhile contribution. By the teacher's believing in them, they are helped to believe in themselves. The following are a few suggestions for children with specific disabilities.

Deaf children, whether they are partially hearing or totally deaf, can participate in many theatre arts activities.

1. Use the movement and pantomime activities in the book.

2. Use a drum for rhythms, or a stick, like a broom handle, marking time on a wooden floor.

3. Select stories in which the plot can be communicated largely through pantomime.

4. In classes where children are "mainstreamed," consider having the hearing impaired children play the characters, signing and gesturing as the characters would, while hearing and speaking actors stand to the side and speak the dialogue at the appropriate time as the character would.

Vision impaired or blind children are generally comfortable with language.

1. Begin with sound and simple dialogue lessons.

2. Use rhythmic activities in a barrier-free space. One of the needs of this group is to become more comfortable with their own bodies and their relationship in space.

3. Begin movement activities which are confined to the area they are standing in, and then gradually increase the amount of space to move in. Moving freely in space is a special luxury that many will not have experienced before.

4. Encourage them to work in pairs, holding hands or touching in some way. Working with a partner may help them feel more secure.

5. Keep the setting constant for any given story. Blind children can dramatize stories, but the setting needs to be carefully delineated, so that a chair, for instance, is always in the same place. When they feel secure in the setting, they will be able to concentrate on the action and dialogue of the story.

Children with *limited movement capabilities* can also participate in drama.

1. Use rhythmic movements with any part of the body that can move: fingers, elbows, eyes, nose, mouth and so on.

2. "Dance" with a wheelchair! A mobile person manipulates the wheelchair in a rhythm.

3. Use puppets. They are particularly effective with those whose movement is limited. The puppet becomes the "alter ego" who can do everything the person with the disability cannot do, and, in fact, the puppet can do things that no humans can do!

4. Adapt stories so they can accommodate a person in a wheelchair. For example, there isn't any reason that Tommy has to "skip down the road." He could "move down the road," or roll, or go, or amble along.

Children with Behavioral Problems

The discussion here does not refer to severely emotionally disturbed individuals, but rather to those children with behavioral problems who are still able to be in a regular classroom setting. The behavior of such children is often either very inhibited or very aggressive. Participation in drama activities can be very helpful, but using drama does not imply that the teacher should play "therapist." There are trained drama therapists for that. The teacher can guide drama activities, however, which may help inhibited children feel more confident to express themselves, and help aggressive children control their actions.

Inhibited or shy children often are lost in the classroom, because they do not cause any problems, nor do they demand attention. It is easy to become aware of them only when they are asked to respond verbally or to interact with others in some way. Classmates frequently "rescue" the child by saying, "He is shy, he won't talk," and then provide the answer for him. Such a child may have a very difficult time communicating ideas, which can be frustrating for the child, the teacher and the rest of the class. A great measure of patience and support is necessary.

The following are a few suggestions that may help shy children become involved. Once they allow themselves to become involved, they generally participate with no reluctance.

1. Begin each session with a movement warm-up that is exactly the same each time, or has only minor variations. This establishes a ritual which children respond to—they know what to expect.

2. Use rhythmic movement activities where everyone in the circle holds hands while moving.

3. Use rhythmic activities in which partners hold hands. You act as the partner for the inhibited child. Or, become the partner for two children, and during the activities have some excuse to move away and let the two children continue the movement, without you.

4. Ask the inhibited child to help you in small tasks, such as passing out something or turning on the lights.

5. Use puppets. Frequently, inhibited children learn to act freely when they can hide behind a puppet, or a mask.

6. Give gentle encouragement and positive reinforcement.

Very *aggressive* children present a different kind of challenge to the teacher. These children usually demand, and receive, attention for unacceptable classroom behavior. They need a lot of reinforcement for positive behavior. A few hints follow.

1. Plan many different activities, because these children usually have a short attention span.

2. Let them know that you want to have fun but you also mean business and will not put up with fights or playing around. If necessary, have them sit out for awhile, and permit them to return only so long as they obey the rules.

3. Use some activities in which individuals may volunteer to pantomime something for the group. Praise and applaud all volunteers. They need to feel better about themselves.

4. Always begin with a movement activity. As with inhibited children, aggressive children find security in ritual.

5. Ask the aggressive child to be your "assistant" sometimes.

6. Present a problem and ask the child for suggestions. For example, "We need to show that the crocodile is eating the monkey. How can we do this without touching? Susie, what do you think?" Then try out the idea offered by Susie, or use it to build upon.

7. Touch them occasionally on the back, or shoulder or arm, when they have done something well, or have tried to cooperate.

8. Speak calmly. If they misbehave, they pay the consequences by having to sit out. Speak to them matter-of-factly, and with sincere sympathy. For example, "Oh phooey, James, you forgot the rule. Sit over there for awhile. I'll bet you'll remember better next time." Then go right on with the rest of the group.

Children Who are Economically Deprived

Children, from all cultures, who are economically deprived often have not been exposed to cultural resources, such as literature, art, performances, trips outside the community and so on. Such children are like any other children, they just have a few special needs. A few suggestions follow:

1. Try to approach drama with the children from where they are in their daily lives. Many of them have never been exposed to anything but television and movies.

2. Start slowly; they will soon catch on to the idea of drama and delight in it.

3. Choose material that might seem slightly older than their actual age level. Many children from low income families are much more "street wise" than other children—they have had to fight for themselves. Don't ever talk down to them.

4. Choose stories with lots of action.

5. Don't let them shock you. Some will try with the things they say.

6. Keep abreast of the current trends and fads in music and clothes within the culture. Such awareness will help you understand the children, and, in turn, you will gain their respect.

7. Let them know that you want to have fun but you also mean business—you will not put up with fights or playing around. If necessary, call a halt to the drama if they behave in unacceptable ways. Ordinarily they are so hungry for a creative outlet that calling a halt will be enough to keep them quiet and behaving.

8. Give them as much caring attention as possible. Many get very little individual and personal attention in their daily lives.

9. Honor the traditions of the cultures from which they come by includ-

ing drama activities centered around cultural festivals, and literature, art and music based on their heritage.

It is common knowledge that no two snowflakes are alike. Upon close examination, one can see the unique qualities of each and appreciate the intricacy of the formations. In like manner, no two human beings are the same. Each one is special. When a child is looked at with close attention, one begins to appreciate the unique qualities of that human being. Teachers have the opportunity to bring out the specialness of each child, so that the child and others can recognize and appreciate the gifts each has to offer.

Chapter VI:
ASSESSMENT

Teachers employ evaluation strategies daily, making decisions that have a direct effect on the learning that is both possible and probable. In order to make valid judgments about what has been achieved both in teaching and in learning, there must be a clear understanding of objectives and the learning that is expected. Explicit evaluative criteria must be developed to ensure that evaluative decisions are educationally sound and communicate clearly to others.

In the theatre arts curriculum, evaluation should focus on individual growth as it is reflected in how the student participates in the creative process, what the student produces, and how the student responds to aesthetic experiences. Students should be measured against their own potential, recording where they start and how far they progress, rather than comparing students against each other.

There are basically two types of evaluation, "ongoing" and "summative." Ongoing evaluation helps teachers plan appropriate work for students, maximizing their strengths and identifying skills to be developed. Judgments about the student's work are applied directly, by talking with him or her about strengths and weaknesses, and indirectly, by structuring new experiences aimed at building upon previous achievements. The Assessment section at the end of each lesson in this book is intended to provide ideas for ongoing evaluation. Depending on the lesson, it will include such things as questions about the accomplishment of the drama objective, and the suggestions for oral, drawn, or written application of the lesson's content. Ongoing evaluations can provide a base for summative evaluations.

Summative evaluation documents the individual student's achievement at a specific time. Although ongoing evaluation is far more prevalent, summative evaluation is given more importance, causes more worry, and is thought of as "the real thing" by many students, parents, and administrators. Audiences for the two types of evaluation are normally different. Ongoing evaluation is employed in the everyday relationship between the student and teacher, whereas summative evaluation is used to inform parents about their child's progress and to determine promotion. It is, therefore, important for all concerned to know the precise purpose of any evaluation and to whom such information is directed.

EVALUATION STRATEGIES

When evaluating students in a theatre arts curriculum, the teacher is looking for behaviors which indicate the student understands certain aspects of the art form. Sometimes such behaviors are readily displayed during the acting out of a piece of literature or an improvised story. If a student performs well, one can deduce that he or she understands the concept being taught on some level. However, evaluating on performance alone would bring one perilously close to grading a student on the merits of artistic talent, which is not the intent of the theatre arts curriculum. Therefore, the teacher strives for a balance between evaluating what the student does while improvising and other behaviors which reveal the student's understanding even if she or he is not a gifted performer.

There are a number of evaluation strategies which are appropriate to use and which can help achieve the balance one is looking for in the theatre arts curriculum. They include class discussion, audio and videotape recording, problem solving projects, role playing, oral and written critiques, oral and written tests, drawing, journals and criteria checklists. Although the Assessment section at the end of each lesson recommends certain strategies, each teacher will want to choose those that seem most important for a given class of students.

Class discussion is one of the most commonly used strategies. In fact, teachers will note that class discussion is part of the creative drama process called "reflect" or "evaluate," and is built into every lesson. The goal of such discussion is for students to learn how to evaluate their own and one another's work in a constructive manner. The discussion is based on questions from the teacher, some of which relate directly to the objective of the lesson.

Periodic use of **audio and videotape recordings** can help the students evaluate their own work more clearly, as well as help the teacher evaluate the students' progress. After two or three times, students will become accustomed to the camera and will behave as they normally do.

Problem-solving projects require application of knowledge, critical choices, and decision making. Such activities are open-ended creative endeavors centering on the process rather than on preconceived products. Consequently, the teacher's personal values should not restrict student creativity. An example of such a project might be the following assignment: Develop a plot in which the conflict deals with people vs. the environment.

Role playing is related to problem-solving projects. The student reveals understanding of a concept by applying it in action. For example, if the objective is to understand that the character's attitude often determines how he or she does something, the student might be assigned a certain character and a certain action, such as a mother baking cookies. The student then plays the role in several different ways: happy, because an old friend is coming to visit; irritated and rushed, because she was just informed she had to bring cookies to a meeting in an hour; tired and out of sorts, because she is coming down with a cold.

Oral and written critiques of both student work and professional productions can assist in the student's aesthetic growth. Oral critiques by the students themselves can be started earlier in the grades than one might expect. The oral critiques grow out of class discussions where the tone is positive and constructive, rather than negative. Such critical analysis needs to be based on established criteria. Sometimes half the class may be pantomiming something, for example, and each person watching is assigned to focus on one particular person and comment on something specific, like what the person did to show he or she was walking through a thick forest, or a dark cave. Written critiques can be done in a similar manner, as the students develop writing skills.

Oral and written tests can be used to evaluate students' understanding of terminology and such concepts as plot structure and character objectives. A written test might even take the form of writing a story with the intent to show clear plot structure, for example, or to describe the sequence of events in a story that was just acted out.

Drawing, or other visual art applications, can convey whether or not a student understands a concept, even when he or she may not be able to put it into words. Although teachers already tend to use drawing in the primary grades, intermediate grade teachers should consider its use, too. For some students, drawing is a preferred mode of expression and teachers are often surprised at how much a student who doesn't talk much knows.

Journals can be a very effective way for older children to reflect on the content of the lessons and on their own aesthetic and artistic growth. Journal writing can be directed or non-directed. The journal suggestions given for sixth graders in this theatre arts curriculum are directed. Specific assignments are made which relate to the lessons. Frequently several options are given, which may be selected either by the teacher or the student. A journal could include reflective drawings as well as writing. Teachers read the journals periodically and note how well the student is grasping the concepts being studied. Some teachers rotate their reading of the journals by collecting five, for example, at a time, thereby avoiding a large number to deal with at one time.

Criteria checklists can be very useful for evaluating individual student progress and achievement. Criteria focus on specific theatre art objectives, as well as individual and group behaviors necessary for effective work in theatre arts. The same criteria for pre-assessment, ongoing, and summative evaluation can serve to document student progress toward mastery of stated objectives.

Whether the teacher chooses to use one method of assessment or several, notation of students' progress is important for planning future lessons. Since the teacher is actively involved with the students during a theatre arts class, observations will usually be recorded after a session. Periodic records rather than daily notations are usually adequate, with the first and final sessions of a grading period being useful for revealing a continuum of progress toward mastery of the essential elements. Notations about every student may be made following one session, or the teacher may find it more manageable to evaluate different groups of students in different sessions. Observations may be all inclusive or limited to selected behaviors for different activities. (Use the "NA" to indicate which behaviors are not being evaluated.)

The teacher may use a checklist format or a rating scale format. A very simple method is the checklist, in which a check mark indicates desirable behavior has been observed, and a blank space indicates the need for improvement.

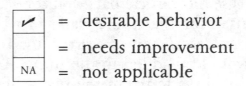

If a more detailed continuum of development is desired, a rating scale of 1–4 can be used, rather than a check/no check.

1	= poor
2	= fair
3	= good
4	= superior
NA	= not applicable

Teachers may choose to keep individual records for each student, or class records for specific lessons. Teachers may also want to consider asking the students to evaluate themselves periodically, using the same form as the teacher. Students in the intermediate grades can begin to reflect seriously on their own behavior and how it matches the expectations of the classwork. Their self-assessment can be compared periodically with the assessment made by the teacher, and any discrepancies can be discussed.

Sample forms for ongoing behaviors follow which are somewhat more detailed than the behaviors listed on the first page of each grade level chapter. Teachers can use the form for whatever level of specificity seems most appropriate for their classes.

There are also forms suggested for the evaluative criteria of the three essential elements. The evaluative criteria forms may be used for an individual student, in which case the vertical bars would be lesson titles and dates; or the form may be used for the whole class, in which case vertical bars would be added and students' names written in. In the latter case, the lesson title and date would be added to the form. Again, teachers should feel free to adapt any of these forms to the needs of their particular classrooms.

DATE: LESSON TITLE:

	STUDENTS																
ON-GOING DRAMA BEHAVIORS																	
CONCENTRATION																	
follows directions																	
sustains involvement in activity																	
IMAGINATION																	
contributes original ideas																	
reacts spontaneously																	
solves problems creatively																	
incorporates imaginative detail																	
COOPERATIVE INTERACTION																	
contributes to group effort																	
listens courteously to others																	
takes turns																	
assumes role of leader																	
assumes role of followers																	
accepts group decisions																	
NONVERBAL EXPRESSION																	
uses appropriate gestures																	
uses appropriate movement																	
VERBAL EXPRESSION																	
speaks clearly																	
speaks expressively																	
improvises dialogue																	

355

EVALUATION AND CRITICAL ANALYSIS

makes constructive contributions to discussion and evaluations																				
incorporates improvements into playing																				

ATTITUDE

cooperative, involved																				
shy, inhibited																				
disruptive, hostile																				

356

STUDENT ─────────────────────── PROJECT ───────────────────────

CLASS/PERIOD ─────────────────── EVALUATOR ────────────────── DATE ──────────

CRITERIA	− +	COMMENTS
	1 2 3 4 NA	
	1 2 3 4 NA	
	1 2 3 4 NA	
	1 2 3 4 NA	
	1 2 3 4 NA	
	1 2 3 4 NA	
	1 2 3 4 NA	
	1 2 3 4 NA	
	1 2 3 4 NA	
	1 2 3 4 NA	
	1 2 3 4 NA	
	1 2 3 4 NA	
	1 2 3 4 NA	

1 = poor   2 = fair   3 = good   4 = superior   NA = not applicable

ESSENTIAL ELEMENT

Acting: Expressive Use of the Body and Voice

CONCEPT

Movement

EVALUATIVE CRITERIA

Repeats movements with precision						
Synchronizes movements						
Moves in various kinds of rhythms						
Moves body parts in isolation						
Creates contrasting movement patterns						
Moves easily in small and large spaces						
Knows a variety of locomotor movements						
Knows the difference between heavy and light movements						
Falls down safely						
Creates the movements of a variety of animals						
Interprets the movements of a variety of inanimate objects						

ESSENTIAL ELEMENT

Acting: Expressive Use of the Body and Voice

CONCEPT

Sensory Awareness and Pantomime

EVALUATIVE CRITERIA

Responds appropriately to directions						
Describes sensory details of objects which are present						
Describes sensory details of objects which are not present						
Allows the senses to stimulate the imagination						
Clearly communicates animal movements						
Clearly communicates sensory properties of objects:						
size						
shape						
weight						
texture						
temperature						
Clearly communicates being in a specific place						
Clearly communicates specific activities						
Clearly communicates character movements and actions						

ESSENTIAL ELEMENT

Acting: Expressive Use of the Body and Voice

CONCEPT

Sounds and Dialogue

EVALUATIVE CRITERIA

Imitates animal sounds							
Imitates environmental sounds							
Creates character voices							
Speaks clearly and distinctly							
Communicates different meanings by changing							
intensity							
pitch							
volume							
rate of speed							

ESSENTIAL ELEMENT

Acting: Expressive Use of the Body and Voice

CONCEPT

Emotional Recall

EVALUATIVE CRITERIA

Recalls and describes different feelings								
Uses body to express feelings								
Uses voice to express feelings								
Expresses appropriate feelings while acting out situations								
Expresses contrasting moods as a character other than self								

ESSENTIAL ELEMENT

Playmaking/Playwriting: Collaborative Improvisations

CONCEPT

Dramatize Literary Selections Using

Sensory Recall, Pantomime, Dialogue

EVALUATIVE CRITERIA

Sensory Recall								
Responds appropriately to directions								
Describes sensory details of objects which are present								
Allows senses to stimulate the imagination								
Pantomime								
Clearly communicates animal movements								
Clearly communicates sensory properties of:								
size								
shape								
weight								
texture								
temperature								
Communicates being in a specific place								
Communicates specific activities								
Communicates character movements and actions								

362

continued

Dialogue

Creates character voices							
Speaks clearly and distinctly							
Communicates meaning by using vocal							
intensity							
pitch							
volume							
rate of speed							

Emotional Recall

Uses body to express feelings							
Uses voice to express feelings							
Expresses appropriate feelings while acting out situations							

Improvisation of Plot

Develops stories with clear beginning, middle, climax and ending							
Understands the three major sources of conflict							
Shows how the setting affects a plot							
Shows how time affects a plot							

363

continued

Characterization

Shows physical characteristics							
Shows characters' objectives							
Shows characters' attitudes							
Uses dialogue and voice to reveal character							
Listens and responds appropriately to others							
Sustains concentration / characterization							
Enacts scenes from various points of view							

ESSENTIAL ELEMENT

Playmaking/Playwriting: Collaborative Improvisations

CONCEPT

Dramatize Literary Selections Using

Puppetry and Shadow Play

EVALUATIVE CRITERIA

Constructs simple hand, body and shadow puppets						
Acts out the story or poem using						
appropriate movements for puppets						
character voices						
clear and distinct speech						
appropriate intensity						
appropriate pitch						
appropriate volume						
appropriate rate of speed						

ESSENTIAL ELEMENT

Responding and Constructing Meaning:
Development of Aesthetic Sensibilities

CONCEPT

View Theatrical Events

EVALUATIVE CRITERIA

Player-Audience Relationship and **Audience Etiquette**						
Arrives promptly						
Talks quietly before performance						
Remains seated during performance						
Does not talk or eat during performance						
Responds attentively to performers						
Applauds at appropriate times						
Waits for turn to exit						
Characterization (Describes the following in relationship to the performance seen)						
physical characteristics						
objectives of characters						
how attitudes affected action						
actors' use of the voice						
actors' use of movement and pantomime						

366

continued

Plot

Describes the major conflict						
Describes how the setting affected the play						
Describes the time affected the play						
Predicts plot resolution						
Suggests alternative courses of action						
Staging (Describes how the following contributed to the production.)						
the set						
the lights						
the costumes						
the sound						
any special effects						

Evaluates and Makes Aesthetic Judgments

Discusses general response to theatrical event						
Gives reasons for comments, based on						
characterization						
plot						
staging effects						

ESSENTIAL ELEMENT

Responding and Constructing Meaning: Development of Aesthetic Sensibilities

CONCEPT

Recognize Similarities and Differences in

Television, Film and Live Theatre

EVALUATIVE CRITERIA

Describes similarities and differences with regard to						
setting						
acting						
time of action						
special effects						
camera angles						
position of the audience						

368

THEATRE ARTS GLOSSARY OF TERMS

ACT—That part of the creative drama process in which the children portray characters in a scene or story.

AESTHETIC GROWTH—Increased understanding and appreciation of the art of drama.

CHARACTER—A person, animal, or entity in a scene, story, or play with distinguishing physical, mental, and attitudinal attributes.

CHILD DEVELOPMENT—Theatre arts help children develop awareness of themselves as physical beings, creative beings, social beings, organizers of experience, and active participants in their environment.

CHILDREN'S THEATRE—Plays presented for an audience of children.

CLOSING ACTIVITY—A quiet activity or discussion that is calming and helps prepare the children to participate in their next subject or activity with control.

COMMUNICATION—The process of interacting with another person or persons to give and receive messages, either verbally or nonverbally.

CONCENTRATION—The ability to focus and keep one's attention fixed on the matter at hand, to the exclusion of distracting factors.

CREATIVE DRAMA—"An improvisational, non-exhibitional, process-centered form of theatre in which participants are guided by a leader to imagine, enact, and reflect upon human experiences." (As defined by The Children's Theatre Association of America.)

CRITIC—A professional theatre critic is a person who attends a performance and reviews it for a newspaper, radio, or television, describing the strong and the weak points of the production and/or the script.

CRITIQUE—A written or oral review of a performance which describes its strong and weak points.

DESIGNER—In professional theatres there are often several designers: a set designer, who plans what the stage will look like for each scene; a costume designer, who plans what the characters will wear; a lighting designer, who plans how the set will be illuminated and how different effects will be achieved; a sound designer, who plans any sound effects or music that might be desired.

In small theatres, often one designer will fulfill all the design functions. Frequently the designer will build the sets and/or the costumes, as well as design them.

The designer(s) works as a member of the production team with the director and other people involved in getting the play ready for an audience.

DIALOGUE—The words used by the characters.

DRAMA AS AN ART — Teaching in order to help children understand and appreciate the art of drama, which is a story told through action and dialogue.

DRAMA AS A TEACHING TOOL — Using drama as a teaching technique to enhance, extend, and deepen the understanding of concepts in other subject areas. Using drama in this way allows children to learn physically and kinesthetically, as well as mentally and emotionally. It helps total learning so that concepts are likely to be remembered.

EMOTIONAL AWARENESS — Activities to heighten awareness of feelings both in oneself and in others.

EMOTIONAL RECALL — The ability to remember feelings in order to recreate them with honesty and sincerity when playing a character.

EVALUATION — That part of the creative drama process in which personal efforts and efforts of others are reflected upon and appraised, after acting out a scene or story.

FANTASY — The use of imagination to create strange, unusual, or non-realistic characters or settings, such as creatures from outer space, or toys that talk.

GESTURE — An expressive movement that communicates an idea, a feeling, or state of being.

IMAGINATION — The process of forming a mental picture of what is not physically present or of what has not been personally experienced. Or, the process of combining images from previous experiences.

IMITATIVE SOUND — Imitating sounds, such as wind, thunder, animals.

IMPROVISATION — The spontaneous creation of a character through action and speech in a particular situation.

INTERPRETIVE MOVEMENT — Movement used to depict non-human roles or abstract concepts.
      Examples: fire, wind, power, love.

INTRODUCE — That part of the creative drama process in which the teacher presents a motivating activity or discussion, preparing the children for the activity or story to follow and helping them to identify with a given character or situation. An effective introduction stimulates the children's thoughts and their feelings.

ORIGINAL DIALOGUE — Improvising the dialogue for a character.

PANTOMIME — Action, movement and gesture, without words.

PERCEPTION — The process by which people use their senses to gain information from the physical environment. It may be as simple as identifying the color of a fabric or the tone of a sound, or as complex as describing a plot line or creating a character.

PLAN — That part of the creative drama process in which the teacher asks questions to help children understand the action and feelings of the characters and the sequence of the plot, in preparation for acting it out.

PLAYING — Improvising or acting-out characters in a scene or story.

PLAYING IN ROLE — A technique used by the leader during the enactment, in which the leader plays a role that allows for some authority and control, to heighten and advance the playing.

PLAYWRIGHT — The person who writes the play. Often a playwright will work directly with a theatre company while they rehearse the play, and make changes in the script during the rehearsal period.

PLOT — The story revealed through the action and dialogue of the characters. Plot structure usually includes a beginning, middle, and end; it has a problem, complications, climax, and resolution.

PUPPETRY — The animation of objects to create characters in dramatic situations.

QUESTIONS — Open-ended questions that begin with why, what, when, where, how, and who encourage discussion. Closed questions that elicit yes-or-no responses discourage discussion. Examples: How did the character show her power? (open-ended) Did the character show her power? (closed)

RAP — A type of music which became popular in the late 1980's, in which lyrics are spoken, often rapidly, to a strong rhythmic beat.

REACTION — Responding to a stimulus. Drama is built upon the action and reaction of the characters.

REFLECTION — Thinking about the meaning of something one has done, or witnessed or read, relating the event to one's own life.

REPLAYING — Enacting the scene or play again, making improvements, and sometimes changing roles so that the children have the opportunity to play more than one character.

RHYTHMIC MOVEMENT — Activities that have a certain rhythmic pattern.

ROLE PLAYING — Enacting a role (character) other than oneself in an improvisation based on a given dramatic situation.

SCENARIO — An outline of the action of a play, without the dialogue.

SENSORY AWARENESS — Experiences to sharpen perception and open senses to heightened awareness.

SENSORY RECALL — The ability to remember sensory experiences in order to recreate them accurately.

SHADOW PLAY — A form of puppetry using flat puppets, hands, or human silhouettes presented behind a backlighted sheet.

SIDECOACHING — A technique used by the leader during the playing, or acting, in which the leader offers suggestions or comments from the side of the playing area, to heighten and advance the playing.

SITUATION ROLE PLAYING — Improvisations which focus on understanding the viewpoints of others.

SPATIAL PERCEPTION — Activities which focus on how the body moves in space and how characters move in relationship to one another.

STORY DRAMATIZATION — Improvising a story based on literature.

THEME — The main thought of the improvisation or play, developed through the plot and characters.

WARM-UP — An activity in which the children focus their attention on limbering up their bodies and/or voices.

Appendices

Appendix A

IDEA STARTERS

These activities can be used as jumping off places for your own ideas for dramatization. Or they can be used, as written, for those one to five minute interludes which often occur during a day, or when the children need an action-break from other classroom work. The suggestions are not placed in any sequential order. Use those which seem appropriate for your class situation.

HOLIDAYS AND SEASONS

A. Halloween

1. Build a dramatization around the witches' chant, from Act IV, Scene 1, of *Macbeth*, by William Shakespeare:

Double, double toil and trouble,
Fire burn and caldron bubble.

Fillet of a fenny snake,
In the caldron boil and bake.
Eye of newt and toe of frog,
Wool of bat and tongue of dog,
Adder's fork and blindworm's sting,
Lizard's leg and howlet's wing,
For a charm of powerful trouble,
Like a Hell brother boil and bubble.

Double, double toil and trouble,
Fire burn and caldron bubble.

2. Ask students to imagine that it is midnight on Halloween. They are in their beds, sleeping, when they feel a spell being cast on them. They feel very strange. In slow motion they change into something else. Instead of being evil, however, they find they are a powerful force for good. They are given one hour to accomplish the thing that would be most helpful to the world.

B. Thanksgiving

1. Ask each student to think of one thing he or she could do that a particular family member would be thankful for. They pantomime the activities.

2. In small groups, students act out a scene evolving around something they are thankful for.

C. Winter Holidays

1. Brainstorm ideas about how the winter holidays could be happier for people less fortunate than they are, for example, people in nursing homes, people without homes, children in hospitals. In groups, students act out what they might do to make the holidays happier for a particular group of people. Later, they may even decide to follow through in reality!

2. Students take turns pantomiming their favorite activity of the winter holidays.

D. Fall

1. They pantomime activities that take place in the Fall. Football, for example, is more than just the game. There are marching bands, drill teams, twirlers, people selling food and programs, to name a few.

2. Fall signals the start of a new school year. Students act out one of their favorite things about school. If you are willing, they can even act out their least favorite thing!

E. Winter

1. They pantomime something they like to do best in the winter.
2. Dramatize the Greek myth of Demeter and Persephone.
3. Act out what they like least about winter.

F. Spring

1. They pantomime games they like to play outside in nice weather.
2. They pantomime flying a kite on a windy day. What happens when it gets caught in a tree?
3. Each one pretends to *be* the kite.

G. Summer

1. What are some activities they are looking forward to doing in the summer? They show their ideas, rather than telling.

2. They go exploring in the woods and come upon something very mysterious. What is it and what will they do?

3. They are bored; there doesn't seem to be anything to do. Suddenly they look up and see a strange light flashing all over the room. Whatever the light is, it wants to take them on an adventure. What will the adventure be? How will they get there?

H. Birthdays

1. They think of a present that begins with the first initial of the birthday person's first or last name, or the month in which he or she was born. They pantomime the presents. For example, Manuel Garcia might get a motorcycle, a mouse, a mermaid, a gorilla, a glove, a garbage disposal. This activity can be done individually, or in groups.

SENSES

A. Touch (They should keep their eyes closed to help focus on the tactile sense.)

1. Students touch various parts of their chairs and describe the way it feels.

2. In pairs, they find something for their partner to touch. The partner describes it and tries to identify it.

3. They touch selected objects with various textures, and tell what other things have a similar texture to what they are touching.

4. In pairs, they explore their partner's hands by touch. Then eight or ten students form a circle. One person is in the middle and, with eyes closed, tries to locate his or her partner by touching the hands of the people in the circle.

B. See

1. Play "Twenty Questions," with something clearly visible in the room. One person decides what the object is. The others ask questions about it that can be answered "Yes" or "No." They must be able to identify the object by the time twenty questions are asked.

2. After looking at a picture for thirty seconds, they write a list of all the things they remember about the picture. Compare lists.

3. Crumple a plastic garment bag, such as you get from the cleaners, into a small ball. Then open your hands. While the plastic changes form, students tell the various things it reminds them of.

4. With eyes closed, students "see" an alligator walking down the street toward them. Give them one minute to use their inner vision to see what happens. Talk about it.

C. Hear (eyes closed)

1. Make some sounds, such as adjusting a window blind, turning pages in a book, pouring water in a glass. Ask students to identify the sounds, in the order in which they heard them.

2. In pairs, students make a series of sounds for their partners to identify in sequence. They begin with three sounds, then keep increasing the number of sounds until they can't remember them in sequence.

3. Ask students to recall a family member's voice. How does it sound when the person is excited, when he or she is angry? They describe the voices.

4. They listen to a piece of music and raise their hands when they heard either a certain instrument, a particular melody, when the drum came in, and so on.

D. Taste

1. They pantomime eating their favorite food, noticing how it feels in their mouths. They describe the way it feels and tastes.

2. They think of something with a hot temperature and pantomime eating it. Then they think of something that is "hot," such as a jalapeno pepper, and imagine they are eating that. What are the differences? Does the hot sensation occur at different places in the mouth in the two different experiences?

3. They imagine they are eating something very cold. Describe the taste and feel of the food.

E. Smell

1. They think of their favorite smell and the environment in which they smell it. As they imagine the environment, they will recall the smell.

2. Discuss smells that are peculiar to certain places or situations. Examples might include the woods after a heavy rain, outside on a hot summer day, freshly cut grass, a room with people smoking, the ocean.

ADVENTURES

1. They go on a rescue mission. Where? In space, underwater, in a cave, in a burning house, on a lake, in the mountains, in the woods, at a circus, in the desert, in a grocery story, on an airplane?

2. They are explorers. What are they looking for? Treasure, secrets to a lost city, the secret to eternal youth, the cure for certain diseases, the key to world peace?

3. They turn back the clock of time, or turn it forward, to discover what it was like (or will be like) in other times and other places. They can use this chant while rotating all together in a large circle, with arms on each others' shoulders. They move either clockwise or counter clockwise, depending on whether they are going forward or back in time:

378

Time, time, go away,
We want another place,
We want another day.

Repeat the chant three times, increasing the volume each time. Where will they go? Who will they be? What will they do? Will they journey to prehistoric times, revolutionary times, the Old West, Hiroshima, the United States in a thousand years, a new planet?

PROBLEM SOLVING

(You describe the situation, the students either respond immediately, or they can work in groups to act out the situation.)

1. What would you do if you came home and discovered your house had been burglarized?
2. What would you do if you were new in school, and no one would play with you?
3. What would you do if a fire started while you were babysitting at a neighbor's house?
4. What would you do if there were no schools to attend?
5. What would you do if it was the holiday season and your family had no money for presents?
6. What would you do if you got lost in the woods, just as night was beginning to fall?
7. What would you do if your pet suddenly started talking to you in your own language?
8. What would you do if you were told you could have three wishes?
9. What would you do if you had to make dinner for your favorite television actor? What food would you prepare? Whom else would you invite? What would you talk about?
10. What would you do if, suddenly, your best friend wouldn't speak to you?

RELAXATION

(The following are images which can aid relaxation. Students may have others to add.)

1. The sound and sight of waves rolling up on the beach.
2. Being in a boat, alone, on a nice, calm day.
3. Being a lump of clay that someone is shaping lovingly and carefully.
4. Floating on a cloud.
5. Lying in the sun, with a gentle breeze blowing.
6. Listening to your favorite music.
7. Standing on a mountain top, surveying the world.
8. Watching a bright light that slowly gets dimmer and dimmer.
9. Sitting by a stream, watching the sun play on the water and small fish swimming about.
10. Being a lazy cat, sleeping in the sun, on a hammock gently rocked by a breeze.

Appendix B

CHILDREN'S LITERATURE: AN ANNOTATED BIBLIOGRAPHY

Anthologies and Collections

Anderson, Bernice G. *Trickster Tales from Prairie Lodgefires.* Nashville, TN: Abingdon, 1979
Tales from Blackfoot, Kiowa, Crow, Ponca, Dakota and Cheyenne tribes.

Appich, Peggy. *Tales of an Ashanti Father.* New York: Dutton, 1981.
Anansi stories and "how and why tales" from West Africa.

Berry, James. *Spiderman Anansi.* New York, Holt, Rinehart and Winston, Inc., 1989.
Twenty Anansi stories, beautifully told, fun to play.

Bierhorst, John. *Doctor Coyote: A Native American's Aesop's Fable.* New York: MacMillan Co., 1987.
Twenty fables in which coyote is either the trickster or the tricked. The morals are witty and pithy: "If you don't need it, don't do it." "It doesn't hurt to be clever, if you're too small to be anything else." Fine satires of the human condition.

Brown, Dee. *Teepee Tales of the American Indian.* New York: Holt, Rinehart & Winston, 1979.
Tales from a variety of Indian tribes, which are set in times when animals lived as equals with people.

Buck, Pearl. *Fairy Tales of the Orient.* New York: Simon and Schuster, 1965.
Many tales worthy of dramatizing from China, Japan, India, Turkey, Russia, Persia, Arabia and Egypt.

Corrin, Sara. ed. *The Faber Book of Modern Fairy Tales.* Winchester, MA: Faber and Faber Inc., 1982.
A collection of 15 fairy tales written over the last hundred years.

DeWit, Dorothy, ed. *The Talking Stone: An Anthology of Native American Tales and Legends.* New York: Greenwillow Books, 1979.
A wide variety of stories from several tribes. Includes *porquois* stories, creation myths, humorous tales and hero tales.

Dobie, J. Frank. *Tales of Old-Time.* Boston: Little, Brown and Company, 1955.
Includes tales about well known characters, such as Jim Bowie, Sam Bass, Sam Houston, as well as tales about animals.

Dolch, Edward W. and Marguerite P. Dolch. *Stories from Japan.* Champaign, Illinois: Garrard Publishing Company, 1960.
Folk talks rich with potential for dramatizing. Many favorites are included, such as "Momotaro, the Peach Boy," "Little One-Inch," and "Urashimo."

Fitzgerald, Burdett. *World Tales for Creative Dramatics and Storytelling.* Englewood Cliffs, NJ: Prentice-Hall, 1962.
A fine collection of less well-known stories, grouped geographically, with cross-referenced recommendations according to age groups.

Foster, John, compiler. *Let's Celebrate.* Oxford: Oxford University Press, 1989
Festival poems from many countries for all times of the year. Lovely photos and illustrations.

Garner, Alan. *A Bag of Moonshine.* New York: Delacorte Press, 1986.
Twenty-two stories from England and Wales. Some are humorous, some are eerie and suspenseful.

Goss, Linda and Marian E. Barnes. *Talk That Talk.* New York: Simon and Schuster/Touchstone, 1989.
An anthology of African-American stories, including animal tales, history, sermons, contemporary stories, tales of ghosts and witches, humorous tales, and raps, rhythms and rhymes.

Green, Lila. *Tales from Hispanic Lands.* Morristown, NJ: Silver Burdett, 1979.
Nine tales from Spain, South America, Mexico and Puerto Rico.

Hall, Robin. *Three Tales from Japan.* New Orleans: Anchorage Press, 1973.
The dramatized folk tales include "The Magic Fan," "The Princess of the Sea," and "Little Peach Boy." Although intended to be produced by adults for children, older children would enjoy the challenge of acting them out themselves.

Hamilton, Virginia. *The People Could Fly.* New York: Alfred A. Knopf, 1985.
Twenty-four American black folktales, from animal tales to slave tales of freedom. Beautifully told and illustrated. Many are excellent for dramatization.

Jagendorf, Mortiz. *Folk Stories of the South.* New York: Vanguard Press, 1972.
A compilation of Indian myths, ghost stories, strongman tales, border episodes, and noodle-tales.

Jagendorf, Mortiz and Virginia Weng. *The Magic Boat and Other Chinese Folk Stories.* New York: The Vanguard Press, 1980.
Folk tales from the People's Republic of China, reflecting the land's many minorities and the cultural history of the people.

Kipling, Rudyard. *Just So Stories*. New York: Shocken Books, 1965.
  These wonderful "why" stories are excellent for dramatizing and also for stimulating the children to develop their own "why" stories.

Lester, Julius. *How Many Spots Does a Leopard Have and Other Tales*. New York: Scholastic, Inc., 1989.
  Of the twelve stories, nine are from Africa, two are Jewish, and one is a combination of variants from African and Jewish folklore.

Lindsey, David L. *The Wonderful Chirrionera and Other Tales from Mexican Folklore*. Austin, Texas: Heidelberg Publishing, Inc., 1974.
  Droll stories with imaginative endings, accompanied by striking woodcuts by Barbara Mathews Whitehead.

Lobel, Arnold. *Fables*. New York: Harper and Row, 1980.
  Original fables that are silly but provocative. Some are good for dramatizing. They could provide impetus for children to create their own fables.

Lyons, Grant. *Tales the People Tell in Mexico*. New York: Julian Messner, 1972.
  Includes delightful tales, as well as a glossary and a section detailing the background of the stories.

Mar, S. Y. Lu. *Chinese Tales of Folklore*. New York: Criterion Books, 1964.
  A collection of ancient Chinese stories. Historical notes precede each story, relating each tale to a definite period and real people of the past.

Ritchie, Alice. *The Treasure of Li-Po*. New York: Harcourt, Brace and World, Inc., 1949.
  Six stories which capture the humor and dignity of the Chinese people.

Sheehan, Ethna. *Folk and Fairy Tales from Around the World*. New York: Dodd, Mead and Company, 1970.
  Stories from many countries, including Spain, Brazil, East Africa, India, Japan, China.

Siks, Geraldine B. *Children's Literature for Dramatization: An Anthology*. New York: Harper & Row, 1964.
  A leading authority in the field has collected and written poems and stories which are especially good for dramatizing. She makes suggestions about their use in creative drama classes.

Ward, Winifred. *Stories to Dramatize*. New Orleans: Anchorage Press, 1986.
  This book first appeared in 1952 and has been a favorite with teachers since that time. Stories and poems are grouped according to age levels.

Wyndham, Robert. *Tales the People Tell in China*. New York: Julian Messner, 1971.
  Classic illustrations grace this book of stories based on old tales, but written for contemporary children. The tales reflect all levels of Chinese society, customs, and religion.

Books for Intermediate Grades

Some of the plots in these stories may be too complex to act out in their entirety. There are, however, many scenes from the stories which can be singled out for dramatizing.

Aiken, Joan. *Far Forests*. New York: Viking, 1977.
Mysterious and fantastic characters people these tales of romance, fantasy, and suspense.

Anderson, Hans Christian. *Dulac's Snow Queen, and Other stories from Hans Andersen*. New York: Doubleday, 1976.
A beautifully illustrated book of the famous Andersen tales. Children can easily empathize with many of the characters in these stories.

Beachcroft, Nina. *Wishing People*. New York, Dutton, 1982.
Martha received a wonderful present on her tenth birthday—a weather house she had been pining for. She is amazed and delighted when the figures come to life and give her ten wishes. She finds out, however, that wishes can be very tricky.

Blumberg, Rhoda. *The First Travel Guide to the Moon. What to Pack, How to Go, and What to See When You Get There*. New York: Four Winds, 1980.
A spoof that provides great impetus for the imagination.
Also refer to her book, *The First Travel Guide to the Bottom of the Sea*, 1983.
Students could create their own travel guides for other journeys, based on fact or fantasy or a combination of both. (Example, "The First Travel Guide to the Circulatory System.")

Bodelsen, Anders. *Operation Cobra*. New York: Lodestar, 1979.
An exciting tale, set in Copenhagen. Frederik discovers his family is being held hostage by three terrorists. Frederik and his friends cleverly solve the problem.

Bossom, Naomi. *A Scale Full of Fish and Other Turnabouts*. New York: Greenwillow Books, 1989.
Paired statements with accompanying illustrations are amusing. For example, "Race for a train" shows passengers running to catch a train. "Train for a race" shows three runners. Children could make up their own turnabouts and act them out.

Bradbury, Ray. *Halloween Tree*. New York: Knopf, 1972.
Trick-or-treaters encounter Carapace Clavicle Moundshround who explains the origin of Halloween by taking them on a fantastic journey. At the end, he asks "Which was it—trick or treat?" There is no hesitation—"Both."

Brittain, Bill. *Wish Giver*. New York: Harper & Row, 1983.
A delightfully funny and suspenseful story. The characters' wishes do come true, but not as they had intended. There is a play on figurative versus literal language.

Budhill, David. *Snowshoe Treck to Otter River*. New York: Dial, 1976.
Three short stories about two boys who camp in the wilderness. Adventures include an encounter with wild creatures, falling into an icy river, and building a lean-to camp.

Evslin, Bernard. *Hercules*. New York: William Morrow and Co., 1984.
A re-telling of the Hercules myth. It takes place in a "terrible magical world" that is also "like ours in some ways." Many scenes are suitable for dramatizing and for exploring the journey as a metaphor for personal growth.

Harding, Lee. *Fallen Spaceman*. New York: Harper Row, 1980.
An exciting science fiction story. A human-like alien crashes through space onto Earth. Two boys see the fall and go to investigate. One of the boys slips into what seems to be a huge space suit and it takes off into the forest.

Hooks, William H. *Mean Jake and the Devils*. New York: Dial, 1981.
Three stories derived from the Jack Tales of North Carolina. Good Halloween stories.

Jacob, Helen Pierce. *Diary of the Strawbridge Place*. New York: Atheneum, 1978.
The Strawbridge Place was an underground railway stop operated by a Quaker family. This is an exciting tale with many episodes, including a hunt to round up slaves who escaped from Kentucky. Dire circumstances prevail.

Krensky, Stephen. *Castles in the Air and Other Tales*. New York: Atheneum, 1979.
Five stories are plotted around a phrase or cliche: Castles in the Air; A Fine Kettle of Fish; The Last Straw; Too Clever for Words; A Barrell of Fun. The stories are good motivators for children to design their own stories and act them out.

Lane, Rose Wilder. *Young Pioneers*. New York: McGraw-Hill, 1961.
The trials of pioneer life are depicted. The characters face grasshoppers devouring their crops, blizzards, loneliness, and attacking wolves.

L'Engle, Madeleine. *Wrinkle in Time*. New York: Farrar, Straus & Giroux, 1962.
Meg and friends are taken to another world by three extraterrestrial beings. They find Meg's father, but undergo many trials before they can free him from captivity.

Mendez, Phil. *The Black Snowman*. Illustrated by Carole Byard. New York: Scholastic, Inc., 1989.
A boy is disillusioned and unhappy about being black. He and his brother make a snowman from sooty slush and drape it with a bright cloth they found in a trash bin. The cloth turns out to be a **kente**, a lovely, bright African cloth, which is said to have magical powers. The black snowman comes alive and helps the boy find pride in his heritage, as well as his own self-worth. A touching story with several scenes worthy of dramatizing.

Mendoza, George. *Gwot! Horribly Funny Hairticklers*. New York: Harper & Row, 1967.
Three scary stories from American folklore. The reader, or listener, has to decide what happens at the climax of each story. Groups of children can dramatize their ideas of the climax.

Montgomery, R. A. *A Journey Under the Sea*. New York: Bantam, 1979.
In these stories, the reader becomes the main character and determines how the plot evolves. Excellent for dramatizing and learning about plot.

Norton, Mary. *Borrowers Avenged.* San Diego, CA: Harcourt Brace Jovanovich, 1983.
Another in the series of books about the Clock family who are tiny people, no taller than a pencil. They escape from a wicked couple and find an old rectory to live in.

Ride, Sally. *To Space and Back.* New York: Lothrup, Lee and Sherpard Co., Inc., 1986.
Fascinating details of a space journey. Facts will provide a believable base for enacting a space adventure.

Sceiszka, Jon. *The True Story of the Three Little Pigs: by A. Wolf.* New York: Viking Press, 1989.
A wonderful retelling of the tale from the poor wolf's point of view. A good spoof that could prompt children to re-tell other tales.

Schwartz, Alvin. *Scary Stories to Tell in the Dark.* Philadelphia, PA: J.P. Lippencott and Co., 1981.
Good for choral reading and dramatizing. See also, *More Scary Stories to Tell in the Dark*, 1984.

Slote, Alfred. *My Robot Buddy.* Philadelphia, PA: Lippincott, 1975.
This story takes place in the future—where robots are common-place. Some robots act as companions for children. Danny gets such a robot for his tenth birthday—and the excitement commences.

Van Allsburg, Chris. *The Mysteries of Harris Burdick.* Boston, MA: Houghton Mifflin Co., 1984.
Subtitles for the pictures give clues, but each picture is a plot waiting to unfold. Excellent stimulus for writing and acting.

Walsh, Jill Paton. *Green Book.* New York: Farrar, Straus & Giroux, 1982.
A good science fiction book about a group of colonists who are fleeing the dying Earth. They go to a new planet. The children are able to cope better than the adults, and they discover the secrets to survival.

Winter, Jeanette. *Follow the Drinking Gourd.* New York: Alfred Knopf, 1988.
A story about the Underground Railroad, including the songs taught to the slaves. Excellent illustrations and good dramatic action possibilities. Music notation included.

Appendix C

ADDITIONAL RESOURCES

Creative Drama

Cottrell, June. *Creative Drama in the Classroom. Grades 1–3/Grades 4–6.* Lincolnwood, IL: National Textbook Co., 1987.

Both books provide a strong theoretical base along with activities to use in the classroom.

Ehrlich, Harriety W., ed. *Creative Dramatics Handbook.* Urbana, IL: National Council of Teachers of English, 1974.

This book is made up of a series of practical lesson plans written by Philadelphia teachers. Many of the lessons use creative drama to teach other subjects, such as language arts, mathematics, and Afro-American history.

Furness, Pauline. *Role-Play in the Elementary School: A Handbook for Teachers.* New York: Hart Publisher, 1976.

Fifty role-play lesson plans are presented which could be helpful in everyday classroom situations.

Goodridge, Jane. *Creative Drama and Improvised Movement for Children.* Boston: Plays, Inc., 1970.

Many specific lesson ideas are presented, as well as helpful suggestions about evaluation of class progress.

Heinig, Ruth. *Creative Drama Resource Book For Kindergarten Through Grade 3/For Grades 4–6.* Englewood Cliffs, NJ: Prentice-Hall, 1987.

Pantomime, improvisation, songs, story suggestions, and games are arranged to demonstrate simple to complex techniques in the two volumes.

Kase-Polisini, Judith. *The Creative Drama Book: Three Approaches.* New Orleans, LA: Anchorage Press, 1989.

Clear descriptions with ample examples of drama based in the playmaking approach, the theatre games approach, and the educational drama approach. Teachers can experiment with the different approaches to find their own styles.

McCaslin, Nellie. *Creative Drama in the Primary Grades/In the Intermediate Grades*. New York: Longman Inc., 1987

These are comprehensive books which cover almost all aspects of drama with children. The teacher will find many useful activities. The author has written many books on creative drama and children's theatre.

McIntyre, Barbara. *Creative Drama in the Elementary School*. Itasca, IL: F.E. Peacock, 1974.

Specific classroom suggestions are given for primary and upper elementary teachers.

O'Neill, Cecily and Alan Lambert. *Drama Structures: A Practical Handbook for Teachers*. London: Hutchinson, 1982.

Clearly presented plans for using historical and social issues as a basis for developing a drama. The emphasis is on the content of the drama rather than the form the drama takes.

Pierini, Mary Paul Frances. *Creative Dramatics: A Guide for Educators*. New York: Herder and Herder, 1971.

This is a resource book with verbal and visual ideas to stimulate drama in the classroom.

Polsky, Milton. *Let's Improvise*. Englewood Cliffs, NJ: Prentice-Hall, 1980.

Ideas are presented for people of all age levels and for all levels of experience.

Schwartz, Dorothy, and Dorothy Aldrich, eds. *Give Them Roots . . . And Wings!* Revised edition. New Orleans: Anchorage Press, 1985.

Lessons specifically designed for teachers, with goals, activities, and evaluation suggestions.

Siks, Geraldine Brain. *Drama with Children*. 2nd ed. New York: Harper & Row, Inc., 1983.

This is a book for those who are interested in the theoretical basis behind child drama, as well as activities which illustrate the theory.

Spolin, Viola. *Theatre Games for the Classroom: A Teacher's Handbook. Grades 1–3/Grades 4–6*. Evanson, IL: Northwestern University Press, 1987.

Activities from her earlier works for adults have been refocused for working with children in the classroom setting. Many fine ideas are included.

Stewig, John Warren. *Informed Drama in the Elementary Language Arts Program*. New York: Teachers College Press, 1983.

Specific ways are given in which movement and improvisation assist in the development of language skills.

Stewig, John Warren. *Spontaneous Drama: A Language Art*. Columbus: Merrill, 1973.

Drama is used to motivate reading, oral language development, nonverbal communication, vocabulary development, and listening skills.

Valeri, Michele, and George Meade. *Have You Roared Today? A Creative Drama Handbook*. Rockville, MD: Montgomery County Public Schools, 1979.

Specific classroom activities are listed according to grade, materials needed, procedures, and suggestions for sidecoaching.

Wagner, Betty Jane. *Dorothy Heathcote: Drama as a Learning Medium.* Washington, D.C.: National Education Association, 1976.

    The author carefully describes the methods used by Heathcote, a renowned British drama teacher. Her special techniques include playing in role, questioning, and time for reflection.

Way, Brian. *Development Through Drama.* New York: Humanities Press, 1972.

    This book contains capsulized, practical ideas for all teachers, as well as a philosophical basis for using drama for child development.

Wilder, Rosilyn. *A Space Where Anything Can Happen: Creative Drama in a Middle School.* Rowayton, CT: New Plays Books, 1977.

    The author has written an inspiring, yet practical, methods book. Clear guidelines are given for helping contemporary children do creative work.

Puppetry

Boylan, Eleanor. *Puppet Plays for Special Days.* Rowayton, CT: New Plays, Inc., 1976.
This book provides a collection of short plays that should be welcomed by the classroom teacher who is looking for puppet material.

Brooks, Courtaney. *Plays and Puppets Etcetera.* Claremont, CA: Belnice Books, 1981.
This is a charming book written for those with little or no experience with puppetry.

Engler, Larry, and Carol Fijan. *Making Puppets Come Alive.* New York: Taplinger, 1973.
This book not only offers help in making and handling puppets, it also provides assistance about how to put on the puppet show.

Freericks, Mary, and Joyce Segal. *Creative Puppets in the Classroom.* Rowayton, CT: New Plays, Inc., 1979.
The authors show how puppets can be integrated into the curriculum. Simple techniques and inexpensive materials are encouraged.

Hunt, Tamara, and Nancy Renfro. *Puppetry in Early Childhood Education.* Austin, TX: Nancy Renfro Studios, 1982.
This book deals with all aspects of puppetry. Teachers will find it extremely helpful.

Renfro, Nancy. *Puppetry and the Art of Story Creation.* Austin, TX: Nancy Renfro Studios, 1979.
The book stresses how to create stories with the children, using simple puppets. A section of the book deals with using puppetry with disabled individuals.

Schmidt, Hans J., and Karl J. Schmidt. *Learning with Puppets.* Chicago: Coach House Press, 1980.
This book focuses on using puppetry to help teach aeademic and social skills.

Sims, Judy. *Puppets for Dreaming and Scheming.* Walnut Creek, CA: Early Stages, 1978.
This book has a wealth of ideas, with clear directions, especially suited for teachers of younger children.

Special Populations

Behrn, Snyder, and Clopton. *Drama Integrates Basic Skills: Lesson Plans for the Learning Disabled.* Springfield, IL: Charles C. Thomas, 1979.

A practical text demonstrates ways a drama curriculum can help children integrate basic affective and cognitive skills.

Champlin, John, and Connie Brooks. *Puppets and the Mentally Retarded Student.* Austin, TX: Nancy Renfro Studios, 1980.

This book focuses on developing literary comprehension with the mentally retarded child. Special techniques are described for using puppets in elementary classrooms.

Gillies, Emily P. *Creative Dramatics for All Children.* Washington, D.C.: Association for Childhood International, 1973.

A well qualified teacher discusses drama for the emotionally disturbed and physically handicapped child, as well as those who speak English as a second language.

Jennings Sue. *Remedial Drama: A Handbook for Teachers and Therapists.* New York: Theatre Art Books, 1978.

The author has presented a concise, easy to read, book about the values of drama for special populations.

McIntyre, Barbara. *Informal Dramatics: A Language Arts Activity for the Special Child.* Pittsburgh: Stanwix, 1963.

This book is a practical guide for teachers of special education.

Shaw, Ann M., and Cj Stevens. *Drama, Theatre and the Handicapped.* Washington, D.C.: American Theatre Association, 1979.

A collection of essays by prominent practitioners in the field provides descriptions of the kinds of programs available which encourage participation by handicapped people.

Shaw, Ann M., Wendy Perks and Cj Stevens, eds. *Perspective: A Handbook in Drama and Theatre by, with, and for, Handicapped Individuals.* Washington, D.C.: American Theatre Association, 1981.

A practical collection of activities and resources is presented, representing all aspects of handicapping conditions.

Wethered, Audrey G. *Drama and Movement in Therapy.* London: MacDonald and Evans, 1980.

This book is a practical guide to the therapeutic use of movement, mime, and drama.

Music

The *right* musical accompaniment for a drama lesson can stimulate (or calm) the children, create a mood, and heighten the action. Music should be selected with great care. If you cannot find music that seems right to you, it is better not to use it at all. Be prepared to listen to a lot of music.

The following list is like a "starter"—they are pieces which create certain moods. A number of them have several possibilities on a given album. You will discover your own preferred collection as you listen and imagine the action possibilities.

You will note that the pieces listed are mostly classical, and certainly without words. One wouldn't use a piece of music with words unless the words were a part of what was being acted out. You can use popular music, as long as it suits the action. Just remember that popular music will remind the children of a lot of things that may not be a part of the focus for the intended dramatization.

Bartok, *Music for Strings, Percussion and Celesta.*
Circus Time, Music Corporation of America Records, Ringling Brothers and Barnum & Bailey Circus Band, Merle Evans, conductor.
Debussy, *Afternoon of a Faun.*
Dukas, *Sorcerer's Apprentice.*
Grieg, *Peer Gynt Suite,* No. 1, "In the Hall of the Mountain King," "Morning."
Grofe, *Grand Canyon Suite,* "Cloudburst," "Sunrise."
Holst, *The Planets Suite.*
Kabalevsky, *The Comedians,* "March and Comedians' Gallop," "Pantomime."
Mussorgsky, *Pictures at an Exhibition.*
Ravel, *Daphnis and Chloe,* "Daybreak."
Saint-Saens, *Danse Macabre.*
Stravinsky, *The Firebird Suite.*
Tchaikovsky, *The Nutcracker Suite.*
Varese, *Poem Electronique.*
Varese, *Integrales.*

Literature and Author Index

Behm, Tom, 114
Birds of Summer, The, 66
Bushel of Thanks, A, 77
Fog, 324
Frog Who Wanted To Be a Singer, The, 181
Goss, Linda, 181, 254
Hammer of Thor, The, 286
Jack and the Northwest Wind, 114
Mayo, Gretchen Will, 66
Michell, Monica, 104
Sandburg, Carl, 323
Spread the Word: A Storyteller's Rap, 254
Squire's Bride, The, 198
Stone in the Road, The, 90
Strange Visitor, The, 98
Tug of War, 60
Why Mosquitoes Buzz in People's Ears, 104
Wind and the Sun, The, 85

BIOGRAPHY

Barbara Salisbury Wills received her doctorate in curriculum and instruction and her undergraduate and master's degrees in drama from the University of Washington in Seattle. She has taught drama in pre-schools, elementary and secondary schools, and universities over a span of thirty years.

Wills is the executive director of the American Alliance for Theatre and Education and is on the faculty of Arizona State University, Department of Theatre, specializing in drama for children and youth. In addition, she is a theatre education consultant in curriculum and teacher of professional development classes for school districts across the United States. She has also taught at The University of Texas at Austin, Pacific Lutheran University, Seattle University and the University of Washington.

Wills was Director of Arts Coalition Northwest, from 1979 to 1982, which was a regional program of the Kennedy Center in cooperation with the Seattle Center, providing technical assistance for arts in education programs in five northwest states.

In addition to writing the drama sections of several books for teachers and children, she founded and edited, in cooperation with the Kennedy Center, the periodical for children, *Artsploration.* She also served as senior consultant for the television series, *Arts Alive!* She was on the Advisory Committee for the National Endowment for the Arts' report to Congress on arts education, *Towards Civilization,* 1987–88. And she was on the Coordinating Council for development of the *National Standards for Arts Education,* published in 1994. She is a member of the Board of Directors of the Children's Theatre Foundation of America and a Trustee of the Winifred Ward Memorial Fund, Inc.

She served as president of the Children's Theatre Association of America (CTAA) in 1985–1986. She became president of the newly constituted American Association of Theatre for Youth (AATY) in 1987. Under her leadership, AATY merged with the American Association of Secondary Theatre Educators, becoming the American Alliance for Theatre and Education (AATE), with the motto "Artists and Educators Serving Young People." CTAA presented her with the Creative Drama for Human Awareness Award in 1976 and the Research Award in 1983, and, in 1991, AATE presented her with a Certificate of Appreciation for her work as publications chair.